CROSSING the BLVD

strangers, neighbors, aliens in a new america

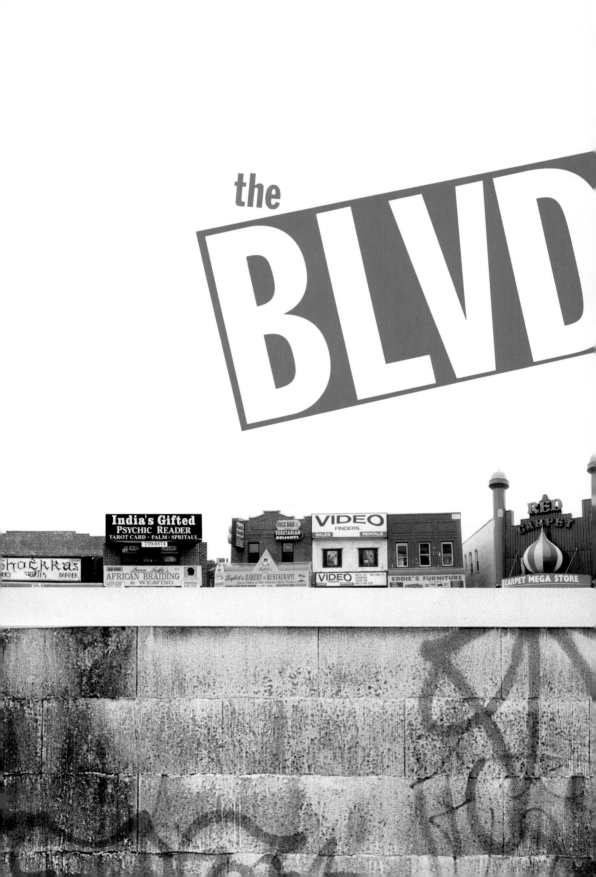

conceived, written, and compiled by .

CROSSING the BLVD

strangers, neighbors, aliens in a new america

. . . WARREN LEHRER & JUDITH SLOAN

based on interviews with participants
in the *Crossing the BLVD* project

photography and design by
WARREN LEHRER

W • W • NORTON & COMPANY • NEW YORK • LONDON

This book was made possible in part with generous support from The Rockefeller Foundation (PACT Grant), Furthermore: a program of the J.M. Kaplan Fund, The Greenwall Foundation, The Puffin Foundation, a V-Day Award, and public funds from the New York City Department of Cultural Affairs, and the Queens Council on the Arts.

Library of Congress Cataloging-in-Publication Data

Lehrer, Warren

Crossing the BLVD: strangers, neighbors, aliens in a new America / Warren Lehrer & Judith Sloan; photography and design by Warren Lehrer

p. cm.

"Based on interviews with participants in the *Crossing the BLVD* project."

ISBN 0-393-05737-2 -- ISBN 0-393-32466-4 (pbk.)

1. Immigrants--New York (State)--New York 2. Queens (New York, N.Y.)

I. Title: Crossing the BLVD. II. Sloan, Judith. III. Title.

JV050.Q44L45 2003

305.9'0691--dc21

2002044353

CROSSING the BLVD

strangers, neighbors, aliens i

WARREN

As a teenager, I used to walk to Crocheron Park on the far eastern border of Queens, find the one little cluster of trees where I couldn't see a parking lot or a baseball field or a fence, and imagine that I was in the middle of a vast wilderness. Really I was near the edge of a cliff above the bumper to bumper traffic of the Cross Island Parkway. I'd sit down, close my eyes and pretend that the roar of cars below was really the sound of a restless, wild ocean, a half a world away. Neither suburb nor city, certainly not the *country*, the borough of Queens, marked by neatly segregated neighborhoods with endless rows of brick apartment buildings, belching factories, little box houses and postage-stamp lawns, was a nowhere land this restless kid wanted to leave as soon as possible.

After living in other parts of the country for more than a dozen years, I find myself again a resident of Queens — now the most ethnically diverse locality in the United States.

[U.S. Census Bureau]

Every day, my wife Judith and I cross the twelve lane gauntlet of speed and commerce that is Queens Boulevard, along with immigrants and refugees from all parts of the globe. **There are those of course who complain** about a place whose residents speak 138 different languages. Once Irish- or Italian- or Jewish- or Greek-American enclaves have given way to neighborhoods that defy predictable aromas, accents, or politics. Occasionally friendships form across cultural divides. Sometimes tensions flair between unlikely neighbors or a shopkeeper and a customer. But for the most part, the choreography of Queens is one of chaotic but polite cohabitation.

I walk five blocks from our apartment to pick up the number 7 train. In a rush, I've walked a quarter mile of asphalt and concrete, past pungent piles of plastic garbage bags, parked cars with multiple anti-theft devices, and anonymous pedestrians. An elderly Afghan woman walks, stops, and waits at each of three median islands, until she finally makes it across the 225-foot-wide boulevard, alive but worn out. After buying saffron rice and other ingredients needed to cook kabuli palau, she knows she will have to make the journey back again. A few dozen Mexican men wait on a work line, hoping they'll be picked to load

John Rocker, the once–Atlanta Braves' ace relief pitcher, achieved infamy for his scathing comments re: the prospect of riding the Queens number #7 train to pitch against the N.Y. Mets at Shea Stadium. "The biggest thing I don't like... is the foreigners... You can walk an entire block and not hear anybody speaking English. Asians and Koreans and Vietnamese and Indians and Russians and Spanish people and everything up there. How the hell did they get in this country?"

I used to think the aging process meant getting wrinkles and developing an accent. As a kid, most of the old people I knew were immigrants, either Italian or Jewish. Born in Brooklyn, New York, both my parents were children of immigrants, and both lived with one foot in the old world and one in the new world. They spoke Yiddish to each other and read the New York papers in our tiny house in a tiny Connecticut town, where I spent my early childhood. We had a vegetable garden, a peach tree, and woods in the back. In the summers I fished around for frogs and gooey things in the swamp near the railroad tracks. My father used to take me down to the tracks to watch the train go by. It calmed me in much the same way all things locomotive calm my young nephews. The Russian man — I called him the caboose man — would wave as the train rolled away. My dad told me, "See, the man was watching us watching him."

From time to time, our family took the train into New York City to see plays, walk the streets, get pickles, and visit my mother's cousins. Most of my father's family perished in the Holocaust. His mother was the only grandparent I knew. The closest I came to having a family reunion was opening a box of my grandmother's old brown and white photographs. *Who were these people I resembled?* The dark eyes, the dark hair, the tell-tale rings under the eyes. My grandmother taught me how to speak English with a Yiddish accent, "Judela, dus is a vinda." I'd walk around saying "vinda." I remember brushing her thick, waist-length hair. Although I have no conscious memory of it, she must have told me stories. Now I imagine I was brushing her secrets into my soul. She died when I was nine. When I was twelve my father died.

For twenty years I made a career of gathering stories, interviewing my grandmother's contemporaries and people who could have been my father. A migrant worker of sorts, eyeball-deep in oral history projects, looking backward to go forward, going forward to see clearly backward; researching, packing, flying, performing; I traveled from Canada to Israel, Hawaii to Scotland to Japan, up and down the east and west coasts and in towns and cities in between.

and unload fifty pound bags of fertilizer. Three generations of sari-clad Indian women pass an Ecuadorean medicine man talking on a cell phone to his long distance mother. I hurry past a woman from Senegal. Her son, entranced by his Pokémon Game Boy, unknowingly brushes up against a classmate from Ireland who's making sure not to step on any cracks in the sidewalk. Across the treeless boulevard, a teenage boy (who could be from anywhere) pries open a parking meter with a crowbar. I

look up and see two billboards on the elevated subway station. The one for Libby's Nectar reads, "Ahora con CALCIO" — CALCIO spelled in letterforms made of tropical fruit. The other billboard, in large white type on a red field reads, "TIRED OF SITTING IN TRAFFIC? EVERY DAY, ANOTHER 8000 IMMIGRANTS ARRIVE. EVERY DAY!! **www.ProjectUSA.org.**" I see my train pass overhead. Exhausted by the daily battle against time and noise and congestion, I contemplate escape. Maybe next year, Judith and I will get out of here. Go somewhere far away. Nepal, Belize, Fiji. Anywhere. We'll take photographs and write about the people we meet on our travels.

Based in Astoria, Queens, **Project USA** *mounts national billboard campaigns railing against open-door immigration policies that they consider disastrous.*

There are several spots underneath the concrete arches of the elevated subway between Bliss and Locusts Streets where sounds reverberate like in a canyon or gothic cathedral. I am in one of these spots. I stop. I listen. Laughter, arguments, prayers, cries and whispers, collect into an echo chamber of a thousand dialects. Looking out from the invisible bubble that separates me from *the other*, I am surrounded by exquisite, storied faces. The world has come to me.

WARREN & JUDITH

We decide to become travelers in our own backyard. For three years we trek between the shadows.

Now I can say I actually live somewhere — in the borough of Queens, in the city of New York. Queens was never on the top of my list of places to live. It wasn't even *on* the list. For eight years the only people I knew in Queens were my husband Warren and my in-laws. I'd go to Manhattan and Brooklyn to perform, visit friends, be inspired and entertained. I never did anything in Queens. What's in Queens? **The post office**, where I stand on increasingly long lines, ashamed at my rage toward foreign-born postal workers who continue to put other people's mail in my box. An apartment we rent from a man who lives in a fishing village in Greece. The Lebanese market with the good goat cheese. The Chinese shoe repair man whose miraculous $5 repairs allow me to keep a pair of boots for nine years. The Sicilian neighbor and his Colombian wife who complain about the newly-arrived Mexicans. The Egyptian woman at the laundromat who tells me how she left Egypt while I'm on the rinse cycle.

I do laundry more often than necessary just to listen to the stories. I get shoes repaired that I don't even want anymore. I start working as an artist in residence, teaching theatre and storytelling in several Queens schools populated by immigrant teenagers. Warren and I begin interviewing people in our community. The ghosts of my ancestors hover around these interviews. Perennially the outsider, I feel strangely at home inside their stories. Separated from their loved ones, their language, familiar paths, skies, smells, all signposts to memory — they are scared, they are courageous, they are (in the words of Camilo Perdomo, 144–161) "new in front of the life."

sign at our **post office**

OUT OF TOWN
MAILS.

...of the block-long superstores that now dominate most of the major boulevards in Queens, down the side streets, into the bodegas, family-owned restaurants, homes, places of worship, libraries, and community rooms — looking for migration stories,

culture,

and soul.

We meet Sergie, a Romanian exile, at the Queens Burger Coffee Shop. "Crossing the BLVD! **It is for me a bitch crossing that boulevard.** Two or three times a day I do it. Ahh. Who cares about the boulevard? Crossing the Ocean — that's the hard thing. That's what you should call your book!"

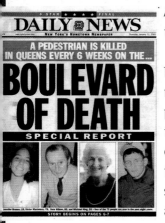

For drivers, **Queens BLVD** *is a ten-, sometimes twelve-lane expressway. For pedestrians, it is a treacherous crosswalk. Cited as "the most dangerous road in New York," Queens BLVD was the site of 73 car related deaths and over 1500 injuries from 1993–2001.*

Inside an unlocked storefront, on a desolate street in a coastal neighborhood of Queens, a Nigerian Pentecostal prophetess presides over an all night vigil of speaking in tongues and trance-dancing, 22–29. A few hundred Falun Gong practitioners, considered dangerous by the Chinese government, practice their gentle exercises in a schoolyard park on the 10th anniversary of their young but burgeoning religion, 40–51. Five nights a week, a woman from Vietnam with a New York gift of gab, works as a bar maid in a strip joint in order to support herself and her Amerasian daughter, 110–119. A former aviation lawyer from Colombia delivers food with his partner a year after they escaped anti-gay vigilante groups who were determined to "socially-cleanse" the streets of Bogota, 144–160. A once-state-sanctioned performing artist known throughout the Soviet Union, moves her dance studio out of her one bedroom apartment, into a subway station storefront in a neighborhood where 30,000 fellow Bukharan Jews have settled, 230–241. On an unsuspecting Father's Day morning, the owner of an empty lot discovers his property is being used for a Mexican Rodeo and calls the cops, triggering the pursuit of a 2,000 pound bull as it runs horns-first, past a terrified crowd on Northern Boulevard, 270–281. Enduring the frigid winter air, a Haitian exile leads a demonstration outside the white stucco home of the former leader of FRAPH, the paramilitary force allegedly responsible for the murder and torture of countless Haitian civilians, 300–309. Five nights after the September 11th attack on the World Trade Center, an Egyptian Coffee Shop in Astoria is smashed up by four young Americans at three o'clock in the morning. The police catch the perpetrators, but the café owner decides not to press charges. He says he understands their rage. An hour later, the four young men are back, 320–329. Two flights of stairs above the intersection of little India and little Colombia on Roosevelt Avenue, is a florescent-lit hall where semi-professional ping-pong players from all hemispheres of the globe — grunt, whack, and slice 40mm balls from deep inside the zone, 332–345.

AZTECA

CROSSING the BLVD documents these and other signs of migratory life, normally hidden within the seemingly mundane, sometimes hideous urban landscape of Queens. First-person narratives, culled and edited from audio-taped interviews, reveal stories of crossing — displacement, expectation and readjustment.

How different are these **new immigrants** from those who came here as "foreigners" in the distant past? Is this crossroad of the world a pot where cultural identities melt? Or do they boil over, overlay, transmutate? Or simply co-exist? What compels so many to leave their homeland and come to this place of great promise and contradiction? As documentary artists and excavators of personal testimony, we look into the eyes of each of these tellers, and take their words at face value, not as the only truth, the absolute truth, but their truth as they lived it back home, in America, and in between. The 79 individuals featured in this book do not represent their ethnicities or countries of origin, but many reveal the human toll wrought by the machinations of post colonial empires, played out in the hot zones of a cold- and post-cold-war world.

Our close-to-home expedition began in the fall of 1999 and continued through the fall of 2002. The horrific events of September 11th, 2001 occurred a little past our midway point and became part of our project. For most U.S.-born citizens, 9-11 is a day that forever changed the world, but for many of the people we interviewed, it is one of several geo-political calamities that altered the course of their lives. Collectively, these strangers, neighbors, "aliens" form a group portrait of a new and not-so-new America. Crossing the BLVD focuses primarily on a wide array of new immigrants: from those who came with networks of support and sponsorship > to those who arrived like shrapnel flung from distant wars, often fueled by American foreign policy > to those who attained refugee/asylum status > to those who came as skilled professionals or remain "undocumented workers" displaced by the horns of a bullish global economy. Above all, Crossing the BLVD is a celebration of resilient, prismatic character — in search of home.

By **new immigrants**, *we mean people who came to the United States after the 1965 Immigration and Nationality Act Ammendments. One of the major Civil Rights Acts of the time, the '65 law mandated an end to discriminatory immigration policies that gave preference to "white," Western Europeans. That legislation vastly increased the numbers of immigrants from southern and eastern hemispheres, forever changing the make-up of the American population, particularly in the cities, undeniably in the borough of Queens. A majority of the people reflected in these pages came to the U.S. after 1990.*

CROSSING ⊞ BLVD

juxtaposes multiple perspectives:

individuals and families who live only blocks apart but come from opposite ends of the earth

different points of view within families/groups

By families we mean:
• traditional "nuclear" families
• non-traditional families.
By groups we mean: schoolmates, co-workers, fellow congregants, bandmembers, etc.

our observations, historical perspectives on countries of origin, changes in United States immigration policy, and other contextual matter

Each person is distinguished by typeface and column placement. Columns are headed by the name of the speaker highlighted in yellow.

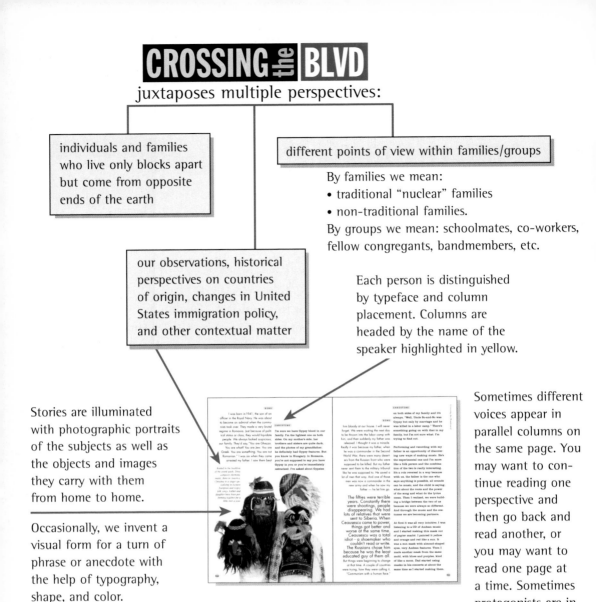

Stories are illuminated with photographic portraits of the subjects as well as the objects and images they carry with them from home to home.

Occasionally, we invent a visual form for a turn of phrase or anecdote with the help of typography, shape, and color.

Sometimes different voices appear in parallel columns on the same page. You may want to continue reading one perspective and then go back and read another, or you may want to read one page at a time. Sometimes protagonists are in conversation with each other.

Queens is home to both Kennedy and LaGuardia airports — the **Ellis Island** of the *new* new century. Got $5 in your pocket, where do you go? The next block. Maybe you can't afford the $30 cab ride into Manhattan. Maybe you can't figure out how to get anywhere else. Or maybe, like so many other financially strapped residents of New York looking for a place that is larger than an endtable, you are pushed into the boroughs into the only apartment you can afford. Or maybe, like Bovic Antosi, **74-85,** you escape your country within an inch of your life, only to find yourself locked up by the Immigration and Naturalization Service (INS) at a detention center near Kennedy Airport.

Between 1892 and 1954, twelve million immigrants came through **Ellis Island***. In great numbers they populated the neighborhoods closest to their point of arrival in lower Manhattan. The second great wave of immigration into the United States occurred between 1965 and 2000. In the 1990s alone, over one million foreign-born people migrated to New York City, largely through the airports.*

Divided into **FIVE MOVEMENTS**, Crossing the BLVD begins with contemporary pilgrims in search of an America that is known both as a bastion of religious freedom and a place in need of spiritual healing. The second movement features asylum seekers who fled imprisonment, war, ethnic cleansing, death threats, and/or political persecution. We move next into family ties: of brothers and business partners; of families separated and reunited; of generational gaps; of traditions abandoned, rediscovered and made new. In a movement of neighborhood stories, community members share their own perspectives on near-legendary events, environmental hazards, the emergence of demons from back home, and surprising acts of reconciliation. We end with unlikely coexistences, collisions, and collaborations between athletes, classmates, political activists, and musicians.

Some of the stories in the book were featured in the **Crossing the BLVD radio documentaries** produced for New York Public Radio's nationally syndicated program, *The Next Big Thing*. www.nextbigthing.org

A majority of the people we interviewed are not native English speakers. For some, English is a second language — for others, it's a third, a fourth or a fifth. In shaping these stories we've attempted to retain the rhythm and syntax of speech. While we could have cleaned up the English just to get to the story, we delight in the unexpected word combinations and often poetic phrasings that pop from the hybridization of language. In cases where the teller speaks very little or no English, the stories are translated.

The audio CD that comes with the clothbound edition of this book (available also as a stand alone CD through W.W. Norton), is a collaboration with composer, Scott Johnson. Original music and audio collages form a soundtrack where speech becomes music and music is speech. The recording features Scott Johnson and an electric-acoustic ensemble, as well as music and voices from Crossing the BLVD participants.

The project continues on **www.crossingtheblvd.org**, an interactive website that includes a timeline of U.S. immigration policy; audio clips; an opportunity to contribute your own crossing stories; information on the exhibition and performances; and links to the radio pieces, EarSay, and other resources.

At 112 square miles, **Queens is the largest** of New York City's five boroughs, with 55 neighborhoods, 58 boulevards, and a dizzying web of intersecting avenues, streets, parkways, roads, drives, places, lanes, terraces and courts. (We live near the corner of 43rd Street and 43rd Avenue. Not to be confused with the corner of 43rd Place and 43rd Road.) Populated by two million people, made up of over one hundred nationalities, Queens has the largest mix of immigrants and refugees in the world.

In 1683, the British reorganized a cluster of previously Dutch-ruled towns into a county and named it Queens in honor of Catherine of Braganza. In 1898, the New York State Legislature created the Greater City of New York, consolidating Manhattan, Brooklyn, Staten Island, the Bronx, and Queens as **boroughs of a single city**.

itinerary

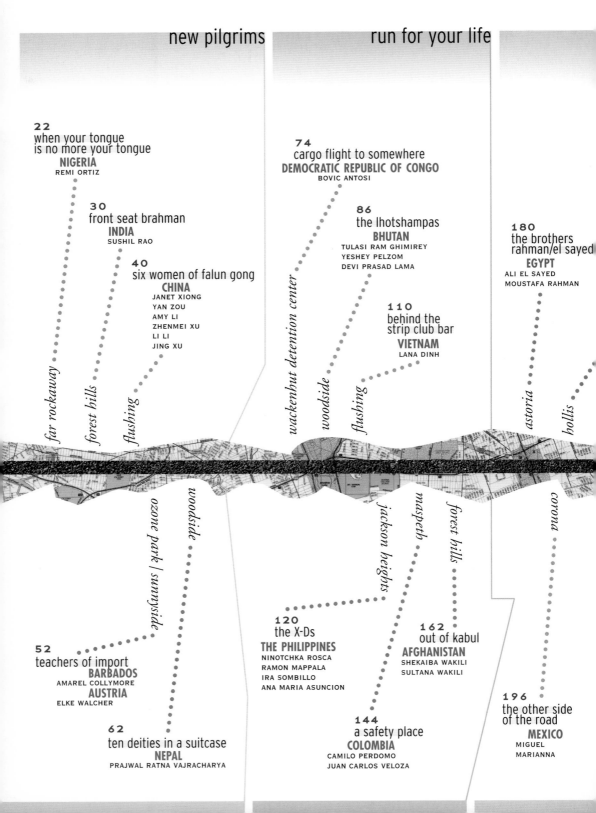

new pilgrims

run for your life

far rockaway *forest hills* *flushing* *ozone park / sunnyside* *woodside* *wackenhut detention center* *woodside* *flushing* *jackson heights* *maspeth* *forest hills* *astoria* *hollis* *corona*

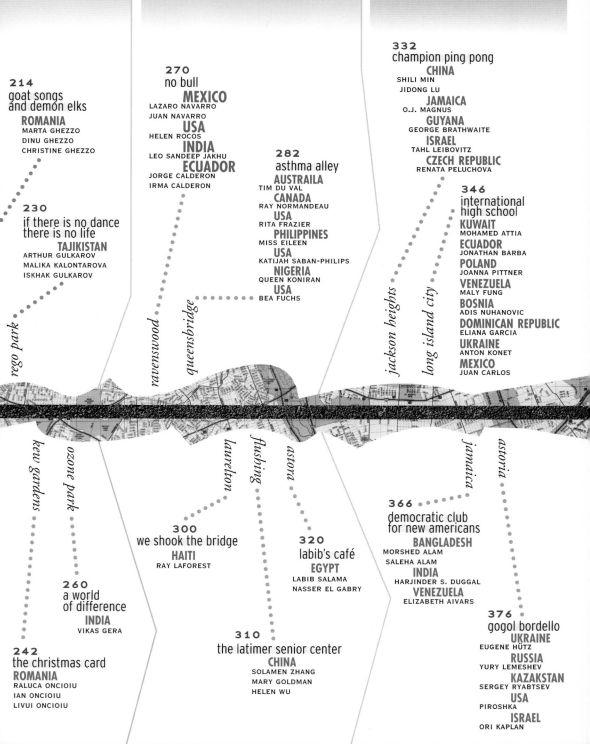

new pilgrims

when your tongue is no more your tongue

front seat brahman

six women of falun gong

teachers of import

ten deities in a suitcase

when your tongue is no more your tongue

A Sunday morning in April. Walking on broken glass, down broken sidewalks, we wander onto a quiet street off of Seagirt Boulevard in a low-income section of Far Rockaway. The salty sea air mixes with the smell of baked chicken and spilled beer. A few doors down from the Hasidic-run kosher market and the out-of-business Medical Center, across from a vacant lot and a hair-braiding salon, is a storefront with a sign that reads LIGHT OF GOD MINISTRIES. We tiptoe into a service of percussive rhythms, ecstatic dance, speaking in tongues, and rapturous song. We are in a Nigerian Pentecostal Church. The women are dressed in brightly patterned cloth and tribal headwear. A few of the men wear dashikis; most wear dark, Western-style suits with crisp white shirts. Throughout the three-hour plus service, children are running around, playing, dancing, occasionally folding into the laps of their parents or other adult members of the congregation. A four-year-old boy strokes Warren's hand and asks, "Are you a ghost?" We are the only white people in the room. Remi the prophetess welcomes us.

Father in heaven,

I put your people before you. I pray for a shield over every one of them. I pray for the cab drivers, that you protect them from accident, from robbery, from receiving unnecessary tickets, and help them to keep their job. I pray for the nurses, that they will not give wrong medications, that they will not be sued or contract diseases. Holy Spirit, I pray for all the children of this church that you will give them wisdom and understanding, that they will be grade A students.

During the service, many congregants come up to the pulpit, give testimony, lead a prayer or a song. Not so much a preacher as she is a spiritual consultant, Remi concludes a Sunday service asking the Lord for protection.

I come against sickness. I come against
death in Jesus' name. I pray against poverty,
for those who are not doing well; they
should not give up hope. I pray for those
that are in business, that they will prosper,
Lord, that you will be their business part–
ner, that they will be safe on the street,
that they will not be pushed into the
subway track, that you will shield them
from bullets and police that misun–
derstand who they really are. Oh
Lord, let no gunshots come near
them, no guns shall come near
them. I pray that this will be a
week of favor, and by next week
we *all* will have cause to give
you glory. I praise you for what
you have done. In Jesus'
name I pray.
Amen.

*Remi has an unusual sense of time. Sometimes she
shows up a few hours late for an appointment; sometimes
a few days late. She is always candid with us. Often
laughing at herself, our conversations are filled with
interruptions. The phone at the church is always ringing.
People are coming in looking for her. If they need counsel,
Remi will talk with them — for hours if necessary.*

I don't know how it happened. I was not even that strong
a Christian really. One morning I was in my home in
Nigeria when I fell. Fell on the power of the Holy Spirit.
For seven days I did not eat. I was sweating like someone
poured water over me. Words started coming out of my
mouth before I knew what they were. When God takes
over you, your tongue is no more your tongue. You don't
know where you are. I would not see you like I am seeing
you now. I will recognize you, but you will look different,

like shadows covering you. I could open my mouth to talk, but I could not eat, as if my teeth were chained down.

This is not the life I planned. I owned my own restaurant in Nigeria. I had a swimming pool, a flower yard, even a Mercedes. When I was young I had to carry stones and water to sell for a chance to go to school. I studied four years in college and then I ran my own business with sixteen people working for me, I was not looking to change that.

After I fell on the power of the Holy Spirit, people started rushing to my house. I pray for them and tell them what is going to happen. Most of the things I said came to pass. *And that scared me.* So I ran away to the city of Lagos. Then it starts to happen again that people are coming to me for advice. That's when God spoke to me, that I must go to the United States. But I don't know what I'm to do there.

I see myself in a dream.
I am begging for food.
I have no clothes to wear.
I have no money.
So I work for God and God gives me a room
and makes sure I have food to eat.
If it was up to me I would be doing something different.
I would be rich maybe.
But if I don't do the work of God,
I will die.

"The streets in the United States are made of gold."
That's what people say in Nigeria. We call it "God's own country." That means, God favors America. When I got here I was a little disappointed with what I saw. I see some ghetto, some people begging, and I say, "There are places like this in America?" We thought everyone here is enjoying,

is wealthy like Babylon. That's why so many Nigerians go back home. After nine years here, my brother went back with his wife and children. When I'm through with my work here, I'm going back too.

I was in Queens for one year working in a restaurant, and everything was okay. Then some Nigerians came to see me. They said, "Let's start praying together." God spoke to us that we will plant a church. We found an empty store. We bought some good metal chairs with padded cushions at a downtown closing. We put in carpet. We got musical instruments one by one. It's almost two years now and some weeks there isn't enough room to fit everyone. There are preachers who know how to preach very well, but my gift is planting.

In the beginning I wasn't taking care that everything is growing evenly. Some people said I was favoring one over another. Almost half the church left. They thought I was Yoruba. Really I am from a small tribe in the Middle Delta. Now, most of the congregation don't know where I'm from. Each week I make sure to wear the dress of a different tribe. Last week I had on Yoruba dress. This week I am wearing the dress of the Ibo. In Nigeria if you are Yoruba you cannot stay in Ibo land. They will discriminate against you. There are some towns in Nigeria, only three miles away and they cannot understand each other. Luckily I speak many lan- guages. But I don't allow a lot of native songs in the church. I want there to be unity. The songs we sing are Nigerian, but the words we use are English. Only if someone wants to give thanks to the Lord – then they can use their native tongue, so they feel at home. Also the dancing is native. Yoruba people dance with their waist. Ibo, they dance with their chest. And the Hausa, they dance like they are hopping.

I don't know how to dance. I'm very shy. Before I worked for the Lord, I didn't even talk to people. I just look and smile.

It was God gave me the boldness to speak and the boldness to run a church.

For this I am also thankful to America. Here a woman can be anything. In Nigeria so many men treat their women like slaves. Even if a woman is pregnant, she has to carry all the load on her head. The man will just follow and carry the hoe. At any time the husband can tell her, "Wake up. Move out." They can tell you to leave all the kids and then they pick another wife. Some men marry thirty wives, some marry twenty, some marry four. My mother was the second of eight wives. She did not know my father before the day she married him. Later she became a slave to the other wives. That's why so many Nigerian women choose the Pentecostal. The Pentecostal only marry one wife.

I come to this church in the morning and someone is waiting to talk to me. One woman came to this country after her husband lost his farm to an oil company. Now her baby has asthma. A man won the visa lottery to come here. He sold every-thing he had. After two years he cannot pay the rent or feed his family. He had nothing to go back to Nigeria with. So he jumped into the river. I am praying for the family they don't jump into the river too. Some people run for their lives to come to this country. Just now there is a civilian government in Nigeria, but when the military comes in, they dictate. Talk against them – they come in the middle of the night and kill you. Some people come here for education. Other people come for a better life. There are times coming to America can make you rich. Sometimes it makes you wretched for life. There are times, I will be listening to a church member, they call me *the prophetess*, and I think, what am I doing – how can I counsel this person? It isn't Remi that knows what to tell them. That's why I must fuel this power by reading the Bible, by fasting and praying.

REMI

You are the only Jewish people I know. I say hello, but the Jewish
people here, you can't penetrate them. They are always following
each other like snails. That's why I was surprised when you said
you were Jewish and you knew what kind of bread to buy in the
market. One or two times I went in, but I don't know what to
get. We used to have a white lady who came to services, but she
wasn't Jewish. She left after a few months. Sometimes we have
black Americans, but they are never steady. Some of our church
members look down on black Americans. And some members
don't want *any* outsiders coming to the church, but I am comfortable with whoever comes. Jesus our Savior didn't call you
by your color. Wherever you were born, whatever color
you are, you are a human being.

Tell me again – what do you call the name of that bread?

front seat brahman

We visit Sushil in the house he shares with a few other people in a suburban-esque section of Forest Hills. We talk as he prepares dinner. Whatever subject comes up in our conversation, this Hindu monk turned cab driver, poet, and now small-press publisher always manages to bring things back to matters of the spirit. Whether he's standing over a pot of simmering vegetable soup talking about boiling everything down to two funda-mental truths, or driving a customer to the airport as he ponders the difference between the road and the destination, Sushil appears to be in a nearly constant state of parable-producing awe and metaphysical inquiry. Originally from Bombay, he lived in Miami for many years before coming to Queens.

PAKISTAN

CHINA

Delhi

NEPAL

INDIA

Mumbai
(Bombay)

FOREST HILLS

YELLOWSTONE BLVD

QUEENS BLVD

BAY OF BENGAL

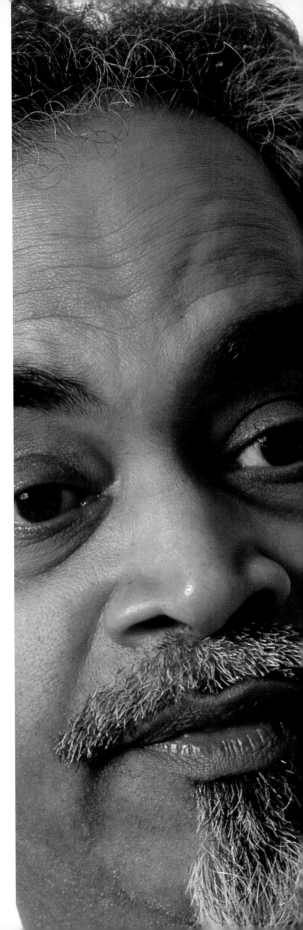

It was the mid-sixties. I was a teenager
living with my family in downtown Bombay,
disillusioned by all the urbanization going
on. Bombay is an island like Manhattan, and
it reached the point, they could only expand
vertically. In place of gardens, modern buildings were going up everywhere. I remember
thinking, if the trucking industry went down,
Bombay would die within days.

One day, I opened a copy of
Time magazine and saw all
these photographs of American hippies in blue jeans
who left the cities and went
back to the earth to become
farmers. I thought, that's
what I want to be — a hippie
farmer! I went away to agriculture college to learn how
to be a farmer, but they
made me dissect frogs in a
botany class – so I quit. Why
should a vegetarian have to
cut up little animals to learn
how to grow mangos and
spinach? So I enrolled in a
philosophy college. A year
later, my father died and I
was kind of out of control.
I quit college and became
a traveling hippie.

At nineteen, I met my spiritual teacher in North India on a bank of the Ganges river. I became a monk in an ashram in the holy city of Haradwa. For three years, I lived without money or sex or any material possessions. Those were the happiest years of my life. All I owned were two pairs of unprocessed cotton pajamas and three T-shirts. I slept on the roof of the ashram with very few blankets, and before I went to sleep I would drink a lot of water, so by three o'clock in the morning if I didn't wake from the cold, I would be forced to get up and take a leak. Once I was up, I would go down to the rose garden and meditate. My favorite job at the ashram was harvesting the roses. Everybody should get a chance at least once in their life to work in a rose orchard. If you're lucky, you can get up early just to sit still amongst the roses. Of course it's not considered a wise thing to sit in there because of the thorns and the snakes. I remember sitting there after meditating for an hour, gushing with admiration and gratitude that something in me was able to drink the beauty of the rose orchard and the smell and the feeling of privacy. Imagine you're in a corn field with fully grown corn – only it's a rose orchard – with rows and rows of red and pink and white roses spreading out for miles and miles, and right behind the orchard is a tributary of the Ganges, and there's quite a lot of mist coming off of the cold water, and maybe you hear a dog barking or the the sound of an automobile coming from somewhere far away, and the feeling you have is that this field of roses and the mist and all of nature has been created to nudge you toward God. Even the terrifying things in nature like a tiger killing a deer or a monsoon storm or the fear of a poisonous snake biting you in the darkness reminds you how awesome God's creations are.

After being alone like that for an hour or two, the sun would come up, and some of the other monks would arrive, and we'd pluck the roses together in silence. Whatever roses didn't go to market we sold to worshippers as garlands to put on the Hindu idols that dotted the city.

At first, the message of my teacher seemed obscure. I'd ask a practical question about a meditation technique, and he'd say, "Somebody can give you a really beautiful car, but if you don't have direction, you're just going to go around in circles." I'd ask something about God, and he'd say, "A human being needs to reach something that is not mundane within themselves."

After a while, I felt the presence of something inside my chest. I knew I could not reach it, but I knew it was there. That's what gave me direction. I was told it was a seed inside me and if I took care of it, one day I will get fruit. It's true what I was told.

Nine out of ten people who sit in my cab, the first thing they ask me is where I'm from. And four out of five will say, "Oh, India is a very *spiritual* country." So naturally, I steer the conversation in a direction to provoke a better understanding. I might say something like:

"How can a country be spiritual? Really, there are only a few people in India who are genuinely spiritual. Percentage-wise, I really don't think America is any lower. You can go to India and meet a dozen very insincere people and you will see terrible corruption. You can't get anything done if you don't bribe someone to do it. And you will come back and you will **never** say that India is a spiritual country. But I tell you, if you find a sincere person in India, you'll find them to be **exceptionally sincere** and very informed − not in the way Americans are informed through formal education and media about a million pieces of information − *they* will know the stories of heroic deeds and heroic people − stories that were passed down to them from individual to individual. Like how my dad talked passionately about doing civil disobediences alongside Gandhi in India's struggle for freedom, or like my grandfather's sister, who I knew as a toothless old woman, but she used to tell me stories about the characters in the Bhagavad Gita like she knew those people her whole life, or my aunt who used to talk about her husband (my father's brother), how he lived a very simple life, but never lied, and always did what he promised and commuted to work every day for an hour each way, eating only a fruit for lunch that he grew and peeled himself and was grateful for every bite.

The most popular of the ancient Hindu Vedic scriptures, the Bhagavad Gita is one of many sacred texts that Sushil refers to in the course of conversation.

No, I cannot call a country spiritual − even a holy book cannot be spiritual. I don't care if it's the Bible or the Mahabarata or…" At this point, my ride may be looking at me like I'm a heretic or something. I try to make contact with them through the rearview mirror, or if it's safe, I might half turn around and say something like:

SUSHIL

"If you came to my house thirsty for water and I started reading books to you about water, **very intelligent, Nobel Prize-winning books about water** – it won't do the trick. What you need is water. Eventually you're going to go to my neighbor and ask for water, and you're going to say, 'That guy next door, all he does is talk.'" I drop the person off at their destination, and so many times they will ask the cab company, the next time they need a ride, "Can Sushil be my driver? Make sure it's Sushil." If I was actively writing poetry, and it was a long fare, they probably heard a poem, whether they wanted to or not.

"I wrote this poem one time when I was think-ing about miracles, you know like water or wine coming out of a rock. To me, it is much more miracu-lous that I am alive! With eyes to see and fingers to touch and all the things this incredible body is capable of. Wine I can buy from a store, but I can't buy life! This is a poem to God:

what an imagination
you must have had
to envision me alive
and feeling like this

"I live on a planet that has water. Rare, incredible water.
What great luck!
In the coldness of space, we have a beautiful sun to warm us.
It's incredibly intelligent that our heat comes from the sun and not from the interior of the earth. Houses burn down when they have stoves inside them. Here we get all the advantages – the heat, the light, the vitamin D."

Sometimes a ride will ask me, if I care so much about the earth, why don't I fight against what man is doing to it? Join Greenpeace or some group like that. It's a good question – can any of us afford to focus on our spiritual life in the face of holes in the ozone? To this I might say something like: "People destroying the environment is like a man sitting on the branch of a tree and sawing it. Eventually he's going to fall. The tree won't fall, but...."

Better yet, I might say, "If my hands start choking my throat, my hands will give up before I die. Because my hands are depending on my breathing. We are human beings doing stupid things, choking ourselves, polluting ourselves, but it's going to stop. We're going to faint before we die.

"For the first five centuries of Christianity, Rome was at its peak, and England was totally barbaric. England was to Rome what India or Africa was to Europe fifty years ago – a primitive colony. A few hundred years later, England was the ruling power and other countries like America were the colonies. Now America is the ruling power, and guess what? A hundred years from now, it's all going to reverse. The oppressed are fighting back and they're getting stronger. The oppressing classes are spending all their energies oppressing. They will topple and the cycle will keep going on and on like that. I don't want to be a part of that cycle."

I'm not driving a cab these days, but when I did, I heard more talk about technology than religion. It's the new religion — technoism. I'd often throw a pebble into the conversation, see where the ripples lead. "What about the technology of pure water? The Arabs use all their petro-dollars to come up with ways to desalinate the ocean water so they can have cities in the desert. A lot of money and a lot of brain power and effort goes into that. Meanwhile, billions of gallons of water are purified for free every year by the technology of rainfall. It's an ingenious system! First the sun causes mega-amounts of dirty water to evaporate. Once it's lifted up and purified as vapor, it's delivered drop by drop as rain, stored as snow, for everybody's benefit. All the mosquitoes, the ants, the tigers, the humans, the elephants, all creatures are dependent on this technology of nature. Whenever it rains, I look at those raindrops. I see something very precious."

A young couple comes into my cab on a rainy day. They say, "Oh man, it's miserable out there." I say, "That is the water of our life." They ask me what I mean. I tell them, "You can live without food for days at a time. But water you need almost every four hours. Water is like diamonds. Our life depends on it!"

In the mirror, I see the expressions on their faces start to change. "Our bodies – 95% water. That can of Coke you have there – 99% water. The other 1% is the technology of marketing and artificial flavors. What you need is the water! Believe me, you will get tired of the Coke. One day you will thank God for the water." They're not sure if I am crazy or what.

We wake up every morning with this vacuum inside us. That's what gets us out of bed – that longing, that thirst. We think it's sex, it's money, power, youth, technology. We think it's Coke. We go for all these things and still something is unsatisfied. You're a millionaire. You have a gorgeous wife and three kids and bionic parts implanted inside you that are guaranteed to keep you alive for 150 years, and *still* you have this vacuum saying,

"Fill me.

Fill me."

But the only thing that can satisfy you is invisible. Then you experience something like Psalm 23, where you say, "My cup runneth over, my cup overflows and I feel no want."

You say, "Thank you God, it is raining! It is pouring so damn hard, I am drenched from head to toe,

and I adore you for it."

Driving a cab is the only *real* job I've ever had in this country. It's not all that different from harvesting roses. Every day before I'd go to my cab, I would meditate, so by the time I had contact with my customers I had a very spiritual feeling, and the cab became like this sacred vehicle for me. Transporting people to where they wanted to go.

Now I'm in the publishing business. But I had to drive for 15 years before I could get into it. I followed my mother to Miami after she left India. South Florida is a lot like South India – you can swim all year 'round, it's tropical,

and the mangos are even more plentiful than they are in India. There's lots of pilgrims there too – every kind of spiritual seeker you can imagine. When I wasn't driving a cab or meditating, I spent a lot of time cooking. I even developed a reputation for being a very good cook, which is silly because I'm just an ordinary cook, compared to my mother. But the people down there were bananas about my cooking. This friend of mine told a friend of his in New York about me, and one thing led to another, and before I knew it I had agreed to cook for a big party in Forest Hills, Queens.

My friend was at this party and he was boasting about what a great cook I was, but it got to be a problem because I was running about a half a day late driving up from Florida. By the time I got to the party it was already ten o'clock at night and everybody was starving. Ever since I was in the United States, I avoided New York. I come to this house in Queens, which didn't fit my picture of New York because there were trees around and little gardens, and I'm greeted by about 70 hungry people. I'm completely exhausted, but I go into the kitchen and I see there's a pile of cauliflower sitting there, and a bunch of garlic and broccoli, and I realize this whole thing about me being a great cook had somehow mutated into me being "a world-famous chef." Tired or not, I just thought, *okay, I got to do this thing.* So I got a couple of people to help. We closed the doors to the kitchen, and we cooked a nice meal which everybody enjoyed. The next morning, Alex, the guy who owns the house, says to me, "If you can cook like that, you're welcome to stay here for as long as you like."

He and I talked for a couple of days about a lot of things and then we made a deal. He had a house with an address, and good business skills (which I am sorely lacking), and I had a lot of ideas about publishing. So we started a little publishing company out of the house. That was six books and two years ago.

A two-person publishing venture, Hrdaipress Press publishes books of "devotional poetry" by ancient Sufi, Buddhist, and Hindu authors, and by Sushil Rao. Border on opposite page from Sushil's notes for a translation of a Kabir poem.

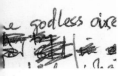

ਰ ਮੇਰੀ ਸਿਮਰਨੀ ਰਸਨਾ ਊਪਰਿ ਰਾਮੁ ॥
ਦਿ ਜੁਗਾਦਿ SUSHIL ਗਤ ਤਾ ਕੋ ਸਖ ਬਿਸਾਮ ॥ ੧॥

A friend came to visit the other day. He said after we die, we will come in front of God. I asked him, from where will we come? From behind God? From His left side? His right side? Where are we now? He can't see us? You want to be in front of God? Look in the mirror. ॥ ੨॥

six
women of
falun gong

JANET XIONG
YAN ZOU
AMY LI
ZHENMEI XU
LI LI
JING XU

A few hundred people, mostly Chinese, gather in a schoolyard park to celebrate the 10th birthday of Falun Gong. They appear as one, as they move in slow motion gestures to a recording of a hypnotic gong. Falun Gong, a.k.a. Falun Dafa, is a practice of exercises and meditation established in 1992 by a 41-year-old former government clerk, Li Hongzhi. His teachings are based on a mixture of Buddhism, Taoism, Chi Gong and other traditional Chinese beliefs and practices. He also writes about the existence of alien life, levitation, and supernormal powers. In 1995, the Chinese government gave him the Award for Achievement in the Science of the Mind and Metaphysics. In 1999, a Chinese government survey showed that 70 million people were practicing Falun Gong — more people than belonged to the Communist party. Almost overnight, the government outlawed the practice of Falun Gong. According to Amnesty International, thousands of practitioners have since been imprisoned and tortured, and hundreds executed.

Li Hongzhi lives in exile, purportedly in Queens, in secrecy and tight security. In the course of trying to have a private meeting with "Master Li," we end up getting to know six practitioners, all living in Queens. We meet them in various apartments and out in the park where they do their exercises alongside brightly-colored banners. We wonder how a government can portray the spiritual practice we observe through these women as a dangerous cult that threatens to bring down a society of over a billion people. Continued persecution has turned their belief in "forbearance" into a patient but persistent form of civil disobedience and non-violent activism.

RUSSIA

Jilin

Beijing ●

CHINA

Shanghai

Hubei

Guangzhou

INDIA   Shenzhen   TAIWAN

I'm not a person politically driven. I love the homeland from my childhood. But when you see something different from what the government has been telling you, it is a shock. I was in New York to study for an advanced degree in International Relations when June 4th, 1989 took place. What would you feel if you see on TV your own government crushing the innocent people and students? Right away we ran to the street in front of the Chinese Consulate to protest what was happening in Tiananmen Square. Everyone was crying.

When I finished my degree I had to decide whether to stay in America or go home. I wanted to go back but I realized I wouldn't fit into that society anymore. During the past ten years I've been searching to find a career that I would really enjoy. I tried many things. Foreign affairs. Real estate. Insurance. I was lost. *Spiritually.*

Janet Xiong is the coordinator of Queens Falun Gong practitioners. She says she didn't have a religion growing up in the central Chinese province of Hubei. "Communism was my religion." *She works as a legal researcher for a New York City public entity.*

A poster of Li Hongzhi on the wall of Janet's apartment. Regarding his whereabouts, and his role in the lives of practitioners, Janet says: We are told that Li Hongzhi lives in Queens, but I cannot say for certain. I've never been to his house. Sometimes when we have an Experience Sharing Conference, he will come out and answer questions. He doesn't want to be seen as a guru. If we call him Master Li or hang his picture on the wall, it's only out of respect for everything his teachings have done for us. He won't take our money, so we show our gratitude in other ways.

JANET

My husband had a serious problem with his back. Sometimes he had to lay in bed for days at a time. All the doctors told him there was nothing they could do. So he went on the Internet and found something called Falun Gong. He tried it and started getting better. At that time I was very suspicious of everything. After my husband fully recovered, I figured maybe I should give this Falun Gong a try. We started going to seminars at the YMCA on Queens Boulevard. Now a group of us go to each other's apartments to do exercises and read the book. Sometimes we go to the park. If you practice every day you discover a lot of phenomenons.

Truth

Compassion

Forbearance

We call it Human Body Science. Just imagine for five years of practice you become a very healthy person without any medication. Through the principals of Truth, Compassion, and Forbearance you begin to discover the true meaning of why you are a human being. You begin to discover the existence of different dimensions other than what we see with the naked eye. Many scientists in physics believe in four dimensions, even five and six dimensions. This is what we're trying to explore in Falun Gong. When you are sick you think, *I can take some pills to make it go away.* Falun Gong teaches you the reason you are sick is because of karma built up from the past. In this life or in past life. Once you endure the hardships from your past, the pains will be removed little by little. As long as you keep practicing, all the myths of life will be revealed in front of you. Are we the only intelligent beings in the universe? There are many Americans urging the government to release documents about aliens visiting the earth. Can we deny all those people their own experiences with aliens? Sometimes I look at ants creeping on the floor. To the ants we must seem to have superpower capabilities. We're living on the same surface but in another sense we are in different dimensions. There are still so many phenomena science can't explain. Hundreds of years ago when the microscope was not yet invented, some people told the Queen of Britain that there were viruses and bacteria smaller than insects inside our bodies and she had their heads cut off. Nobody believed such a thing was possible. Nowadays people take for granted that bacteria and viruses are facts. It tells me to keep my mind open. To study and explore what is the truth of this whole universe.

Yan Zou is an herbal doctor from Jilin province in Northern China, near the Russian border. She now lives and practices in Queens, where she told us her story of transformation.

YAN

After the surgery remove my left breast, the doctor told me the cancer already spread. Then I try to find something to tell my son and daughter. "If mom die, she will go to the beautiful place." But I don't know where is that place. I went to China to say goodbye to my family, but my sister refuse to say goodbye. Instead she introduce me to Falun Dafa. I think I'm not going to believe it because I already tried Buddhism. I already tried different Chi Gong practices and different meditations. When I try Falun Dafa meditation, I start to clean myself and I know this is for me.

Before, I drink and smoke all the time. When I got drunk I crying, crying. Talk to people about my miserable life. After I learn Falun Dafa, I quit everything. Before if my son or daughter say some bad words to me, I will turn the corner and weep. Now nobody can hurt me. My mind is very strong. My body very healthy. No cancer anywhere. Before I am just skin and the bone. Now I worry if I get too fat.

YAN

I never use ad in the newspaper telling people I am herbal doctor. All my patients spread my name mouth to mouth. First someone comes to me, I give the treatment. I spend a lot of time telling them what food is good, what food is bad. I teach them some exercises and say, "Do this every day and you don't need me anymore." If I don't see them again I know I am doing my job.

Now my sister is in jail. I send letters to her that she doesn't receive. The Chinese government pay the people to report on their neighbors. Everybody knows who is practitioner of Falun Dafa. Police catch my sister doing peaceful practice. For that she is a criminal.

Tiananmen Square has become the place of choice for Falun Gong practitioners to assert their right to practice, no matter the consequence.

First ten years in America the bad dreams follow me. Somebody knock on the door, it will shock me. I think it's Cultural Revolution again when they took my parents and my two brothers to jail and send me to work in countryside far from my own babies. After Cultural Revolution, my father told me, "Use your whole energy to go to America. That is country for freedom." When I came here in 1987, I swear never to go back to China. I only went back because I was dying. After the government crush down on Falun Dafa, I went again to tell the government Falun Dafa save my life. The policeman at Tiananmen Square ask me, "Are you a practitioner of Falun Dafa?" I say, "Yes!" At the police station they question me around three hours. Then they send me back to America. Now I am on a list that I can never go back. They search my everything. They call everybody in my phone book. One friend answer the phone. "No. I am not practice Falun Dafa." Now that guy come here. He said, "I cannot live in China anymore. They always bother me because my number is in your book."

We tell Ann her story reminds us of the anti-Communist mania of the 1950s. It's hard for her to believe that such a thing could ever happen in the United States.

JANET

When I first heard the Chinese government declare Falun Gong to be a political threat to the system, I thought, **what is the matter with these leaders? Are they stupid?** This is a simple practice that helps you to be a better person, a better citizen and employee. The first instinct is to say, okay, let's go tell them our personal experiences. That is why Falun Gong practitioners go to Tiananmen Square and the U.N. and every other place to tell the Chinese government they are wrong about us. We don't show any action, any movement or even any words that are against the government. We just exercise and read our books in silence.

One week after the July 1999 crackdown, I was arrested for doing my exercises in the park. The police interrogated me, but I didn't take them seriously. I said to the policeman, "There are other people in the same park doing Tai Chi exercises. Why don't you arrest them?" With Falun Gong exercise you move your hands up and down. With Tai Chi you move your hands side to side. "Is side to side legitimate and up and down against the law? Is this a joke?" The policeman wasn't laughing. He said, "Why don't you learn something else, like aerobics?"

Amy Li loved her job as a fashion designer and manager of a women's clothing company in Guangzhou city, but was looking for something to relieve the stress of supervising 17 employees while raising a young daughter, being a good wife, and having very demanding relatives. She attained the relief she was looking for after a neighbor lent her a copy of the Zhuan Falun book. A few years later she faced a whole new set of challenges.

Gathering at a park in Flushing on the 10th anniversary of Falun Gong

AMY

My husband had a Master's degree in law and I started reading his books on Chinese law very carefully. I began writing letters to the government appealing my arrest, telling them what Falun Gong is all about and reminding them that Articles 36, 37, and 38 of the Chinese Constitution guarantees the right to practice freedom of religion. The letters were not responded to, except I noticed I was being followed. I went to the nearest Appeals Office which was located right in Guangzhou City. Upon arriving there I was arrested. With two arrest charges to my name I went to the Beijing Appeals Office and was arrested a third time by a random police stop. On that day they were approaching every pedestrian in Beijing questioning them if they are a practitioner of Falun Gong. I answered yes, so they threw me in the police van and started beating me, asking me to give them other names. They beat me again at the police station until I nearly fainted. In three days they arrested 3,000 people. I overheard one of the policemen complain that he hadn't had a chance to sleep in three days. Many of the policemen didn't know what to do. They were simply following orders which were changing day to day.

Traditionally, when the Chinese government decides to repress and persecute a particular group, within a short period of time, that group will disappear or acquiesce to the pressure. With Falun Gong, this did not happen. They arrested us, but we still appeared. The government had never seen a situation like this.

For eleven days they tortured me at the police station.
"Who taught you the practice of Falun Gong?
...What is the whereabouts of this person?"
They used all kinds of devices to try to get me to speak. They deprived me of daily necessities including toilet paper and underwear and pads for menstrual flows. They were furious that I refused even to tell them my own name. If I told them they would search my home and fine my family with a heavy punishment. Eventually they found my personal information and transferred me into the custody of a detention center in Guangzhou. Still I refused to answer their questions so they brought my husband and my daughter and my parents into the detention center to use them as a kind of sentimental torture. They got my husband and daughter to cry and beg me to give over the names and addresses that the police were asking for. If only I did that, they would release me.

The manipulation of my family was even more severe a torture than the physical beatings. Still, I didn't give any of the information they wanted. I simply forebeared it. When I was finally released from the detention center, they sent me to brainwash class to have my brain washed. For fifteen days they kept me in a six-meter room with other Falun Gong practitioners. They forced us to take hallucination drugs. Then they let my little girl into the room. They took her away screaming and crying so everyone could see what could happen to their families. They forced us to watch videotapes that defame Falun Gong. I asked to see a lawyer. They said, "No, you don't have the right." So I went on a hunger strike for five days. They said, "Sign this paper saying you will never practice Falun Gong or we'll have to send you to a labor camp." My husband's work unit put up a bond for me on their guarantee that I won't practice Falun Gong anymore. Of course I still practiced Falun Gong so my husband's work unit put pressure on him to divorce me. One night he was taken to the police station and interrogated for six hours. Upon such unbearable mental torture, my husband had no other choice but to divorce me.

Zhenmei Xu came here from Beijing in 1986. She always tries her best to make the weekly protest in front of the Chinese Consulate in Manhattan. We first met Zhenmei after a demonstration in front of the Waldorf-Astoria where the annual meeting of the World Economic Forum was being held.

After her divorce, Amy moved to an apartment that would be a studio/home for her and her daughter. As soon as she moved in, the police came to tell her she wasn't welcome. They shut off her water and electricity.

There was one policeman who hadn't yet lost his soul. He was kindhearted enough to warn me: "Go away as far as you can or in a couple of days you'll be living in a labor camp." I knew then I had to leave. My apartment was on the fifth floor. I couldn't use the front door because my place was being watched at all times, so I prepared a thick rope long enough to escape out the window in the middle of the night. I sent my daughter to stay with my mother, without telling either of them my plans. If they knew, they would have to report it. If they didn't report it, they would be breaking the law.

I escaped my apartment at four o'clock in the morning. All I had was a tiny backpack with some underwear and a few photos. Nothing related to Falun Gong. My experiences at the airports were very eventful. I don't want to recall them. I am only glad that I made it to a place where I can do my spiritual practice without hiding or shame.

Amy's ability to contact her daughter and family is extremely limited, yet she remains determined to reunite with her daughter sometime in the near future. For now, she is part of the extended family of exiled Falun Gong practitioners. In China she designed women's clothes in a modern style. In New York she's got a job designing men's sportswear with cartoon character patches. It's not her dream job, but at least it's in her field.

All of us stood outside the meeting of World Economic Forum. We don't protest. We just practice and hold a banner that says Falun Dafa. So many groups tried to get a permit to protest, but they were not allowed. We usually get a permit because the police are very relaxed with us. They always say, "You are very peaceful group. You never make problems."

I am a U.S. citizen now, but my face is still Chinese. If I go to China I would be in danger just sitting on a park bench reading Falun Gong book or sitting naturally with my legs crossed one on top of the other. Even if a white American would go there and sit with legs crossed, the police will be demanding answers. If they are not satisfied with your answers they will throw you in jail. That's if they let you in the country in the first place.

I went with my fifteen-year-old son to China to visit my father, who was very ill. Customs stopped me at the Beijing airport because my name is on a list from being at Tiananmen Square for the Chinese New Year in 2000. They put me in detention overnight and let my son go by himself. Because of this experience, my son refuses to ever go back to China.

Not a swastika!

Surrounded by four rotating yin/yang symbols, the ancient Buddhist "wan" sits at the center of Li Hongzhi's "Falun emblem," which represents a continually revolving, multi-dimensional universe.

The wan symbol itself represents Buddha consciousness and good luck. Adolf Hitler flopped the symbol, perverting its use and meaning for his own twisted ends.

*Li Li and her husband had a successful
textile import-export business in the city
of Shenzhen in Mainland China. She
became a Falun Gong practitioner in 1996.*

L I   *translated from Mandarin*

I know there are many people come to this country to become rich.
      But I was successful in my country already.
          My husband and I had several houses in China.
      We had two cars and a house attendant to help us with the chores.
   My daughter was receiving a wonderful education.
If I gave up my belief in Falun Gong we could still have all that life success.

          Now we have a small apartment in Elmhurst and,
      well, I don't want to make deeper comments about the life here.
I don't yet know this culture, but I am
            free
      and that's what's important.

Translated from Mandarin, Jing Xu describes the life of a banished citizen, who for years tried everything she could to reenter her country.

December 1999. After I participate in Falun Dafa conference in Hong Kong, I snuck back into China and was arrested. My name was already on the blacklist. The police searched my bags and then stamped CANCEL on my passport. The policeman was very kind to me. After he released me, I tried many other ways to get back into China. I tried through Japan. Through Pakistan. No matter how I tried I was denied by my own country. I ended up living as a homeless person in Thailand, where I had no friends or relatives and no clothes even to change. I can still remember watching some doves eating pieces of bread on the ground and my mouth watering from hunger. During the days I would look for other suffering people to let them know how beneficial Falun Dafa could be. At night I was squatting on a second floor above a store that made bean curds. The room was so cramped and so hot. When I practice Falun Dafa I was able to cool down the room. The boss of the bean curd store was very nice to me. He would come up to give me food and say, "How come your room is so cool when the rest of the place is boiling hot?" I told him it's because I'm practicing my faith.

Jing Xu's cancelled passport

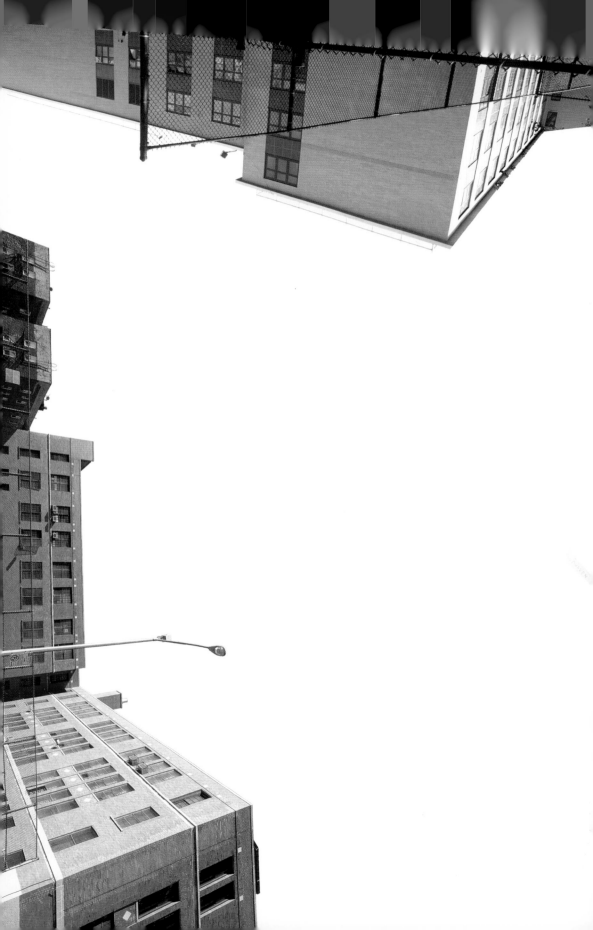

AMAREL COLLYMORE
ELKE WALCHER

teachers of import

In 1997, due to a severe teacher shortage, the New York City Board of Education began recruiting teachers from Austria, where there was an overabundance of qualified science and math teachers. What began as a modest program with 31 science and math teachers from Austria soon expanded to a multi-national recruitment program focusing on college graduates from Germany, Sweden, Canada, and Spain. By 2000, the recruitment program expanded to Barbados, Jamaica, Trinidad, and Tobago.

Amarel Collymore is an English teacher from Barbados. She came to New York with decades of teaching experience to join the teaching staff at a Middle School in Ozone Park. Elke Walcher is from Austria and teaches science. She began her teaching career at the Queens Vocational High School.

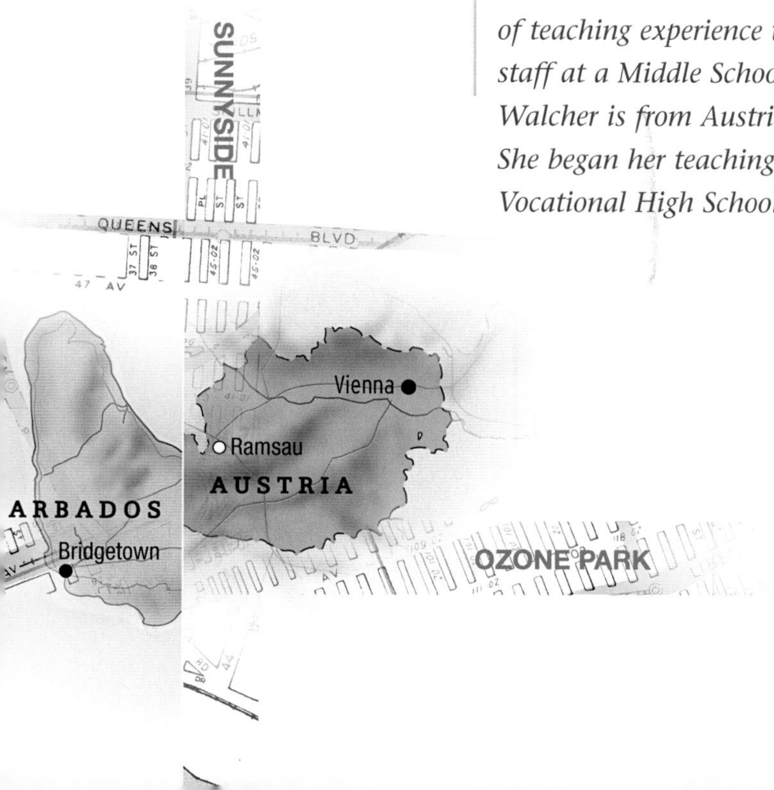

SUNNYSIDE

QUEENS   BLVD

47 AV

Vienna

Ramsau

AUSTRIA

ARBADOS

Bridgetown

OZONE PARK

We meet Amarel during the last few periods of a school day at the Middle School where she teaches in Ozone Park. Built for a capacity of 1,200 students, the school currently enrolls 1,650. By the time we make it through security, it's a period change. Amarel leads us through the mint-green hallways densely packed with young teens en route to their next class. We find an empty classroom with peach-colored walls, filled with evidence of student projects. Our conversation is marked by a neverending succession of bells, alarms, barely audible announcements, and loud hallway activity. While we find it hard to concentrate, Amarel appears completely unfazed by the noise.

Congratulation

Dear Scholar/Teacher

AMAREL

I started teaching here September 3rd [2001]. The first day I got myself in the wrong stairwell and got caught in the rush during a period change. The sheer urgency of the movement made me think I could be trampled. In Barbados the kids move in an orderly fashion. These children just burst out of the class into the halls talking and being themselves. They have only four minutes to change from one class to another. Now I know the best thing is to stand at the door of your room to supervise the movement. Except if you're what they call a "travel-ing teacher," you have to move all your materials from room to room. The only benefit of that, you get aerobic exercise running from floor to floor in time to put your lesson on the board before the students get there.

n your recent receipt of a New York City ped

In Barbados, if a student acts up, they get put out the door right away. When I first started teaching here I thought the kids were raging all the time. Then I figured out it's just normal for them to curse and swear. Back home you save your swear words for special occasions.

September 5th, there's a rap on my door. I open it and see these big, tough-looking guys looking down at me. Eighth-graders. All my 32 years of teaching I've had kids bigger than me. But these guys were giving me this menacing look. I looked up at them and said, "You know something? The three of you look just like my three sons!" Well that just melted them.

"You have three sons?"

"Yes. And they're all older than you, and I love them to death."

There were times that first week I was tempted to pack up and go home.

Week Two. September 11th. The first period, I'm having a class of seventh-graders write compositions introducing themselves to me. I'm starting to break through to the kids, but I'm still intimidated by the building and all the different accents and all the paperwork I have to do and don't yet understand. Second period, I go to the teacher's lounge and the principal comes on the loudspeaker. **"A plane just crashed into one of the World Trade Towers."** The guidance counselors got busy trying to reach the parents who

AMAREL

worked downtown by the Towers. The teachers got busy trying to keep the kids calm. I was doing that, but in my mind I was thinking about my brother who worked for the Transit Authority close to the World Trade Towers, but I wasn't sure exactly where his office was. I kept pushing him out of my mind. My job was to focus on the kids. Some of them were break-ing down. Third period, I go back to the teacher's lounge and the TV is on. As I walk in I see the second plane hit the other tower. That was around 9 A.M. As I stood there watching the replays, I began feeling scared. I tried calling my brother but nothing would go through. How was I going to get home if the buses weren't running? The newness of everything made it worse. Why was I in America at this time when I could be in beautiful Barbados, where I walk on the beach every day and I have a comfortable job as Dean of a very good school and I have a wonderful family and friends? What is wrong with me? I saw an advertisement in the newspaper saying New York recruiters were coming to Barbados to look for teachers. Instead of passing over it like anyone in my position would ordinarily do, I went for an interview. When I told my friends, they said I was crazy. We see all these shows about New York schoolchildren having no respect for their elders and doing whatever they please. "Why would you want to put yourself through that, Amarel?" Suddenly I was thinking they were right.

The next few months were very scary with all the anthrax and the media getting me more and more depressed. There were many times I thought I might go back home, like so many other people from the International Teacher's Program. I can't remember when I changed my mind, but I don't think about going back anymore.

Whenever I get a new class, I know it's just a matter of time before I break them. By break them I mean get them to understand that I care about them. It happened here around Christmastime. I told my homeroom class,
                    "When I went to school we didn't have busses.
                    We walked to school."
"You mean two blocks?"
                        "More like three miles. An hour and a half each way.
                        But it was fun because everybody was doing it."
I tell them what it was like growing up in a large family with a mother who was Panamanian and a father who gave all of us unusual names.

AMAREL

"My father always dreamed of being a teacher himself, but his father died when he was ten years old. Being the oldest he had to leave school and start working to support the family. That's why he was so focused on mak– ing sure we got an education. He prevented us from speaking Bajun around the house. If we said something like, 'Gimme da book,' he would make us say it again in English. Barbados was an English colony for a long time and Bajun is the Barbadian dialect that is predominantly spoken by people of African descent. And Barbados is predominantly comprised of people of African descent. Bajun is a mixture of African dialects and English. If I say to you, 'Give me a scotch, dere.' What would you do?"
"Give you a drink."

"Right. But in Barbados, we would be asking you to move over and give me a part of your seat."

Once the students have some information on my background, it's amazing how much they share about their own experiences. Soon they're writing compositions about being in foster care and coming to this country when they were small. Little by little they're building up their vocabularies.

Even the roughest kids, deep inside, are good people. When the boys get mad and start acting out, I say, "A handsome face like that and you're misbehaving." They break out in a smile. You can't smile and be angry at the same time. My feelings about the Board of Ed are another matter. They never held their promise to find us places to live. And they said

ther quickly to American life. they would finance a second Master's degree, and it turned out that was only true if you taught in a school that is *under review.* They fingerprint you and examine every hair on your head like you're some kind of criminal. But the thing is – I've gotten accustomed to these kids. *I really have.* The Lord brought me here for something. I'm not yet sure what it is. I know now if I had to, I could teach anywhere. But I'd like to teach here again next year if I can. I want to see these kids get into college and then soon I want to see some signs on their door, MANAGING DIRECTOR of someplace. Knock on their office door and say, "Do you remember me?" Like I do in Barbados.

We meet Elke at the vocational high school where she's been teaching for a year and a half. Her school is also overcrowded and noisy.

ELKE

All my life I wanted to be a teacher.

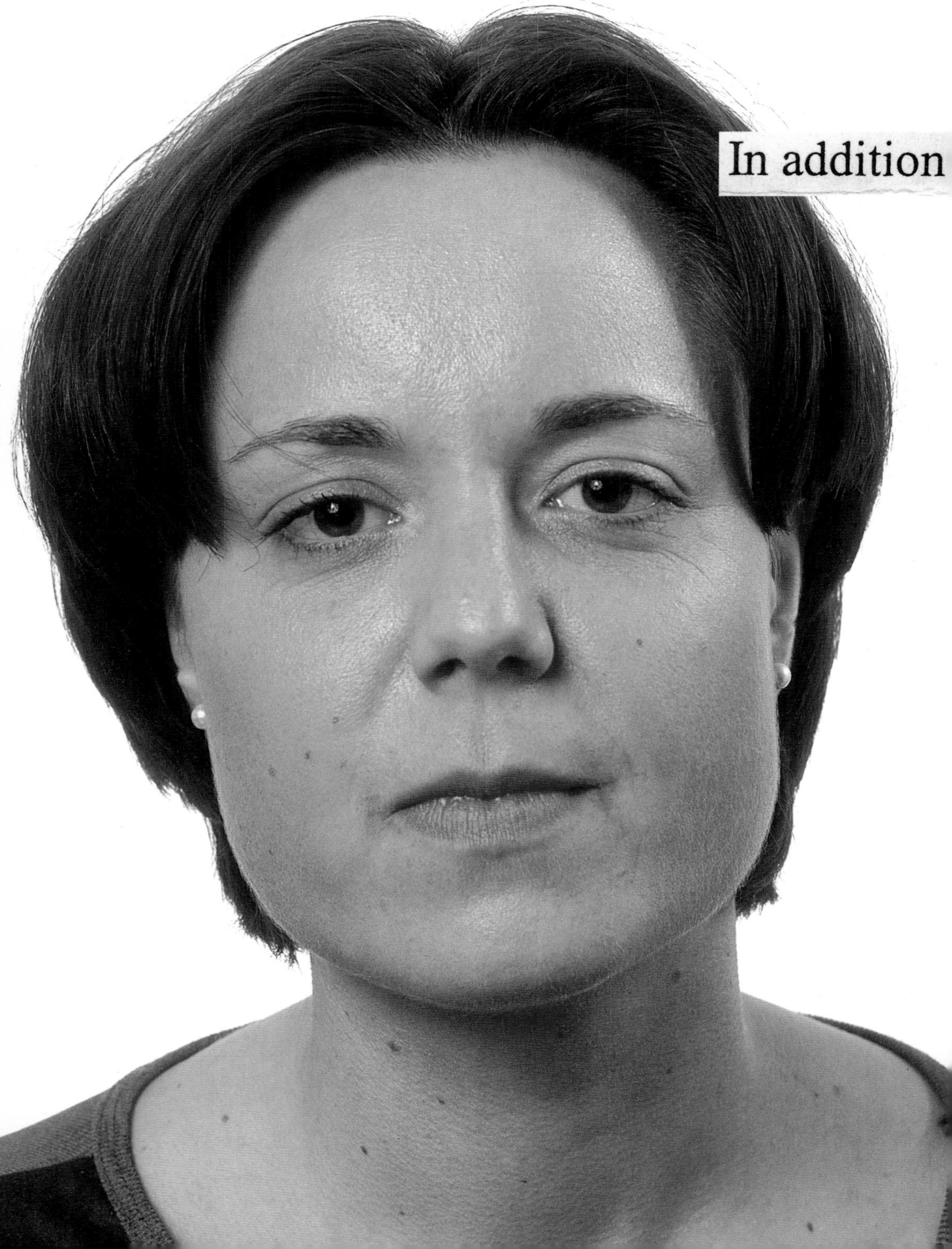

In addition

Then I finished teacher's training college and couldn't find a job. I was like, *Arrgghhh!* There are just too many academics in Austria and not enough students. That's why I wrote down the address when I saw the man on TV from the Austrian Board of Ed saying New York is offering a program to hire Austrian science and math teachers. I'm a travel person anyway, so I was instantly like, *Yes!*

bmitting licensing and employment application

When I got to New York I thought I'll never survive here. I come from a country village high up in the mountains where every second person's last name is the same as mine. I get here and everybody's a different color and nationality.

I started two years ago with 60 Austrian teachers. A lot of the guys said, "I want to teach in the Bronx. See how rough it really is." Everybody in Austria, if they hear *the Bronx,* they think a very dangerous place. Too many blacks there. It's a prejudice Europeans have against blacks any- ways. I have to admit that. The movies give the impression that all blacks are criminals and they all live in the Bronx. That's why so many men in the program thought it was a macho prize to prove they could handle it. Come back home, "Oh, I've been teaching in the Bronx."

First day teaching at Queens Vocational High School, I couldn't believe, the class was half black. I walk into the classroom and close the door. There are 36 students crammed into a very small room. Six rows of seats, six seats in each row. Most of the guys are wearing gang jackets and bandanas. They're checking me out from my toes to my head. Some of them sit with their feet up on the chairs and their head back like, "What do you want?" When they stood up, those boys were two, three heads larger than me. I was like, *Oh my God, I don't know if I can do this.* I got scared. The girls are wearing lots of make up and really long artificial fingernails. I figured, vocational school, all the girls take cosmetology. They don't have much incentive to learn science. First time I take attendance I see they don't have regular American names like James or John. They've got names like Rashida and Shaniqua.

ELKE

Faculty

Right away, they're complaining,

"MISS. THAT'S NOT

HOW YOU SAY MY NAME."

"I'm sorry, but you probably can't pronounce my name either."
I'm thinking to myself, this is the biggest mistake of my life.
This wasn't just my first class in America. This was my very first class as
a professional teacher.

commencing service,

When I told the students I'm from Austria, immediately they asked, "Oh, where the kangaroos are?" I said, "No, not Australia." Most of these kids don't have a clue about Europe. Not just the kids I have to say. Switch on the news here — it's 95% about America. I dare to criticize, but where I come from, we're very interested in the rest of the world. In school we had to learn all 50 American states by heart. Including the capitals! Ordinary everyday Austrians think they know everything about America. Like all Americans are fat, they just eat fast food, and every other woman has fake breasts and plastic surgery. And of course, all blacks are criminals.

eager to make this a smooth and comf

Out of the 60 Austrian teachers, 12 to 15 usually go back home after the first few weeks. Some of them can't adjust. Some of them don't have enough English language skills, and you know, words are the only power you have in the classroom. I'm not sure what I did, but there was a moment during the first semester when the ice broke. I might have said something very honest, or I let my guard down, and all of a sudden I felt comfortable in the classroom. From that point on, there was a connection between the kids and me. Still, there's a line I had to find between being myself and being a figure of authority. If you're older that border is there automatically. Here is the teacher. Here is the student. That's why I insist they call me by my last name. The other obstacle I had to overcome — I'm a biology teacher, but the school assigned me earth science. The first semester I had to study every single night for three hours preparing for the next day's lesson. I'm glad they didn't give me physics or chemistry. Earth science, at least the kids already know something about volcanoes and earthquakes. To teach them the theory of relativity or mitosis — that's a bigger challenge. Astronomy they love. Anything to do with rocks they hate. They hate

120 120

Lehramtsprüfung für Hauptschulen

ELKE

geologic time scales. They always ask, "Miss Walcher, when is it finally over?"
But black holes, exploding nebulae, they can't get enough of. In the city you
don't see too many stars, so I show them movies about stars. Most everything
else, they don't see the point. They do the work because I ask them to do it.
Science is not their favorite subject, especially at a vocational school. I see
myself as one-third psychologist, one-third parent substitute, and one-third

ly appointed staff also must complete a "Ne

teacher. I might be giving a lesson on plate tectonics or oceanography, but
I'm also trying to figure out why the girl in the back row has so much anger
and aggression inside her. I end the lesson a little early so I can talk to her.

A lot the girls with the long fingernails are actually in plumbing and electrician
programs. I asked them how they do that work with long fingernails. "No,
Miss. It's no problem." The shop teachers say, "You should see them at work.
They're very good." I think if they take off their fingernails they feel like a
part of them is missing. It's a very American thing — nails. I live in a blue col-

able transition for you. lar neighborhood and every
other corner there's a nail
studio. Life is more money-oriented here and so fast pace. Just
to survive and have nice things, both parents have to work. By
the time they come home in the evening they want to be left
alone. If the kids don't get that new pair of jeans or $200
sneakers, they're depressed. I ask myself where the heck do
they get the money? The kids in computer tech, the day they
graduate they get jobs for more money than their teachers.

Teaching is a calling. If you do it just for the money you won't
last. Especially in New York. Some of the teachers look at me like
I'm nuts whenever I talk with my great enthusiasm for teaching.
You do have to be a little insane to be a teacher. All the good teachers are
going out for jobs in the suburbs. They want to stay in their profession, but
they can't take the low pay. If the city doesn't figure something out, they
will lose all their good teachers. Add to that so many teachers are planning
to retire. What's the Board of Ed going to do? They can't keep recruiting
Austrians! At one point we're going back home. They need to find a long-
term solution so the kids of this city can get a decent education. Otherwise
you'll have a stupid population. And you know how fast that circle goes.

our regular appointment to a position in the New

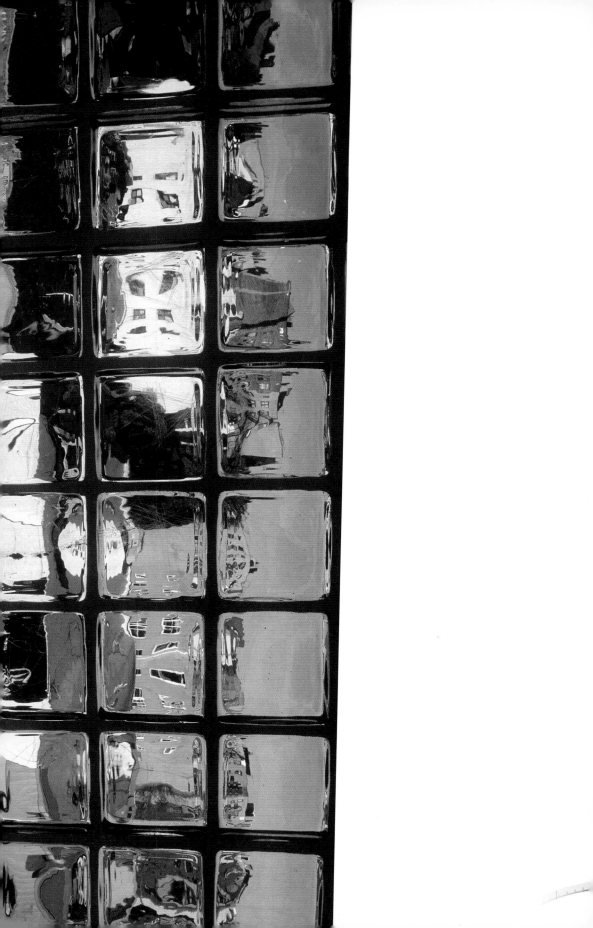

ten deities in a suitcase

New Year's Eve. We're attending a program of traditional and contemporary Nepalese music and dance at a newly-built Hindu temple with a few friends from Bhutan. The temple has a mall-like quality, with clean architectural lines, cushioned movie-theater seats, and that new building smell. One of the performers, Prajwal Ratna Vajracharya, a master of an ancient Tantric Buddhist dance tradition, performs a dance of a wrathful but compassionate deity. We don't understand all the symbolism in the dance, but we're moved by this incredibly focused and commanding performer. We introduce ourselves. It turns out, Prajwal [which is Sanskrit for "framer of light"] is living a few blocks from us. His room is so small he has to rehearse by means of visualization. Charged by his father to pass on the knowledge, Prajwal is a roaming ambassador of Charya Buddhist dance. He teaches, performs, travels a lot, and considers his work a devotional calling, not an entertainment. We find him charming and mercurial. His demeanor alternates between being wistful, passionate, and matter-of-fact.

CHINA

TIBET

NEPAL

Kathmandu   BHUTAN

ROOSEVELT

INDIA

There are one hundred gods and goddesses in Charya Buddhist dance tradition, but I only bring ten here. Ten different costumes. And the masks, and every small bell and string of beads I need because if one is missing, it is not right for the dance. Most people think being a dancer is just a lot of fun, going here and there. Wherever I go I have to carry 60 kilograms of stuff. I used to travel with three big bags, but the airlines made me pay an extra $150. Now I take one very huge suitcase with everything in it. When I put on a

According to Prajwal, Vajra Yogini is the super-highest deity in the female aspect. She is more gentle than most gods or goddesses, healing through emptiness or nakedness of mind.

costume, it's not me anymore. You see me dancing, like the other night at the temple, it's not me dancing. It's the movement of the god or goddess that is dancing with my body.

The first time I toured out of my country, I went to Hong Kong with my father. It was the first time I see the modern way of living. I go in front of a door — it opens. I couldn't believe it. More than thirty times I go back and forth to see it open and close. I never saw an elevator before either. We went into one of those glass elevators. In only one minute we're on the 30th floor. We go up and down and up and down. *This is very interesting life.* Then I tour Japan and India. Germany five times. Switzerland three times. Many different countries. The first time I came to New York I performed at Tibet House. I didn't learn anything because I have a translator with me all the time. The second time I came here I was alone. All I did was stay inside the hotel. I couldn't speak English. I didn't know my way around. I call a friend I know from Nepal who was living in New York. The lady at his office says, "Do you have an appointment?" I know this guy my whole life. "Sorry, he's busy. Call tomorrow." I call tomorrow. "Oh he's busy."

Next day I call again. "Oh sorry, he's busy."

He doesn't have two minutes to talk. Everything is busy here. The mind is busy. There is busyness all around. So I stay in the hotel room watching TV. I call the Asia Society to see if they got my videotape. Someone introduced me to the director at a party. I remember she said to me, "Oh, I'm looking forward to getting together with you." She never returns my calls. I don't want to talk to a person like that. I call my friend this time at his home in Astoria, Queens. He doesn't have time to see me. **"I come all the way to America and you can't see me."** I had to beg him for a visit. We get together at his home. He's blaming me the whole time, he's losing a hundred dollars just to visit with me. Giving me food. To see an old friend is losing. That is New York City. Friendship is loss.

In Nepal, if someone is visiting from another country, immediately I will drop what I'm doing and run there to see them.

"Oh, I'm happy to see you."
Here, everyone is too tired.

I was born the last of five sons to a very poor family in Kathmandu. We sleep all six boys in one room. When my father's books came out about Nepali dance and culture, we were no longer very poor. My father is my great master. He started teaching me how to dance when I was eight years old. When I was twelve I start to perform. For two thousand years the teaching of this dance was kept secret to just a few people. The masters used to cure themselves using these teachings. No other medicine. Then in 1957, there was a World Buddhist Conference in Kathmandu Valley and they decide to bring the dance out to the public. More than anyone, my father dedicated his life to making public this sacred dance. Move a finger with the proper gesture and your liver or your lungs will be healed. If you don't learn properly, you can do harm to the body. I saw people here in Queens doing Nepali dance they learn from video-tapes. I asked them if they know the meanings of the movements they are doing. Most of them have no idea.

Every day of his life my father was learning. Except he didn't learn that smoking gives you cancer. We told him all the time to stop smoking but he didn't listen. That's karma. He smoked two packs of cigarettes a day. He said, "I can't write if I don't smoke." He finally learned when it was too late. We knew for six months that he is going to die. We had a homeopathic doctor who gave him a very strong herb to take the pain away. No morphine. No opium.

He was totally clear. We brought him oxygen into the home. We also had an ayurvedic doctor treating him. Anything to make him happy. My father was not willing to die until his biggest book was published. He was so happy when he saw it. Thirteen hundred pages all about the stupas [temples with large eyes on the steeple] in Nepal Valley. Two weeks later he was dead. He died on the roof of our house, in the treetops with a fresh wind blowing and his family all around him. More than a thousand people came for the ceremony.

I wouldn't want to die in America. They are always trying to bring you back to life. In Nepal, if you are about to die, they take you to the fields, to the temple, lay you into the river. Now it's time to die. Then you can go to heaven. You shouldn't die in the hospital. Take you to nature to die. No more suffering. That's why I don't want to stay here too long. In Nepal, even if you get to be 80 years old, and you can't work, your family takes care of you. Here, you sit in the hospital, in the nursing home. *Oh, where's my son? Where's my daughter?* If you want to die happily, you've got to go to Nepal and make a family there.

The Buddhist principle is that you are reborning and reborning again and again until you have no more trouble with life. Then you go to heaven. Some people in Nepal say, "If you have to be reborn, be reborn as a dog in America. Or a cat." In Nepal if you're reborn as a dog, it's hell. If you're a pigeon they will treat you better. But a dog or a cat, they will kick you. There are mostly street dogs running around in Kathmandu. In America, they give you luxurious life. Stroke you all day, shampoo you, take you to dog doctor. Love you more than wife or husband. *Unconditional.*

I'm here in the United States as an ambassador of Sanskrit way of healing movement. Every day I'm serving my father's life getting this knowledge to the public. When I teach, it's a very slow process. One step, then another. Low level teaching is *get there right away.* My way of teaching is not physical. I don't say copy this movement, this way, that way. Straighten out your feet. No. I teach minimum six hours about what is the meaning of a single gesture. If your first finger meets your thumb in a circle, what is in your mind? If you see someone who is so completely poor they don't have any-thing, can you feel a blessing with your heart for that person? What position is that feeling of compassion? Can you see it in your mind? Now get it out. You must feel it inside your heart before you move. This is unusual approach for American students, to talk about compassion and harmony in dance class. When they hear we're not moving to learn the dance, they don't understand. "What do you mean we sit softly and meditate?" First time I teach in New York, seven people came. Next day only one person shows up.

Getting a regular job without the proper paper is hell. I got a job as a busboy. One day fourteen, one day sixteen hours job. Standing up the whole time, holding everything. Being a new person, they want me to carry all the heavy things. Catch the chair. Bring the table. Put it there. Okay okay. Come home, I couldn't sleep all night. When I wake up my hand stays like holding a tray. It doesn't move any other way. My feet are in so much pain. I'm thinking I'm going to die. I got $500 in tips for the week, but I had to go for medical treatment. I spent $500 to see the doctor. So I quit. This is not my life. I stay home, gather many students.

Finally, I figured out how to be happy in New York.

Expect nothing.
Have nothing.
Instead of staying in Manhattan,
I decide to live in Queens with other Nepalese.
Five people, one bedroom apartment. Just like
growing up with my brothers. Queens is won-
derful place with all Asian people living here.
Nepalis and Pakistanis and Indians. I never have to speak English
language. I can go to the store and speak Newari [the mother
language of Nepal] or Hindi or Nepalese. I sent my family some
pictures I took on the street of people in saris and Indian dress.
It's hard for them to believe this is America.

Every day I am learning something new. There is no room in my
apartment to practice dance, so I sit with earplugs and visualize my
dance. Every day I get the energy into my body, so clearly from my
inner heart to my mind, I can see every part of the dance. That is
my way of rehearsing in the present day.

Even when I go outside and people yell at me, I am happy. It is Buddhist teaching: If everybody is liking you — egoness will be there. You are too proud. But if someone doesn't like you, it makes you more sensitive. I want to understand them. Find out what it is they don't like. Even if they're wrong about me, there's truth in their dislike too. I must learn from that. New York is very good for this kind of learning.

So much space. And yet no space.

So far away. A lot like home.

So much criticism and anger.

Much knowledge.

Vajrapani is a male Bodhisattva or compassionate deity. Even though his goal is to help humanity, he takes on a wrathful appearance in order to battle temptation.

run for your life
- cargo flight to somewhere
- the lhotshampas
- behind the strip club bar
- the X-Ds
- a safety place
- out of kabul

cargo flight to somewhere

The United States has served the role of savior in World War II and in a number of humanitarian military interdictions around the world. It has also pursued its geo-political interests (oil, anti-communism, global markets) by initiating coups and supporting military dictatorships and corrupt governments in numerous countries. Ironically, when life becomes intolerable or too dangerous, many people from these countries seek refuge in the United States.

After fleeing the Democratic Republic of the Congo, Bovic Antosi became one of two hundred involuntary residents at the Wackenhut Detention Center, a privately run INS facility adjacent to JFK International Airport. Perhaps the least desirable housing project in the borough of Queens, "Wackenhut" detains its inhabitants for as little as several days and as long as several years in a state of legal and psychological purgatory.

Bovic returned to the unmarked detention center to to tell us about his search for freedom and democracy.

I am sitting on a wooden crate on a cargo flight to somewhere, I have no idea where. It is very cold in the plane and dark. I am cargo. I am secret. My angel is a Russian pilot named Melanov. The plane lands – where I honestly do not know.

By the sounds outside, I don't think there's a war going on. I'm exhausted of war. Melanov hands me a passport and visa with my picture and a made-up name. "From this point on, you are Phiri Christopher and you are from Zambia." He hands me an envelope with a ticket inside. "Go to the destination of the flight and you will be a free man." My angel was no more with me. There was nothing else to do but following his instruction. I give my boarding pass to the steward and see that I am going to JFK International Airport.

My real name is Ideda Antosi, but most people call me Bovic. I am from the Democratic Republic of the Congo, former Zaire – a place of great beauty, and also, I'm afraid, great brutality. My family is of the Yanzoni tribe from the southern province of Banunu, in the city of Kikwit, which is not a city really, with nice highways and all means of transport and banks and things like that. It's more like a town with small shops and everyone knows who you are. You can't imagine how beautiful it is there – so full of palm trees and every kind of fruit tree. In terms of fruit you don't have to suffer for anything. You just climb a tree and you're eating a banana or a mango or an orange.

I studied hydraulics and environmental engineering at the Institute of Building and Public Works in Kinshasa, which also is where I became active fighting against Mobutu dictatorship. Since I was one year old in 1965, all the way to 1997, Mobutu Sese Seko was President of Zaire. Can you imagine all your lifetime experiencing only one president? In the beginning, the population was happy with him because we were newly independent from being a Belgian colony. By the time I went to college there were many demonstrations by students expressing concern against how he rules like a king. Three times I was arrested and beaten up by soldiers for demonstrating. Not by the civilian police —

I'm talking about soldiers who are trained to fight wars against foreign enemies. The kind of people Mobutu sent to put a stop to anybody who was a member of the new opposition party — the Union for Democracy and Social Progress. If you are UDPS they will rough you up or disappear you or kill you straightaway.

After I graduated, the government offered me a job working on the water network. I never wanted to work for the Mobutu government but I did want to provide the population with drinkable water. My speciality is keeping water clean and the water system in my country was totally broken. Always, water is my focus. So I did accept the job in order to practice my profession and to support my wife and our new baby. At the same time I was working undercover for the UDPS. When anyone would be arrested, I would get information where they are being held and transmit it to the opposition leaders so they can focus on that quickly before the persons disappear. This is the double life I was leading.

By the '90s, Mobutu panicked because he was being abandoned by many people who used to support him, including C.I.A. who made him so powerful to begin with. The United States supported him because they needed someone in the center of Africa to stop the Communist movement. When the Cold War ended, Mobutu and his ministers knew their time was soon up, so they took money out of the country and paid us American dollars to build mansions for them in foreign countries.

I didn't want to participate in this kind of work, but those overseas missions were the only way I could make money to support my family. Then in '97 Mobutu impose an obligation – all men working for the government must go into military training so they could stop the coming soldiers of the rebel leader, Laurent Kabila. I did refuse to join the military.

Why should I die for a government like that?

My wife said, "You must hide, Bovic, or they will kill you."

I ran away to the neighboring country, Congo Brazzaville, and stayed there six months until I heard that Laurent Kabila took control of the government. Kabila said, "No more will anyone rule this country as a dictator." He changed the name of the country to the Democratic Republic of Congo. I thought, I can go home now to my family and my job.

When I came back to Kinshasa, I see soldiers of Kabila picking people out of their homes. I get to my house and the front door is open. Everything is turned upside down – the furniture and clothes and everywhere there is broken glass. I'm calling to my wife and daughter. I discover they are not there. Four soldiers come in the door. They search me and in my pocket they find my UDPS membership card. They were planning on arresting me for being on the side of Mobutu, and now they arrest me for being also on the side of UDPS. They say, "You are member of both of these. You are a dangerous person." They locked me up with fifty other former government work-ers. I keep praying to God,

if you can hear my prayer, please help me to be reunited with my family.

After three days I was released thanks to a friend who was working in Kabila government. I search everywhere for my wife and daughter. Where could they be on this earth? Where am I going to go? I took all the money I had and ran again to Brazzaville where there was also now a war going on.

Eight months after being appointed army chief of staff, Mobutu helped overthrow and kill Patrice Lumumba, the first Prime Minister of a decolonized Zaire. Mobutu's 30-year megalomaniacal rule included putting his own face on all paper currency.

I'm sitting at a table with some people, but I am not eating. My mind is somewhere else. For three months I am hiding in a house in Brazzaville. It was not easy to take what was happening, to the extent that my mind was with my wife and daughter or in my ransacked house or sometimes nowhere at all. The food on my plate meant nothing. I made friends with a Russian named Melanov. He asked, "What's going on with you, Bovic?" I tried to cover up, but I couldn't keep the tears from coming out. I read in the paper, Kabila declared the UDPS enemies of his revolution and is killing people just like Mobutu did. I was thinking too much and drinking alcohol too much and there was no appetite at all inside me.

One night, Melanov says, "I will help you get someplace where you can be free. How much money do you have?" I told him I have $3,000. He says he needs $2,500 to make arrangements. Two weeks later, he takes me to the airport in Brazzaville. Because of the war, there were no commercial flights, only cargo flights. That is how I became cargo. Next thing, I am on a passenger plane to JFK. Nine hours, I don't say a word. I can't sleep. I know I'm going to United States, but it means nothing to me.

The plane lands. I go to the Immigration desk and give them the passport and the ticket. They stamp the passport and tell me to go ahead. I went now to customs, and one of the custom officer says he wants to search me. "Sure," I say. He takes me to a small room. He search my bag, and that is where he discovers my documents from Zaire. "You have two different names here. Tell me, which is your true identification?" I tell him, "I'm from Zaire. I'm in trouble and I'm looking for a United Nation Commissioner for Refugees." He tells me there is a law to cover people who are in danger. I could seek asylum right there in the airport.
    I said,

"Yes, I seek asylum in the airport."

He brings me to another room in JFK Airport and handcuffs my hands together and my feet to a stool and leaves me there from three P.M. to eight o'clock the following morning. No food. No water. No sanitation. Ten or eleven other people handcuffed to stools like this. All through the night I'm crying. What is going to happen to me? In the morning, a security guard transfers us to a place where they will process our cases. I ask, "Where are we going to stay? Is it a hotel?" He says, "Yes, we are transferring you to a hotel." He takes us outside in handcuffs. Anyone looking at me will conclude – there is a man that did commit a crime. He puts us in a van, drives us into a tunnel and thereafter we take an elevator to a cage room that says INTAKE. Am I not yet in America? I know I am not in Zaire or Brazzaville. Maybe I am somewhere in between.

A guard tells me to remove all my clothes. He hands me an orange uniform. It looks no different than movies I used to watch with American criminals in orange uniform. I said, "This is not a hotel." The guard laughs, "No. This is a detention center." I ask, "What is the difference between a detention center and a jail?" He told me I'm going to discover it for myself.

I don't know if the system of American jails is that there is no window in them, but the detention center run by the Wackenhut Corporation – there are no windows in there. No access to fresh air or the sun. The only air you have is conditioned air they pipe through the cinder block and iron building. It's a system of five dormitories for men and two for women. Forty people to a dorm. That first day, they took me through so many doors that open and close electronically, and finally to a fully-bedded dormitory with all men who are there in orange uniforms. I thought, surely this is a mistake. In a field of 40 beds, one of them is mine. To my right is the desk of the security officer. To the left, three toilets. No door to give you privacy. The showers, the toilets, the telephone booths, even the prayer station... must be seen by the security official who sits with his eyes on you.

When I was a kid I had dreams of being lost in a strange place. At eight years old, my parents sent me 70 kilometers away to a Catholic boarding school. Of all my nine brothers and sisters I was the most loved of my parents – that's why they sent me away. They could barely afford the cost. It was my father really who wanted me to get a better education. Every time they brought me to the bus it was a tears separation, my mom crying, telling my dad that I was too young to go. At a very early age I learned how to live far away from my family. I learned to live in a place inside myself.

What else is in this Wackenhut universe? A ping-pong table. A TV with some chairs around. A small, maybe three-by-three square meter room that they call a library, but I have

to find another word for that room because most books people needed were not found there. There is a dining area where they give worst-quality corn flakes for breakfast, stale, and for lunch mashed potato with two slices  of bread, and for supper again the same mashed potato with two slices of bread, and if you are vegetarian, they bring also mashed potato with two slices of bread. Once per month they give you chicken. On Thanksgiving Day they come and spoil you with turkey and too much food. Imagine your stomach is already used to a system of eating small and then one day a year they bring you too much food. You cannot eat it. How can you give thanks? But you do give thanks, that all these things in your life, especially the Wackenhut food, have not yet killed you. And oh, there is a tiny courtroom on the second floor where you don't even have to go outside to get judged. And there's always the noise. A thousand times a day or night you hear the airplanes flying freely from one place to another. You never see a plane, but you feel, whenever there is a taking-off or a landing – the building shakes.

I have to explain how the telephones work. Wackenhut is a for-profit business they are making from the sorrow of detainees. It means, if when you came there you did have some money, Wackenhut is going to open up an account for you, and by the time you leave you will have no money. When you are in need of anything, for instance a phone, you have to order a telephone card. The telephone company charges Wackenhut Corporation, then Wackenhut charges you 500% over the cost.

Of all that I have been through, my time at Wackenhut prison is the darkest period in my life.

10.27.97 *In compliance with the 1996 Immigration Act, an INS officer conducts a "credible fear" interview with Bovic. He must show a credible fear of persecution or death or he'll be sent back to his country.*
11.4.97 *Bovic qualifies as having credible fear, enabling him to apply for political asylum.*
11.11.97 *Scheduling hearing with immigration judge.*

The judge says, "Where is your lawyer? I'm postponing your case for two more weeks. You have to look for a lawyer."

11.25.97 *Second scheduling hearing with judge. Still no lawyer. Hearing postponed again.*
12.6.97 *Third scheduling hearing with judge. Still no lawyer.*

The judge asks me, "You have the list of free lawyers?" I say, "Yes. I'm calling them, but they are busy." The judge gave me one more week. "Next time, with or without a lawyer, I'm going to decide about your case."

Bovic calls his brother in London who calls a lawyer friend in New York who calls another lawyer who agrees to be Bovic's lawyer for $2,500.
1.13.98 *Fourth hearing. Bovic's lawyer shows up after hearing begins. He obviously knows nothing about Bovic's case. The judge postpones the hearing again.*
1.28.98 *Fifth hearing. The judge rejects Bovic's asylum. Tells Bovic, "You have the right to appeal." Lawyer tells Bovic he will appeal.*
2.26.98 *INS officers come to deport Bovic back to the Congo.*

I beg to call my lawyer. They let me speak to him for a minute, then disconnect the phone. They handcuff me, put me in the van, back through the tunnel, back to JFK. I am boarding a plane when the guard receives a call in his radio to bring me back again to detention. My lawyer forgot to file an appeal. He says now he will file an appeal.

3.29.98 *Still no appeal filed, INS officers come a second time to deport Bovic. Bovic contacts his brother in London and finds out his wife and daughter are alive and living in Canada.*
4.13.98 *Bovic contacts the office of the United Nations Commissioner of Refugees. While he is on the phone with them, INS officers come a third time to deport him.*

They are putting me again onto the van when another INS officer comes down. "Hold on. There is a lady from the U.N. talking on his behalf." They take me back inside. "You have a file now under Torture Convention."

[The Torture Convention is an international code of law established through the United Nations, but not always honored by the U.S.] Bovic languishes in detention for 14 months with no end in sight. He and 50 other detainees begin a hunger strike.

There are many books written about international law, about freedom, about how the U.S. is superpower promoting human rights all over the world, but I tell you there is no application of those books. There is nowhere in any book saying they are to keep someone seeking asylum for more than eight months in detention, for 24 hours a day with only one hour exercise in a room with a concrete roof so you never see the sky or breathe fresh air. It is a confusion to me. Or maybe the human right is for a certain group of people, not for the other. When you are not yet legal, not part of the citizenship of this country, the human right is not bound on you. That is what I found.

Some of us decided to protest, to express our anger about being locked up with no crime even charged on our record. Maybe the best way to solve this problem is to refuse eating. There were fifty who didn't eat the first day. Thirty-five after the second day. The third day, only seven. If you make it past the third day the body is used to it and you can go further. Seven of us carried out this hunger strike for 21 days. By 19 days, I was very weak. On the 20th day, the officer in charge refuse me to meet with my new volunteer lawyer as long as I'm on the hunger strike. That made me so completely depressed that I lost my mind and was kind of foaming in the mouth, so they handcuff me and take me to Jamaica Hospital. For the first time, I see a little bit of America.

3.19.99 *Bovic's new (volunteer) lawyers make an appeal to reopen his asylum case on the grounds of ineffective legal help.*

Three lawyers came to assist me. One French interpreter and different witnesses who are experts on Zaire. The judge reopened the asylum case and said, "We are going to proceed with the claim right now." In an hour the hearing was over. The judge said, "I will have my decision after a week."

9.10.99 *Twenty days later, still no word of the judge's decision. Bovic's lawyer calls the judge to see what's happening. Later in the day, Bovic is sleeping on his cot in the dormitory.*

A guard wakes me up. "You have to go." I thought they were deporting me again. I said, "Please, can I phone my lawyer?" My lawyer says, "I spoke to the judge. You were supposed to be released eleven days ago. It was a bureaucratic mistake." I start crying. I didn't even know any person in New York. My lawyer came to pick me up. He was crying too. He couldn't believe he was setting free his first asylum case. After two years of darkness and so much artificial light, my system didn't know how to process the sun filling up my eyes. I fell down on the ground with blindness.

For two years I prayed to see the sun and to be reunited with my family. I thanked God after all these years that he did set me free. I asked him now for the one other thing — I pray every day for — *You created a man and a woman to be together. You created a man not to be separated with his family. This is three years now.* I call my wife, "As soon as I find a place to live, you and Bebe will join me." My wife isn't coming to join me. She's living with another man. It's the result of detention. She's sorry. I can come to Montreal and visit my daughter.

I'm going to thank God every day that I did meet so many friends inside that nightmare place, from Sri Lanka, Pakistan, and Santo Domingo, from all over the world. When we can't see each other, we email back and forth. I'm going to laugh now, every time I feel like crying. I'm going to laugh because there's nothing left I have to lose. I'm going to sing now even though I cannot sing very good, because there is no more rule on me that I cannot sing. A guard can't take me to the clinic like I'm a crazy person, say there's something wrong with me singing in the dormitory. I'm going to sing on my bed. I'm going to sing when I'm washing. I'm going to sing walking on the street. If I meet someone new to this country, I'm going to give them hospitality that I did not receive, welcoming the people coming. I'm going to correct more the accent of my English that I do have. I'm going to get a job in my field, and by the grace of God I will make clean the water here too. I'm going to discover America outside those cinder block walls. Discover New York. It's not yet discovered to me. I'm going to bring my daughter to live with me. I'm going to enjoy the life because I have the human right now to enjoy. I have the right now.

While Bovic awaits his U.S. engineering certification, he works as a receptionist at a youth hostel, welcoming people from all parts of the globe.

the lhotshampas

TULASI RAM GHIMIREY
YESHEY PELZOM
DEVI PRASAD LAMA

While some Queens neighborhoods are made up of one or two predominant ethnic groups, it's getting to be extremely rare. Sometimes you'll find a particular community living within a two-block area, sometimes within one or two buildings on a block, sometimes on just one or two floors in a building. Occasionally, the community is so small, they're all living in the same apartment.

Tulasi, Yeshey, and Devi are three of six Bhutanese refugees sharing a one-bedroom apartment in the densely populated, unwooded neighborhood of Woodside. They're all separated from their families, who are scattered between Nepal, India, and Bhutan. Sleeping arrangements in the apartment rotate within a 24-hour cycle and change weekly depending on shifting work schedules. Thrown together by virtue of having to flee Bhutan — after the 1985 Citizen's Act essentially outlawed the ethnic minority of Nepali-speaking Lhotshampas — these apartmentmates are all active members of the Bhutan People's Forum for Human Rights. Most never had telephones while living in Bhutan. Whenever we visit, the one cordless phone rings continuously, and is passed around like a baton in some sort of athletic event. Long-distance calls from relatives or members of their organization in Nepal mix with local calls from immigration lawyers or about job opportunities. Things can get testy in the apartment from time to time, yet, whenever possible, dinner is collaboratively cooked and eaten together, with much conversation and humor.

WOODSIDE

BROADWAY

CHINA

BHUTAN
Thimpu

INDIA

BANGLADESH

When I first got here, I'd call Nepal thinking it was daytime and really it was the middle of the night. I always got so confused. Then a salesman came into the store where I was working. He was selling watches on his arm for very cheap. I already had a watch, but I bought another one from him and now I always wear both watches. The blue one is New York and the green is Nepal. I am from Bhutan, but the only family and friends I can talk to are the ones who are living in Nepal. It's half past three in the morning there now.

I come from a small farming village between steep hills in the southern part of Bhutan near to the Indian border. You can be on the top slope of the mountain and see my village right in front of you, but it will take you four hours to get there. We are fourteen people in my family living in a few huts that my father built not far from the river. We don't require lock and key. No alarms. No televisions for people to steal. The mountains in the south are spotted with Hindu temples and rhododendrons and in the fall everything is orange because the orange trees are all in bloom. Wherever you go you will see people with oranges. In my village they even make wine from the oranges.

When I was 18 years old, I got a job teaching school children in Eastern Bhutan. I caught onto the different ethnic languages so quickly, after a few months they "promoted" me to go teach in a very remote area. I was the first person to open a school there, because the Bhutanese people, especially in remote areas don't have respect for education. If you ask the parents to send their children to school, they will say no. So I went all throughout the village with a bag full of sweets to con–vince the children to come to school. First I would bring them in the playground to play. After five, ten days they became my friends. Little by little I started teaching them. Then I started asking the parents to bring lunch for the children. Most of the parents were very happy to see what I was teaching. So I start-ed teaching parents and children together in the same room. It was grade one and two only. I entered the class in the morn-ing and the sound came, "Good morning, Sir" from voices that were lower than mine. Within two months I collected 60 stu-dents. I taught Dzongkha and English and the basics of math. I taught history and about the different customs of Bhutan and how to show respect for each tradition. After three years of teaching out there, I needed to do something else.

I came to Thimphu, the capital city and got a job working on a large papermaking project with the Ministry of Trade and Industry. After a year of working there I took a vacation to go home for the annual festival near where I grew up. This was October 1990. The hills were blazing with oranges and the people were very upset about how the government was enforcing the Citizen's Act which discriminated against the Lhotshampas. Almost everyone living in the southern part of Bhutan are Lhotshampas. If one third of the population of a country is a *minority*, you could say that the Lhotshampas are an ethnic minority, because we are from Nepalese descent. And we are mostly Hindu, unlike the rest of country who are mostly Buddhists. I don't think most Bhutanese, whether they are Buddhist or not, have anything against Lhotshampas whatsoever, except for the ruling elite, who consist of 16 men that advise the king. In 1985, those men decided the Lhot-shampas are no longer Bhutanese citizens. We are aliens according to them and we cannot practice our religion or wear our traditional clothing or even speak our language. And everywhere we go we have to show our NOC certificate [No Object Certificate] saying that we are non-citizens. It's a very famous word in Bhutan, NOC. Wherever you go, for medicine or to travel even in the inner parts of Bhutan we have to show NOC certificate. By 1990, many Lhotshampas from different villages were angry with all these things, and they got together during the annual festival and organized a peaceful demonstration at the district headquarters in the

south. I participated in this demonstration. We were thousands and thousands of men, women and children holding up protest signs and singing songs and listening to speeches demanding Citizen's Act be revoked. It was a wonderful day, really. Nothing seemed to come of it, but we were very happy that we had this rally expressing our views.

About a week later, the Royal Bhutan Army started going into villages arresting people randomly saying they participated in an illegal demonstration. They don't have prisons around there, so they shut down the schools and converted them into make-shift prisons and army barracks. The soldiers interrogate five or six people and the next day they hand over a dead body. Every day this kept happening in different villages. People were so surprised by this reaction and so scared they started fleeing the country by the hundreds.

I needed to get back to my job, but the army blocked off all transportation going in and out of the south. Everything was shut down. All the farm hands were scared to work on our family farm because my father was a known leader of "anti-government" activities and had already fled the country. We don't have enough grazing land, so we pay a friend of my father's 25 rupees a month in the village across the river to look after our bulls. So my mother asked me to help by getting our two bulls, which we use to plow the fields. I took a friend with me to get the bulls because you have to go through the jungle to get there and wild bears or tigers can attack you at any time.

The mountain is like a V, with a river at the bottom. On one slope is our village and across is the other village. We are two villages many kilometers apart but always looking at each other. By the time we got there it was late so we stayed over-night at the house of my father's friend. In the meanwhile, the army set up a temporary camp on the bank of the river and they were looking up through binoculars and they spotted right next to an orange grove there were six people in a house, the house where I was staying. The next morning they came

and arrested all six of us. They tied us together and marched
us towards the river. Along the way they rounded up ten more
people. Sixteen terrified prisoners in all.

When we got to the river, there were 150 soldiers in the jungle
and the army chief was sitting in a makeshift chair by the
bank of the river with a pistol in one hand and a bottle of
alcohol in the other. The soldiers sat us down, maybe thirty
feet from the chief. They untied one of my fellow prisoners
and sat him on a rock so he was eye to eye with the chief. One
soldier stood behind the prisoner and two others stood on
each side of him. We couldn't hear, but we saw the chief asking
lots of questions. Every time the prisoner responded the soldiers would hit him and kick him. Do you know when you
make an egg cream, the foam that you get at the top? That
kind of foam started coming from his mouth. After a while the
three soldiers picked him up and dragged him into the jungle.
For ten minutes we heard the sounds of him being beaten,
and then we didn't hear anything.

I was the next one to be interrogated. Same thing, except the
chief was standing and the soldiers on each side of me. First
question the chief asked, he pointed to an elderly man who
was one of the prisoners. "That fat old man, he is your leader?"
This was a very simple old man. A farmer probably, who only
knew how to cook and eat. "I don't know who he is." Soon as
I said, "I don't know," one of the soldiers punched me on the
mouth and broke four teeth with one punch. Dizzy, I looked
at the hand that delivered this punch. It had a ring with a
piece of metal the shape of a pyramid. Another question,
"Are you an educated person?"

      "I don't know what you mean."
  "What are you doing?"
      "I am a cowboy.
      I look after the cow."
The soldiers start hitting me with canes over my head and
on my chest and back. After that I was unconscious. They tied
my hands and my legs and apparently they dragged me under

the rope suspension bridge and put me into the river. I remember waking up totally wet and bloody. Three soldiers were guarding me. Out of the fog of my head, I heard one of the soldiers say, "He looks like my teacher." I looked up and saw the soldier was one of my teenage fourth grade students. He was a naughty fellow who liked playing volleyball more than doing his studies. I whispered to him, "Please don't say that I'm an educated person." Because educated people were their favorite targets. Soon as there was any protest against the Citizen's Act, the government officials said, "We spend all this money to educate them and now they are working against us." My student whispered to me, "I cannot open the rope on your hands right now, but I will help you any way I can since you are my teacher."

Later that night all the prisoners were taken to a house in another village. We were kept there for three days and three nights. On the third day, my former student spoke to me in his native language which no one else could understand. "Later tonight, all the prisoners will be taken out and tortured. But I will help you at that time. If anyone asks, tell them you are here to guide the army, to show the way to the different villages." He cut loose the rope on the hands of me and my friend. At one or two in the morning, another group of soldiers came. My friend and I told them, "We are your guides." It was a very critical situation at that moment. To protect ourselves while the other prisoners were taken outside and very heavily tortured. Do you scream for help? Do you try to fight them off? There was nothing we could do. When we went outside, we found some of the prisoners were hanging upside down from trees while soldiers burned chile underneath them. Others were lying on the ground without their clothes, bleeding. Later that night I overheard the officer making plans to come to my village and arrest all people who are 15 years and older. It was my job to show him the way.

We set out early the next morning. To reach my village you need to cross the same river three different times because of

how it winds through the mountain. The first cross there is
a bridge. The second and third cross there is no bridge. When
you cross, the water comes up to your thighs and it's very
slippery because of the rocks. The soldiers said they were tired
and they were working only for the government for not much
pay and they don't want to get their uniforms wet, so they
made me and my friend carry them one by one to the other
side. That's how I came to know there were 150 soldiers. They
said, "If our uniforms get wet, you will be tortured."

After walking a few more hours we reached a mountainside
where my village is fully visible, but still some distance away.
I tell the army officer, "There are two leaders in the village that
are the ones working against the king and because of them all
this disturbance is going on. Let me go to the village. I'll arrest
these troublemakers and bring them back to you. That way
everyone will know you are trying to protect the common
people." The officer looked at his exhausted soldiers and said,
"Okay. We'll meet you by the road in a few hours." I felt like a
bird released from a cage.

My friend and I took a short cut to my village and told the first
ten people we saw to alert everyone in the village that the
army may be coming. Then we took another short cut to a
small foothill where we could see the army. They were without
food or rest. After a day we saw the soldiers going back the
other way crossing the river one by one. We counted all 150
soldiers and the chief. Then we followed a little more until we
saw three army trucks come and take the soldiers away. So we
became relaxed and that night I went to my mother's house
and found out that people in the village are searching for me
because they are suspicious how do I know all these things that
the army is doing. So I went and slept in the jungle for three

days hiding from my own village. On the third night I went back to my mother and told her that I am leaving Bhutan.

When we got back onto the road going north, there was an army check post. My friend was too scared to speak to any more soldiers. So he left my hand and I went alone. I told the checkpoint soldier that I came from my job with the Ministry of Trade and then I fell sick and was one week in the hospital. He picked up the phone and called the number of my job and they told him that I do work there. After I crossed that checkpoint I crossed again to Western India, Bengal thinking how awful things had gotten in my country, and at the same time I was thinking how lucky I was that my student was there. Because of him only, I was not killed.

Tulasi demonstrates how people from different social casts have to wear the traditional Bhutanese dress called Kho. A king shows the most white cuff (tago) — starting at around the elbow. Common persons only show four fingers wide of tago. Tulasi's status allowed him to show five fingers worth of tago.

I am a Lhotshampa only by association. Actually, I am from the east. We are Nimapa Buddhists. In Bhutan there are two different kinds of Buddhism. The Nimapa is the older sect of Mahayana Buddhism and Kajupa is the later sect. I never knew the difference until they started to make it into a political thing. If you're not Kajupa, which is the sect of the ruling class in the north, then you are practically nobody. If you are Lhotshampa or Hindu, you are less than nobody. I always thought everyone was living together as one country and everything was fine. I had never been to the south or to the west or any other parts of the country. Even the college I went to — which is the only University in Bhutan — is in my home town. But my roommate was Lhotshampa and many of my friends were Lhotshampas, including the man who later became my husband. They used to tell me stories about women being forced to cut their hair short and being fined for wearing traditional Hindu wrap or speaking Nepalese. At the time I didn't take it very seriously. The Students Union of Bhutan [SUB] used to collect money to publish pamphlets for making everyone aware of what is going on in the south. I used to give five or ten rupees. Not a big amount. I didn't think I was doing anything against the government to help them out of sympathy. Even now I say I didn't do anything wrong.

One day in 1989, the principal of the college called me to his office and said, "You are not to be too friendly with the Lhotshampas. If you are going out with them, that wouldn't be good for your future. Be careful. Now you can go." I left his office not really understanding what he was saying to me. I thought maybe because I had a boyfriend from the Lhotshampa group he was giving me advice in a fatherly way. I didn't take it in a political sense. Honestly, I didn't take it very seriously at all.

A few days later they had the Durga Puja, the annual Hindu

festival at the college. They have singing and dancing and workshops using big statues of all the Hindu Gods. Everyone is invited, all the teachers and students can come whether or not you are Hindu. In the evening I was there with some of my friends and someone said that my mother was waiting for me in the dormitory. I got out from the middle of the function and I found my mother in the hallway very, very angry with me. As soon as she saw me she started screaming. I couldn't understand what she was saying. She started hitting me with a cane.
"What did I do wrong?" That's all I kept asking,
"What did I do? What's wrong?"

>She said, "Let's go home
>and I'll tell you."

>"No, I need to know
>what did I do wrong?"

>"You very well know what you are
>doing. You shouldn't be asking
>questions to me."

Then she took me by my hair and dragged me outside, hitting me with the cane and abusing me with her words — all the way to our home. Many students were looking at us, *What did Yeshey do to make her mother so upset?* Soon as we got inside the house, which is not even half a mile from the college, she locked the door of my room and started tearing the clothes off of me and beating me. I kept asking, "What is happening?" She wouldn't say.

>"What did I do to deserve this?
>I'm your daughter."

>"You are not my daughter.
>You are a shame to our family."

>"I didn't do anything to
>shame our family."

>"How dare you sit with those
>Lhotshampas. It's a shame for
>a Buddhist to sit with them."

Even though she's hitting me and pulling off all my clothes, at least I had an idea what was going on. My mistake was sitting with the Lhotshampas. I said, "I am not the only Buddhist who was sitting there."

> "Your friends' parents are not here in this community to listen to what they are doing. It's me who has to face all those shameful things that people will say about my family."

She kept hitting me for I don't know how long, and for some reason I stood there bearing it. She pulled an electric cord from the wall and was hitting me with the wire and the plug, screaming over and over, "You are such a shame. It's better that you die. Maybe I will kill you and then kill myself."

She started searching for a knife and at that moment my stepfather broke down the door and pulled my mother off of me. By that time I was blue and black with bruises all over my body. My stepfather threw a blanket to me. I wrapped myself in it and left. My mother calling after me, "Now that you have brought such shame to the family, this is no longer your home."

When I got back to the college dormitory I was very sick. I was taking aspirins for my high fever and the terrible pain in my head. That night I decided to end my life. I was taking aspirin after aspirin and then I thought, no, I shouldn't be doing such a thing, so I started drinking water. Lots and lots of water. I didn't know what I was doing, crying and thinking all kinds of things.

I survived that night and then a few days later I started taking classes again as if nothing had happened. I thought maybe my mother just got angry for a while, so on the weekend I went home. I'm the eldest of four brothers and two sisters. After my father died I was very close with my mother. If I was off for the holiday I would take over her chores, cooking and cleaning and taking care of my grandmother. I was not the type who would stay out late or give my mother reason to be mad at me.

Soon as she saw me come into the house, she started shouting, "I told you not to come back. You are not my daughter anymore!"

"She starts spitting on my face. "You are not my daughter. You shamed the family."

I start to cry, "Who told you such things? How can you forget that we were very very close just few days before and now suddenly you have changed."

"You're the one who's changed! I'm not the one." She's spitting at me. "You're the one who no longer belong to our community. You go back to the Lhotshampas, and you join them."

I ask her who told her these things. She said there was a group of boys who had come to inform her that I had joined the Lhotshampa group. Later I came to find out that the principal had sent the boys.

I tried to come back home several times after that, and every time she wouldn't let me in. To this day I have never again seen my mother or anybody else from my family.

My boyfriend and I left the University and went to live with his mother in the south of Bhutan. Of course I was scared to go there because I never spoke a word of Nepali. The only languages I knew were Tsonka, Sharshu, and English. Even though Manoj's mother and I could only speak to each other with hand language, she accepted me like her own daughter.

Soon after we got there, things in the country started getting very tense. Members of the Student Union of Bhutan and the Lhotshampa students like Manoj who participated in publishing the pamphlets were being arrested for anti-government activities. We were scared, so we went to the capital and got a court marriage certificate to protect both of us that we shouldn't be separated. A few days after we were married, we heard the army was coming to arrest Manoj. He had no other choice but to flee the country.

I was living with my new mother-in-law, learning how to speak Nepali, wondering how everything in my life had become so political. From February to July I stayed inside. After the police found out that my husband disappeared they would come to the house almost every day and interrogate me. Sometimes they would scold me for being married to a traitor. Sometimes they would talk in a very nice

No 077588

ROYAL GOVERNMENT OF BHUTAN

CITIZENSHIP IDENTITY CARD

THE HOLDER OF THIS CARD IS

A BHUTANESE CITIZEN

Yeshey's Citizen Card, certifying her religion, place of birth, marital status, etc.

way and try to convince me to go to India to bring him back. Sometimes they would threaten my mother-in-law for sending her son to join the anti-nationals and she would cry in front of the police officer.

Every night my mother-in-law and I used to peek out from the window curtains to watch the police circling our house looking to see if my husband was sneaking back to see us. Some nights we would stay like that at the curtains and fall asleep in each others' arms. Not a day passed without the police knocking on our door. After a while I learned to talk back to them. Once the army officer said, "Your future is no good." I surprised myself. I said, "Who are you to decide my future? I'll do whatever I want." I said it in a very loud voice. My mother-in-law pulled me into the bedroom, "However much you feel angry or upset, do not raise your voice to them. We are two women living alone in this house. They could do anything they want to us." That's when I broke down and started crying. She also started crying. From the living room the police officer says, "What are you two women gossiping about?" I wiped my tears and in a very polite way I told the policeman, "We are as helpless as you are. My mother-in-law is an innocent widow who misses her son. We do not know where my husband is. If you help us to bring him back to the country we would be very grateful to you." The policeman was taken aback. "Okay. If you get any news from your husband, just let us know." That is what he said and then he left.

There was an Indian peddler who knew my husband since he was a little boy. I asked him in my broken Nepalese, "Do you ever see my husband when you are in India?" Because the village where my mother-in-law lives is very near to the Indian border, and I knew my husband was somewhere over the border in India. The peddler always called me daughter-in-law because in my country they always call you by relations. He said, "I'll try to find him for you." So I gave him a letter to take to my husband, saying that I can't bear it any more without him. I'm coming to India on such and such a bus and you be on the Indian side of the border and wait for me because I don't know where I'm going and I don't speak Hindi.

In my application to travel I wrote that I was going to the capital to continue my studies. I didn't even tell my mother-in-law that I was planning on looking for Manoj. Maybe deep inside she knew, but it was such a serious condition we were in, we were afraid to speak the truth even to each other. When I left, she cried that she was happy as well as sad that I was leaving. "When the police officers come, you always did the talking. Now I'm going to be alone with them and I'm scared." I told her I was sorry and I left.

When I got to the government-run bus station it was heavily guarded by the police. I entered the bus to Thimpu. The route crosses the border into India several times before it gets to Thimpu. I was crying because I felt so guilty for leaving my mother-in-law. It was my first journey out of the country. It was my first journey to anywhere alone. I take my seat and a policeman sits down next to me. I'm already sweating, because I'm wearing a Kira [a heavy traditional Bhutanese dress] and underneath that I'm wearing a Kurta [a traditional Indian dress] that I had bought for the trip. Other than that I just had one bag and

my school certificate and my Citizen card. For three hours of wind-
ing roads through Bhutan a policeman is sitting beside me. A year
before I was a very innocent, obedient girl, and suddenly my
whole life is a political act — I'm willing to risk everything to be
together with my exiled husband. I had no idea whether my letter
ever reached him or not.

I was getting very nervous because every stop the conductor
would bang the door and shout the name of the town.

"Anybody getting off?"

You couldn't sneak off the bus without notice. As we got closer to
the first Indian checkpoint, I was thinking of changing my plans
and getting off on the Bhutanese side of the border, then sneak into
Jaigong and take an Indian bus. Before I knew it, we were already
in India and the bus stopped. I couldn't see my husband. The bus
started right away. I gave up hope. A few meters later the bus
slowed down again and stopped. Several people were getting out.
I stood up and got out with them. I never turned around to see if
the policeman was following me.

My husband was right at the door of the bus. He took my hand and
we ran together for a long while. I have no idea what the place
looked like where I got off. All I remember was being excited and
scared and the feel of my husband's hand. We ducked into a small
tea stall on a corner and there I took off my Bhutanese dress and
the shawl wrapped around my head and straightened out the
Indian dress, and then we ran some more until we caught the first
bus to Siliguri. At the time I still didn't know where we were or
where we were going. We thought maybe the police were following us, so we got off the bus and stuck out our thumbs and luckily
a petrol tanker stopped and the driver let us on.

My husband took me to his friend's relatives in Sikkim, which is a
western state of India. He said he was sorry, but he had to leave
me with them because he was working near the border with other
exiled SUB leaders, planning the first major demonstration
against the Citizen's Act in Bhutan.

When I was a very small boy, my mother died and my
father got married to another woman and ran away from
my villiage in Southern Bhutan. Soon after that, the late
King's brother, his Royal Highness, Namgyel Wamgchuk
came to my school, and the principal told him that I
have no parents now. For some reason, his Royal Highness
liked me and he wrote a letter to the principal saying he
will pay for me to be boarded at the school and during
vacation–time and in the summer, that I should come to
Thimpu and stay with him at the royal palace. That first
summer his Royal
Highness adopted
me as one of his
sons and his royal
palace became
my home.

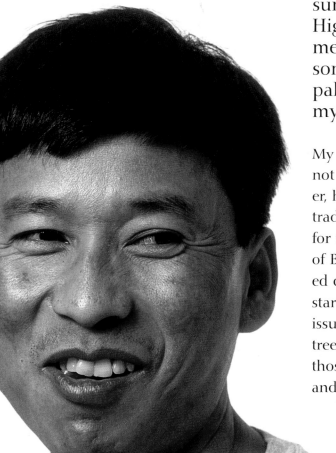

My adopted father was
not only the king's brother, he was the minister of
trade, forest, and mines
for the royal government
of Bhutan. After I graduated college, he helped me
start my own business by
issuing me 500 mature
trees in the forest. And all
those trees I sold to India
and with that money I
became a successful
businessman.

VNINDLAMA<<DEV
TD421056<6BTN6

DEVI

Really I was not a political person or in need of anything for myself. Even though I was Lhotshampa by birth, I was living in the north as part of cultural elite. It wasn't until the King died and his son came to power that the Citizen's Act was passed and treatment of Lhotshampas became an issue. My father told his nephew the King, not to go along with this Citizen's Act. My adopted father treated people very nicely himself. Not only did he adopt me but he had many Southern people around him who are Lhotshampas. But the King did not take his uncle's advice.

In 1989 I started getting letters from a few people in my home town telling me that I had to come help with democracy movement. They said, "Don't think only about your life doing good business. You have to work on behalf of your people. You have to help us because of the contacts you have with higher authority people." I didn't think anything bad can come of this, so I visited them in the south and they made me Unit Secretary of Bhutan People's Party. Firstly I told them we have to organize. We started with one representative from one village and one from another village. At the next meeting we had 25 representatives from every village and we decided to have a peaceful demonstration against the Citizen's Act. Everybody mobilized their villages and the demonstration had people marching from all over. **"WE WANT HUMAN RIGHTS. WE WANT EQUAL JUSTICE. THERE SHOULD BE DEMOCRACY. INDEPENDENT JUDICIARY."** We marched to the subdivisional office and for seven hours everyone was surrounded by the police and the army and their guns pointing at us. I was shocked they would threaten us for speaking peacefully our minds. We gave demands and then the subdivisional officer told us to go back home. With his gun he said, "Please do not come this way any more. Please, go away." Everybody

BHUTANESE
CITIZENSHIP ID
CARD NO 0222039
NAME DEVI PRASAD
LAMA
S O K PRASAD
VILL K RUNG
BLOCK H PUR
DIST S JONGKAR

SIGNATURE OF BEARER

HOTOGRAPH

Chief of Protocol

went back. But during the nighttime the police were asking around who is the leader. They want to capture him and send him to Thimpu to be sentenced to life imprisonment. I got tipped off by a friend in the government that the army was going to arrest me. He said, "Please go before the army comes." I found out later the army opened fire on another demonstration further south.

I fled to a border town in India thinking I could get refugee status there. Instead the government of Bhutan asked the government of India to do a joint operation against me, but I escaped fifteen minutes before they came to the house where I was staying.

I fled to a border town in Nepal with a high fever and not even a single note of money in my pocket. It turned out I had caught malaria. When I got better, I went to Kathmandu and worked for human rights in Bhutan, organizing with NGOs [Non-Governmental Organizations] and United Nations, collecting money to buy 1300 train tickets for Bhutanese refugees to get from India to Nepal. This has been my life ever since. I could be living as a businessman in my own country. Instead I am in a critical position, over ten years now with no status outside my country, separated from my wife and my son. I don't know whether it will be possible to bring them here or not. Sometimes I'm thinking to go back, but how can I? Every intelligence group in Bhutan and India is after me now.

I can't get a job in timber industry because everything here in United States is different. The kinds of wood are different. In Bhutan I have an elephant for bringing timber from the hilly areas and down the river and for loading

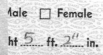

Sonamayee Printing Works, Kokrajhar.

No.

Addi

Rs.

on ac

DEVI

logs on the truck. If the log is skinny enough the elephant can take the log in his teeth. Sometimes three logs at a time. If the girth is more than 36 feet, we tie the log to a big rope and chain and the elephant pulls that. One elephants can load 30 trucks per day. They unload in the sawmill too. If you don't have elephant you have to pay 250 rupees for someone else's elephant. In America, they don't use elephant. They use Caterpillar. You know, tractors. I was an expert in using elephant but I don't know first thing about tractors. My elephant's name was Babulal. I had him from 1971 to 1990. After fifteen years of trunk-breaking work in timber, I had sell him.

There are four agencies in Jackson Heights for immigrants with no working papers. They require $10 registration fee. And then $70 in advance for the job, even if they didn't find a job for you. I told them I'm looking for a night job so in the day I can meet with my lawyer and work with human rights organization. First job he sent me to was a salesman job in clothing store – during the day. He told me you will be paid $310 a week. When I got there, the proprietor said, "No, I will only pay you $280 a week." That job was from nine to nine, six days a week. After that, the agency sent me to a deli. But I do not have experience making all kinds of food for people.

You can't complain to the agency because everyone looking for jobs there has no status. If I get asylum, I'd like to take a course to get some computer knowledge. I used to use a computer in Bhutan, but the computers here, they are completely different.

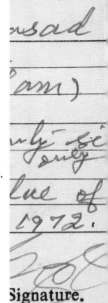

Signature.

ISIONAL OFFIC
HAM BHUTAN.

१। उत्तर
२। दक्षिण
३। पूर्व
४। पश्चिम

रेजिस्ट्री

किन्ने को
नाउ
ठिकाना

किन्ने पछि
१। नाउ
ठिकाना

२। ना
ठिकाना

मन्डल को सहि—

TULASI

Yeshey and her husband had a son in Kathmandu, where over a hundred thousand Lhotshampa Bhutanese continue to live as refugees with no legal status. Yeshey, Tulasi, and Devi came to a conference at the United Nations as representatives of the Bhutan People's Forum for Human Rights. They each applied and eventually received asylum. They all continue to work for change in Bhutan and for the chance to be reunited with their families.

I have fourteen in my family, so I have to work many hours to support everyone. When I was in Kathmandu, people made fun of me because I was always working. When I folded clothes in a church I was Christian. When I worked as an interpreter in Buddhist organization I was Buddhist. When I cleaned a Hindu temple I was Hindu. Any nonsense I can do to help my family.

I put dots on my subway map at all the places I've had jobs so far in New York. I have many dots by now. I ask my lawyer, if they catch me working without a work permit, what can they do to me? He says, they can detain me, but they cannot send me back because I am applying for asylum. Still, I'm scared to work in the daytime. At night I feel safer the INS will not come around.

I'm working right now at a magazine store selling many things, not only magazines. I sell ice cream. I sell newspapers, milkshake, egg cream. Now I know what is regular coffee, what is half and half. When I first got the job, the boss ask me, "Do you know how to make coffee and tea?" I said, "Yes, I know." In Bhutan we had just one regular tea and coffee. First night on the job, a guy came, he was so fat, I never saw such a fat person before. The guy said *"Halfandhalfregular."* He slurred it so fast I couldn't under–stand. Later that morning another fat guy came in and ordered, *"Regularcoffeesweetandlow."* I looked at my boss. He said, "Sweet and low." I didn't know what was sweet and low. I thought to make it sweet and low. So I put in a little sugar and to lower the sweet, I added water. The guy got so mad. Now I know what is Sweet 'N Low.

I never thought there were beggars or even poor people in New York. But when I reach here and I see there are those who are suffering like us, I tell you honestly it made me feel at home. Instead of crying when I feel desperate or mentally upset, I try to feel thankful.

YESHEY

The first thing I did when I came to New York was have pizza. When I was in college, I had a Canadian math teacher who used to kid me all the time. Instead of calling me by my name, Yeshey Pelsom, he would call me Yeshey Pizza. First time he said that, I said, "Sir, what is pizza?" I had no idea what pizza was. He said it was a kind of food he used to eat back home that he missed a lot. I don't really like pizza that much, but whenever I eat it, I think of him.

My son goes to a good school in Nepal, run by Jesuits. Even though I am separated from him and my husband, I think luck has favored me. That's why I have very much faith in God. Not Buddha or some man in the sky, but a superpower that guides us in need. That's what I believe.

I work in an electronic store for a very nice Nepalese man, selling cellular phones. Sometimes the customers yell and curse at me because they have problems with their service. Sometimes I go to a corner in the back and cry. Other times it can be very funny to see how upset people get over a telephone.

It is better for us to work in the United States than in Nepal. We have worked in Nepal for seven years. We have published books and articles and nothing has happened so far. If I get asylum over here I can do something for the refugees in Nepal. Most of them have sadder stories than mine. Many women have been raped and tortured and are in jails in terrible conditions. I have a hope that one day I'll be able to go back to my country and teach the women that they don't have to be so backward and subservient and they can start living a better life.

behind
the
strip club
bar

During the 1990s, the City of New York waged
a zoning war against topless bars and sex
shops, pushing many such establishments into
non-residential neighborhoods. The topless
bar where Lana Dinh works as a barmaid is
across the street from asphalt and cement
factories in a little-trafficked, sparsely populated, industrial part of Flushing. It doesn't get
nearly as many customers as the other places
she's worked, but it's only a few miles from her
home, and the owner's not a creep. A handsome
woman and now a very New York, straight-
talking character, Lana got her start behind
a bar serving G.I.s during the war in Vietnam.
Being on the losing side, soon after U.S. troops
pulled out, Lana, her Amerasian daughter, and
her sister ran for their lives and ended up in
New York. We meet with Lana at the bar where
she works, and at her house in Flushing which
she and her daughter share with Lana's boyfriend and Lana's cousin's family.

CHINA

South China Sea

HAILAND

Phu Bai

VIETNAM

FLUSHING

COMBODIA

Ho Chi Minh City
(Saigon)

If you don't have education, 17 years old, they take you in the Army. The boy. All my family was in South Vietnam army. My older brother, he fight all the time in the mountains. He really good fighter. We never see him. Another brother was a captain pilot. My father was Army too. Growing up we lived in the Army house.

Whenever we heard *whooosh* sound, we know it's bomb coming. We run outside to go under the ground. In the backyard we built big underground house. Pack a lot of dirt with our hands every night. Everybody had big underground bunker because Vietnam family not like American family. Over there we have sometimes ten person in a house. When you marry — brother, sister-in-law, grandparents — all live together one house. When I was 13-year-old, nighttime was very scary. One time, after twelve o'clock at night, something explode so loud, we feel the whole house shaken up. You don't know is it grenade thrown in rice field or a bomb from the sky. All you know, you got to do something. You hear airplane, you scream, "Come on. Let's go. Let's go." You go underground. Now I live right by the airport in Queens. When I come over here it took me a while to get used to all the planes coming so close. You don't want to remember everything. So many bodies die, they have to dig one big hole and just pile together. You know, innocent people.

When I was young, I love American soldier. They give us candy apple, bubble gum, chocolate cupcake. We don't have those things over there. I thought Americans are most beautiful person in the world! I still do. They light skin, blonde hair, blue eye. They all big and tall and good-looking. We all small people, you know, and country. They give you job, like older woman do laundry for them. They shine their shoes. At that time Vietnam very poor country. When I was 16, I start to work as bartender for Americans at the officer's club. They have a lot of clubs for the Army in Saigon. I lie about my age. Tell them I'm 18. They have couple drinks at night. I make couple of bucks.

In America we refer to the war in Vietnam as "the Vietnam War." In Vietnam, they call it "the American War." In over a decade, this undeclared war cost the lives of an estimated 444,000 North and South Vietnamese military personnel and 55,000 American G.I.'s. 587,000 Vietnamese civilians were killed and about 935,000 were wounded.

I first started going around with American G.I.s when I was 14. Every night me and my cousin used to go to the officer's club to watch Hollywood movie with them. Talk to them. We love them. See so many Elvis Presley movies with them. Oh my God, I love Elvis! Every night they show his movies. When he die, it was like a part of me die.

So many Vietnamese people don't like Americans. My father grew up with French. He speaks fluent French. He's comfortable with them. When he got old, American start to come over and he retire from Army. He blamed America made the war get worse and worse. My older brother, he hate Americans. That's why they so mad when I get pregnant.

It was by accident. When I was 17, I date my boss at the officer club. Very nice American G.I. He said he was going to marry me. But Vietnamese people very old-fashioned. You got a date, you have to ask permission from your father. Lot of headache. My parents believe you grow up, you marry your own people. Couple times I brought him to my house. My father refuse even to look at him. My boyfriend told his family about me. He wanted to take me home with him. His parents send me their pictures from America. They write, "You come to America with our son." I told him, "What am I going to do in America? I don't know anybody there." Also I was thinking what if I go to America and he dump me. Right after he left Vietnam, I found out I was pregnant. I feel so alone and scared. That was a nightmare year when I was pregnant.

People make fun of me every time I walk out of the house, calling me whore and talking all the time that I'm pregnant and so young. They know I have no husband. And to be pregnant with an American baby. *Forgetaboutit.* Oh that's a big thing. I didn't tell my parents until my stomach was too big to hide. My father know who the father is. He so pissed off, he find all the pictures of me and that guy and all our letters and burn everything. That's how much he hate Americans.

I say to myself, I can't keep my baby here. Just to walk in the street I have to keep my head down. So I went to get an abortion. I was asking other girls who date American, a safe place to go. So many women die in botched abortion. It's not like over here, you go to a clinic and they know what they're doing. The day I went to the city to get my abortion I was stopped by a soldier to show my ID. In Vietnam they give you ID on a piece of paper. Not laminated or plastic. My ID was all worn out. Where there was supposed to be a number, you couldn't see any ink at all. They thought maybe I was from the North. So they threw me in jail for the night.

When I came home, my brother, the second one, he want me to go away somewhere to hide for a while. I said, "You don't like it. That's tough shit. It's my life. My mistake. It's going to be my baby." A few months later I gave birth to a baby girl. My God, the whole town want to know the baby black or white.

This Buddha bring good luck. The outside one bring money. I believe Buddha and God are the same thing. I believe you do the right thing, you got good thing come along. You live the bad life, always got something haunt you later. Probably all the problem I go through, God gave me the most easy child.

They knew it was American but not what color. "Black or white? Black or white?" If my baby was black I got to go someplace and bow my head forever. She came out light skin, dirty blonde hair. People look at her now, they think she's Latin. My father looked at her, he didn't say nothing. He just sit there killing inside. My mother too. After she come out so beautiful and very pleasant child, they love her. Everybody love her. You want to take a bite, she so chunky and gorgeous. My parents' friends say, "I wish my daughter would go out with American, give me grandchild like that."

After I give birth, I send a picture to the baby's father in America. He never write back. He live with his parents in the Midwest and I

think the mother throw away my letter so he don't know anything. When my cousin came to United States a year later, she call his number and the mother say, "Leave him alone. He happily married now." I don't even think he knows he's got a daughter that lives in New York.

When my daughter ask me, what is she, I tell her she half. That's why her nickname is Lie — means *Mixed* in Vietnamese. Americans always ask, "Why you name your daughter Lie? She lie a lot?" She's proud of being a mix. She knows who she is. She don't care.

Over 250,000 Amerasians, born from relationships between American servicemen and Vietnamese women, live in the United States. The first wave came, like Lana's daughter, fleeing Saigon with their mothers in 1975. In 1987, the Amerasian Homecoming Act granted these children the right to migrate in acknowledgment of the widespread discrimination they suffered in Vietnam, as "children of the enemy." While life in the States is better for most Amerasians, a 1994 GAO (Government Accountability Office) study showed lingering problems assimilating. When asked how they perceived themselves, "44% of Amerasians living in the U.S. considered themselves Vietnamese; 5% said American; and 50%, 'other.'"

Soon as Americans start pulling out of our country, I cried. "Oh my God. What we do without them?" A few days before the Communists take over Saigon, a friend of mine who is a fixit man on a big ship come over my house. He say, "Come on. Gotta take all your family on the boat with me." My mom want to go but my father says, "I'm Vietnam. This my country. I'm die here." A few hours later, me, my three year old daughter, my sister, her older son and my youngest brother got on the ship. And I never seen my country again.

LANA

My pilot brother take one of the bomber airplanes and fly right out of there to Ireland. Then he came to this country. But he hate life here. All he want to do is hang around with Vietnamese people. Sing the old songs. My other brother got picked up by the Communists. He such a good fighter, he have very bad name in the North. They keep him in jail for years and years. Put some kind of poison inside him until his body rotten and die.

On the ship I got one pair of pants, one pair of underwear. An old Vietnamese woman take the tablecloth from the ship and make clothes for us. All Vietnamese on the ship wearing red and white tablecloth! For months and months I wear checkerboard clothes. You wash it by hand, you hang it up, you wear it till it worn out.

Six months in Guam I found an American Indian Merchant Marine who would sponsor us to come to United States. He on the sea all year long so we could stay in his New York City apartment. Not too many Vietnamese go to New York because everybody know it's a cold place. We don't like cold, but we we want to start our life again. I say, "We go anywhere." Our sponsor pick us up at airport and drive us to Manhattan. I say, "Oh my God, the city's so beautiful." Then he drive us up to Harlem. I say, "Oh my God, it's so scary." His apartment on a block every other house was burn down. The stores burn down. We thought America is the most beautiful place in the world. Then we live in Harlem. It look like a war happen there. You start thinking, my God, what am I doing here?

If it wasn't for my daughter I don't know what I would have done. You have pleasant children, you happy. You don't care how poor you are because you been poor already. Only thing you don't know nobody. Don't know anything here, how to get around, how to eat the food. All we know, how to cook Vietnamese food. Little bit rice in the morning with egg. Rice with vegetable at noon. Rice with fish sauce at night. Me, my daughter, my sister eat on the floor.

My daughter start growing up. She got a rough time. She don't speak English too good at first. Kids, they're always making fun of her. They say, "Vietnamese kill Americans." That time, you don't see a lot of Vietnamese people. Very rare you know. They used to beat up my daughter. We stay inside the apartment so miserable, cry. So embarrassing every time I got to go to the welfare building, I make sure nobody look at me. I just, *whooosh,* get inside. At first I thought welfare is good. Like a helping hand for you to get started. But they make you feel so dirty. You buy with food stamps, everybody look at you. You feel terrible.

I made a friend who introduce me for a job at a card shop in the Empire State Building. I was like, "I don't have any clothes to wear." My sponsor know one white guy, Jewish. Very rich. He used to like me. Oh man, he was fifty-something. I was 21. I say to him, "I have a job tomorrow but I don't have no clothes to wear." He give me 50 bucks. In 1977, that was a lot of money. I went to the 99-cent store. I buy all the clothes to go to work. When I got the job I'm so happy, like my second life again. I went straight to welfare office to report to them I don't need their help no more. I work 40 hours a week and bring home 80-something dollar. I feel, Oh I'm rich! I live by my own again.

Every year there's a Vietnamese New Year's Eve party in Queens. I went with my sister and we bump into our cousin. Ever since we came to New York we were looking for her. But there's no address, no phone number. We can't find nothing. We so happy to see her. My cousin says, "Move in with me. I live here in Queens." Ever since then I live here. Send my daughter to the same Catholic school as my cousin's three daughters.

Five years at the card store, I say, "My God, this job don't make enough money." After tax I bring home hundred dollar. Hard to live on a hundred dollar. I met a Vietnamese girl who marry to a G.I. She always had a hot life in the bars, you know what I mean? She done everything in Vietnam. She a money woman. When she come here, she work for a strip bar, dancing. She said, "Come on, let's hang out." She took me to where she worked. I said, "*Whooo.* I never seen so much money. Money flying everywhere! Even the bartender make so much money." My friend said, "You can too." I think to myself, it's time to do something wild and crazy.

I went to bartender school and started working nights at a strip bar two blocks from the World Trade Center. My friend say, "Why don't you dance?" I say, "Nuh uh. I'm too skinny." Back then I weighed about 80 pounds. I was so stressed out, I looked old. I look younger now. Nobody would've wanted to see me naked. As bartender, all I had to do was show my legs, wear a one piece bathing suit and high heels. Man, I couldn't believe how much money I was making. American guy not used to seeing Vietnamese girl. I tell you when I just start out, I love it. So many good-looking guys. To me, that was heaven. Lot of girls say, "Oh my God, how can you work in a place like that? All these terrible guys!" I say, "Yeah, like your husband or your boyfriend." It's not just homely guys either. I thought I'd never get tired of seeing a roomful of men. Now it's nothing to me. Except I like the one on one. That's how you make money too. Bartenders are like shrinks to a man in a bar. They got a problem — they want someone they can talk to. Married problems, girlfriend problems, job problems, punk-low-life problems. I could write a book called:

Make a ton of money.

A lot of the strippers play with men's heads. Some guys fall in love with the girl. Night after night they come back spending all their money. They don't give 20, 30 dollars. They shower them with hundreds and they don't get nothing. The guy thinks she understands him. All she understand is the guy's throwing money at her. At the end of the night the girl's boyfriend comes to pick her up. If she give the guy a number, it's usually phony. I seen a couple guys destroy their business. Fall for the illusion. Spend all their money.

After the World Trade Center bombed, I thought business going to be dead. So many people lose their job. Instead alcohol consumption up 75%. People lost their job — they go out drinking! One guy, he comes almost every night. I wonder, what the hell you doing here? You spend $50 a night, when you don't have a job.

The bar I work in Queens — it's an old-fashioned place. My boss don't allow lapdance, no prostitution. A guy wants to give a girl money, he has to reach over the counter. My boss don't want to go to jail. Don't want no headache. He an old-fashioned guy.

My boyfriend is cool with my job. He a modern American guy, 13 years younger than me. I never attract to Oriental men. In Vietnam, man beat the shit out of you. All you do is stay home, take care of house. Except my mom. She always the boss. She learned to read and write by sneaking into school. Go under the desk and listen to the teacher teach the boys. I don't know what it's like now. I know things change a lot. When my sister say, "Lana, let's go over to Vietnam." I don't want to hear that. I stay here 27 year now. I American now.

My neighbors, I always say hi to, but that's it. Used to be Italians and Irish live around here. Never had any problems with them. Now it's all Chinese or Korean moving in. They take over the place! Americans love to sell to them because they pay cash. Beats me how they got so much money. Honestly, I like more American. They say home sweet home. Chinese and Korean, the way they put the gate on and the steel doors look like jailhouse. They don't believe in take care of the house, fix up neighborhood. The house is just a place they leave in the morning, come home at night. In between make money, gamble, enjoy themself.

I still can't believe the World Trade Center not there no more. That so scary man. You live here, you say, "This can't happen in New York City. This is America. Everybody got good life over here." You can't help but wonder what's going to happen next. In the summertime the airplanes come especially close to my house. Sometimes at night, I see the light from a plane. It so loud. You think wild thoughts. Like the plane going to land right through the room.

the
X-Ds

NINOTCHKA ROSCA
RAMON MAPPALA
IRA SOMBILLO
ANA MARIA ASUNCION

JACKSON HEIGHTS

NORTHERN BLVD

73-02

Manila ●

Philippine Sea

PHILIPPINES

ROOSEVELT AV

SIA
DONESIA

Three Filipino-American friends are having dinner in a co-op apartment in a pre-war building in Jackson Heights. Ramon Mappala helped his friend, the well-known writer Ninotchka Rosca, find the spacious one-bedroom apartment several years ago. As a real estate broker for the past 16 years, Ramon has helped many Filipinos find homes in the Jackson Heights area. Ira (Isabelita) Sombillo, a union organizer for home health-care workers, has been living at Ninotchka's place for the past few years. She waters the plants and feeds the dog when Ninotchka's out of town. These three X-Ds, as they refer to themselves [X as in used to be, D as in detainees], were all imprisoned for their opposition to the Marcos regime during the 1970s and '80s. They are part of a worldwide "family" of 10,000 Filipinos who sued Marcos for human rights violations.

Ninotchka's dog Adobo is barking in the bedroom. The door is closed, but there's no stopping the smell of Ira's incredible chicken and pork guapo cooked with garlic, pepper, bay leaves, and vinegar. The three friends are talking about books and movies and politics, gossiping about old friends, reminiscing about the good old/bad old days back in the Philippines — and wondering aloud how it is American troops are back in their mother country. Here are some of their stories, as well as the story of Ana Maria Asuncion, who received help from Ninotchka and the Gabriela Network, after she was sexually assaulted by her immigration lawyer.

We have a saying in the Philippines. "To win the elections you've got have three Gs. Gold, Goons, and Guns." You pay, you get people terrorized, or you kill people. In the beginning of our little democracy, we had a system patterned after the United States. We had a president who had to run for office every four years, we had a congress with an upper house and lower house, and mayors and governors, and so on. And there were guarantees in the constitution for freedom of expression, freedom of assembly, freedom of the press, all the rights. We never reelected a president before Marcos. EVER! We can't stand our presidents after four years. They're so corrupt.

Ninotchka Rosca became a journalist in the late 1960s in Manila. At twelve years of age, her essay was published in the Manila Times. *She continued winning writing prizes and by 1968 Ninotchka was a full-time journalist and managing editor of a magazine called the* Graphic.

Ferdinand Marcos became President of the Philippines in 1964 and in '68 he ran again. Ninotchka covered the Presidential Palace from '68–'71. In '72, she was assigned to cover Marcos' second reelection campaign.

I'm covering Marcos' second campaign, and I see all these photographers and press people taking envelopes out of their pockets. I say kind of innocently to one of my colleagues, "What are those?" She says, "Didn't you go to the press room?" I say, "No." I was the only one without an envelope. They were all being bribed for good coverage. The public funds were literally flowing out of the Presidential Palace.

I was one of only four or five journalists who really had a following in the Philippines at that time. Everything Marcos did, I wrote about. I wasn't afraid of being outspoken. That was my problem. When you are like that, you walk into trouble.

About a month before the presidential elections, I was supposed to go to Albania to do a story for Reuters and the A.P. The night before I was supposed to leave,

I had a going away party for myself. Around one o'clock in the morning I thought, *Something is happening, something is wrong.* I went out to my balcony. I looked at the guy who was my companion at the time and said, "Something is happening right now to your father." He said, "What would happen to my father at one in the morning?" Everybody said, "Nah, nah," and shrugged it off. I stayed out on the balcony most of the night consumed by this feeling of danger. It was coming from all directions.

In Philippine culture everything has a spirit. The stone, the tree, the river. When you're walking in the forest, you're walking not only in this world but also in a spiritual realm. As a Filipina, I'm very close to that other world that is not apparent here in the United States. We sense another existence, always. Of course it's hard to feel that in New York City, but I still get hunches. Sometimes I can tell when somebody's going to call. I haven't seen any ghosts, except once after my friend died last year. He just came to say goodbye. It may make me sound weird, but knowing things you don't see with your eyes is very normal in the Philippines.

A common icon in the northern mountain regions of the Philippines, the Bul'ol is a gender-neutral god of harvest that originates with the indigenous group known as Igorot. For Ninotchka and many other Filipinos, the Bul'ol works as a protector against evil spirits. Ninotchka has two of these. "One for defense. One for offense."

The next day, we found that my companion's father had been arrested at one o'clock in the morning. It was a case of mistaken identity. He and his father have the same name. They meant to pick up my companion who was also a writer and a very close friend of the young guy who had reestablished the Communist Party of the Philippines. His friend had gone underground and we hadn't seen him for ages. My airplane tickets were useless. Marcos cancelled all travel documents and closed down the airports. Not a single plane was going out of the country. The military had a list of those to be immediately arrested and I was on the list, which really pissed me off.

Nothing about me or my plans even factored into this decision. This cavalier casualness. This total indifference to the lives which were going to be affected. Marcos didn't say, "How will this impact on Ninotchka if I declare martial law?" He just thought, *I want to be President longer. Excuse me while I wreck your entire lives.* Dictators are like that.

In the morning, I got dressed very rapidly and went to my mother's. Manila is a very noisy city. All the cars, the jitneys, the buses, they all have the radio on full blast and people are always chatting. That first day of martial law everything was dead quiet. We took public transportation. Nobody was saying anything. Nobody looked each other in the eye. The most frightening thing of all about martial law is that menacing quiet. As soon as I crossed the gate to my mother's house, all the hairs on my arms and my neck stood up. One of the maids came running. "Two soldiers were looking for you." Right away I ran to my political contacts. But they all disappeared. *Zupp.* Either they were arrested or hiding. So I ran to some of my literary friends. They were not at all political, but I knew they were totally fearless. I go there and they're all smoking dope. I thought, *great, I'm going to get arrested for drugs. I don't need this.*
Suddenly there was nobody in the entire city of Manila whom I could trust.

I went to my aunt's house. Her son (my first cousin) was married to Imelda Marcos' sister. I was at their wedding four years earlier. So was Marcos and all kinds of writers and politicians and intelligentsia. This is the weird thing about the Philippines – right now the population is about 75 million. But 80% are peasants. It's a totally feudal setup. There's a very small ruling class – not even 1%, and we're all related in some way. I grew up in that.

This alligator-man from Papua New Guinea is a ruling spirit with both a good and bad side. Ninotchka says, "Its divinity comes from the complexity of the two sides of the spirit."

My aunt was very nice to me. She said, "Oh stay here, no problem." She was alone in this huge house. Just her and the maid. She knew the military was looking for me.

SHE'S THE MOTHER–IN–LAW OF ONE OF THE MARCOS'. NOBODY'S GOING TO TOUCH HER.

We both thought I'd be safe there, but then her son came home. He said, "You can't stay here. The first place they look is the houses of all your relatives." I said, "I never claimed you people to be my relatives! Not in public, not in writing, never!" My cousin shooed me away. I hate him to this day.

I couldn't figure out where else to go, so I got in touch with a very close friend of mine who happened to be one of the speech writers of Imelda Marcos. She said, "Oh Ninotchka, I've been waiting for your phone call." She suggested I call [Mr. A], this older journalist we all used to go to when we had problems. He said "Ninotchka, I'm very worried that some uncontrollable unit might chance upon you in the street and you could get hurt. Let me arrange for the military to come pick you up. They're just going to clarify certain things and then they'll let you go."
"How long will I have to stay in there?"
"You'll be out in two weeks, tops."
I said, "Okay, I'm going home. This is my address."

The next morning, two guys in plain clothes came to my place. I was living on the top floor of this building. To get to

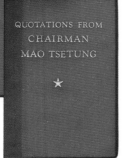

my apartment you had to walk through an open balcony. My wall is all glass. I come out and say, "Could you wait a minute? I have to pack. I haven't even had breakfast yet." They say, "Sure. Take your time." I'm walking along the corridor from the dining area to my bedroom and this huge crate that I'd recently brought back from China had fallen on its side. We have this practice in the Philippines, when you go somewhere, you come back with gifts for everybody. I had recently gone to China and I brought back a crate full of Mao's Little Red Books. It was the simplest thing to bring back from China at that time. All the Red Books were in plain sight! I kept passing back and forth from my bedroom to the kitchen, trying to kick the books back into the crate. Then I looked out the glass wall and saw that one of the guys left a short-barrel assault rifle on the balcony.

They took me to Camp Crame, the headquarters of the Philippine Constabulary, the most notorious arm of the government, in charge of *Internal Security*. They booked, fingerprinted, and searched me. The Colonel said, "Do you know that in a list of 5,000, your number had only two digits?" I said, "First 100. I'm so honored." He took me to a gymnasium filled with double-decker steel cots, stamped: U.S. ARMY. We were given metal trays to eat on, and metal canteens, also stamped: U.S. ARMY.

In 1898, Spain ceded the Philippines (along with Cuba and Puerto Rico) to the U.S. for 20 million dollars as part of the treaty that ended the Spanish-American War. The U.S. sent occupying forces into the islands, headed by General Rafael Crame. Fed up with being occupied, the people of the Philippines resisted. A fierce war dragged on for ten years, resulting in the death of more than 250,000 Filipinos. The Camp Crame military constabulary where Ninotchka was detained is named after the American General. The Philippines remained an American colony with limited self-rule until the Japanese occupied the archipelago during WWII. After the war, the Philippines was finally granted independence, although the U.S. retained military bases and other special rights and privileges.

It turns out, my wise old friend [Mr. A] was a military operative, code-named Gardener. *Whoa man.* As the Gardener, he cultivated relationships, and then he'd get a reward for betraying them later on. He told me I'd only have to stay two weeks, but I was "detained" for six months. In those six months I was interrogated five times. They really didn't know what they were looking for – just fishing all the time. A few months after I got out, I saw the guy who interrogated me. "I have a question for you. Most of the people you interrogated were kept for only twenty minutes. How come you kept me for four hours?" He said, "You were the only one wearing a miniskirt." I thought, *I should really kill this fellow.*

I got very close to some of the people I was in detention with. Since then, I've become close with many other ex–detainees I never even met in Camp Crame. I guess I can thank the Marcos' for connecting me to such a fabulous family of friends.

When I got released from detention, it was very quick and strange. *Bingo, no reason.* One day, I was escorted to the office of Fidel Ramos, who was the head of the Philippine Constabulary at that time. All of a sudden, I'm sitting at this table with a huge baroque silver coffee set and some cookies. Me, five colonels, a general, and a video crew. Very civilized. They'd say, "Oh, Ninotchka." I'd say, "Oh yes, General." They always use your first name. Bloody patronizing, paternalistic bastards. Ramos said, "You know we would certainly

According to Ninotchka, many Filipinos name their kids after characters in Hollywood movies. Ninotchka's mom named her after the beautiful communist spy Greta Garbo played in the movie of the same name.

like to release you, but we're thinking, maybe you should go work for the Office of Civil Relations. I have your release papers right here." I see the papers are not signed. I'm thinking, there's no way I'm going to work for these bastards. I said, "Oh certainly, General. Of course, the Office of Civil Relations – why not?" They made me take an oath of allegiance to the constitution, but didn't specify which constitution, the old one or the Marcos constitution. I took the oath and Ramos signed the release papers. They thought they had me because all of this was taking place for the video, but they could never use that video because if you look at it you'll see I had my middle finger up all while I was taking the oath.

Ramos and I always got along pretty well. I shocked the hell out of him one time when he was the Defense Secretary. I asked him, "How does it feel to be called the number one fascist in the country?" He laughed, "I may be a fascist, but I'm not number one."

"Oh right! That's Marcos." That's why I tell you, being fearless is walking into trouble. I never learned how to be any different.

After I got released, I had to report every day to the military and give them an account of what I did the day before. I was so pissed, sometimes I'd fill 30 pages:

```
7:01  woke up
7:02  wash face
7:03  brush teeth
7:05  brush hair
7:06  think about what to do next
7:07  turn on the radio
7:10  sat on the toilet
```

Sometimes I wrote:

```
Nothing happened today.
```

Just to drive them nuts! After a year they said, "You don't have to report anymore." They thought I had reformed myself. What was I really doing with my time? Naturally, I joined the underground immediately after I got out of detention.

In 1974, Marcos decided instead of having elections, he'll just have a referendum. Do you want President Marcos to continue as President? Yes or no. Anybody who didn't vote would be imprisoned, making all of us complicit in the whole charade. Everybody I knew voted no. The papers said,

The Marcos' were everywhere. He hired writers to write books under his name. You turn on the TV or radio, there he was being interviewed. His kids became actors on the stage. They were constantly demanding that you sing hosannas to them. If I was Lucifer and the Marcos' were God, and that's how God was behaving, I would really rebel.

One day in 1976, I was coming off the bus and this newspaper boy holds up the paper,

DANTE CAPTURED!

I got chills. Commander Dante was the head of the New People's Army. They were the only ones really giving us any hope. When I saw that, I knew I couldn't stay in the Philippines. With the help of the U.S. Cultural Attache, I got a fellowship at the International Writing Program at the University of Iowa. I landed first in Hawaii. I remember stepping off of the plane, thinking, *Ahhh, I can breathe.* While I was there, I gave a talk at the University of Hawaii and said some critical things about the Marcos regime. The next thing I knew, the Philippine consulate in Hawaii was threatening to cancel my passport. I told him, "There were 200 people at my talk. You cancel my passport and you will see what a scandal is."

The state of Iowa is very very flat and very strange. When I first got there I said, "Oy, what is this?" No ocean. No mountains. But I liked being in the company of 26 writers from all over the world.

There was a writer from Palestine and a writer from Israel who were always fighting with each other. The Eastern Europeans were all anti-Communist and all the people from the Third World were anti-capitalist. It was nice. I used the time to start writing literature again and mapped out the structure for my novel, *State of War.*

After the fellowship, I flew back into Honolulu on my way to the Philippines. That's when I found out I was blacklisted by the Philippine government. I had no other choice but to file for political asylum. Two lawyers and five years later my asylum was approved.

One of the Philippines' preeminent authors, Rosca has written six books including State of War *(1988, W.W. Norton). In 1993, she received the American Book Award for Excellence in Literature for her novel* Twice Blessed.

NINOTCHKA

I knew I was going to live in New York eventually. When I was in Iowa, we had a travel allowance and I came to New York with a friend for a weekend. I was so excited when I got there, I screamed, **"Whoa! Fifth Avenue! Whoa! Bonwit Teller! Bergdorf Goodman! Wow, let's tango."** So my friend and I tangoed down Fifth Avenue at seven o'clock in the evening. The amazing thing was – nobody noticed! In a martial law society, somebody is constantly noting what you're doing. In New York, nobody cares. I said, "I need to live in this city."

IRA

Ira has four children, all boys, who are still living in the Philippines. In 1995, she was under surveillance by the Philippine government. She fled to the United States where she received political asylum. She immediately got a job as a nanny, taking care of other people's children so she could send money back to the Philippines to pay for another woman to take care of her children.

One interview. That's all I had. The lady said, "Come back tomorrow." And that was it, I was a nanny. So many Filipinas are nannies. It's the easiest job that you can get here as a woman. You don't need legal papers and there are a lot of nanny agencies in New York. They spell out if you're supposed to be live-in, if you do household chores, whatever the arrangement is. I ended up as a nanny on Park Avenue. When I arrived I don't know what is Park Avenue. My thing is, I need the job.

IRA

Five days a week, I lived with my employers. If they asked me to do seven, I did seven. They pay extra for that. Basically, I take care of the kids and do some light housework. The older one was almost three years old when I started working and the baby was only ten months old. When I left that job, the oldest was nine years old and the little one was six. I really love the children. I don't have a daughter. They're my daughters. A lot of nannies are mistreated, but I am lucky that I had good employers. They sent me to the doctor whenever I got sick and paid the bills. Eventually, they put me on the books and paid my taxes and paid into a retirement plan for me. After all those troubles I had in the Philippines, it was nice to have a good job.

The children of rich people, they're either good kids or they're brats. These two girls could be brats but the parents are real disciplinarians. One time the older one said something bad and the mom talked to her and afterwards the girl said it again. So the mom went to the bathroom, got a bar of soap and washed out her mouth. The girl stopped.

The people I worked for call themselves liberal Republicans. Of course at first I was working for them without the proper papers. Remember Zoe Baird? She was not able to get a job in the President's Cabinet because she hired a nanny that was illegal. I was one of those illegal nannies. I worked for those people for a year before I told them I had been a political prisoner. They ended up respecting me for that. They are kind of protected and don't know many things – certainly not about the Philippines.

Ira was referred to a lawyer from the Center for Immigrants' Rights and received asylum her second year in New York. She soon began organizing Filipina nannies in New York. The nannies see a lot of each other – at the children's school, birthday parties, at the park, in the playgrounds. Some of them get good pay but a lot of them don't. If they get paid $100 a day, it's a good thing. If they are kind of new, they get $60 a day and they're live-in. Please! They don't have any benefits. They're working as a nanny *and* they're doing all the housework *and* they're only getting paid $60 a day! That sucks! Organizing nannies is different from regular union organizing because you don't have a target group of people working for one employer. With the nannies, it's one on one. Each nanny has a different employer and a lot of them are illegal. They might have been nurses or teachers in the Philippines. You wouldn't think they were nannies unless you saw them working as a nanny.

ANR

C1 1 1 3 3 0 0 0 8 0 *

ING SERIES

A-0626CT650P

IRA

After I started organizing the nannies, one of Ninotchka's friends offered me a job organizing home-care workers with the union, 1199. I told the union, I really want the job but I'm not ready to leave the family I work for. Six years with one family, you get very attached to the kids. The union held the job for me till I got the courage to leave the family. I gave the family a month's notice. The children cried, the parents cried and offered me a lot of money. "How much is 1199 paying you? We'll match it." I told them it wasn't the money. Of course, I didn't tell them that I really didn't want to spend my whole life chasing after their kids. Five years working as a nanny is a good job, but after that it makes you dumb. Every day, talking children's talk, reading children's books, playing children's games. The couple didn't under- stand. I think stockbrokers don't know anything about unions. I tried to explain what it means for a home-care worker to get $5 an hour and no benefits and no protection of any kind. One day 1199 was in the headlines, they said, "Oh Ira, that's your union!"

People call me by three different names. I'd never been called Isabelita my whole life until I started working at 1199, even though it's my legal name. My family called me Deedee when I was young, like a pet name. I started calling myself Ira when I was in high school. It was a teenagery kind of thing to do, putting my initials together. I is for Isabalita, R for Rosita, and A for Arnante. My children call me Andi. As soon as I had them, I went underground and I needed to camou- flage myself so I made up a male code name. The rest of my family calls me Ira now. I never get con- fused because I always know who is calling me.

Ira went underground after she got out of college in 1979. She was constantly moving from place to place, secretly organizing workers and peasants against the Marcos regime. In 1983, she was ambushed in a bus station by plainclothes military police. During her three years in prison, she was repeatedly interrogated, but refused to speak. When Corazon Aquino came to power in 1986, Ira was released from prison. In 1992, she became the Secretary General of SELDA (Samahan ng X-Detainees Laban sa Detensyon at para sa Amnestiya), the 10,000 member Society of X-Detainees. A constant thorn in the side of the entrenched military establishment, Ira kept having to relocate until she finally had to leave the country.

In 1986, my friend in California called me and said, "Don't look for any more lawyers!" I said, "I think we can get William Kunstler." He said, "Forget it. I found the best one. His name is Melvin Belli and he's all over the *Guinness Book of World Records*. Just look up the highest palimony reward and you'll see, he was the lawyer. His clients are Mick Jagger, Zsa Zsa Gabor. He had an alimony suit against Lee Marvin and a palimony suit against a man named Kashogi who's a big arms dealer in Saudi Arabia. Millions and millions of dollars in damages." I said, "Whoa."

When he's not with his wife and kids or showing apartments and houses to customers, Ramon Mappala works as a "cultural activist" by producing concerts, plays, and films, and organizing around human rights issues.

Belli modeled our lawsuit on an alien tort law which says if a crime was committed against you in a different country, and now you live in America, you can try the case in the U.S. We thought, Wow! Let's do it, because that's what Americans do in America — sue. So we sued Marcos for human rights violations. The American justice system has one — I don't know if I should call it a flaw, it's just a reality: In order to win a lawsuit you have to get the best lawyer, and the best lawyers are the most expensive. Belli had a Filipina secretary, so he knew all about Marcos. He said "I'll do it. And we're going to win."

There were 18 in our group. We all had different reasons for suing. Some of us were detained. Some were tortured. Some had relatives who were disappeared or summarily executed. By the time the suit went to court, Marcos was dead. Technically then, the lawsuit was against the Marcos Estate. Everybody felt vulnerable reopening their scars. Most of us tried so hard to forget what happened. But in the courtroom we had to tell our stories and convince the jury that all of these crimes were caused by one man. Eventually we joined together with two other groups that filed lawsuits in different parts of the country. Ten thousand people sued the Marcos Estate. Altogether we were awarded a judgement of 575 million dollars that were frozen in Swiss bank accounts, plus about 1.2 billion in damages.

We never saw any of the money. The Philippine government says it's their money. They're still fighting over it. Most of us just wanted to get back at Marcos and teach a lesson to other dictators. Money or no money, we did win our case. In the Philippines you can never win against a person with money or power. I have to admit, the American system of justice is a good system. But for some of the litigants, vindication wasn't enough. Especially the peasants and the farmers who lost their husbands and their children. They needed the money.

I had already seen the good and bad of the American system when I was an exchange student. My last year of high school, I came to live with a nice blonde, blue-eyed Scandinavian family

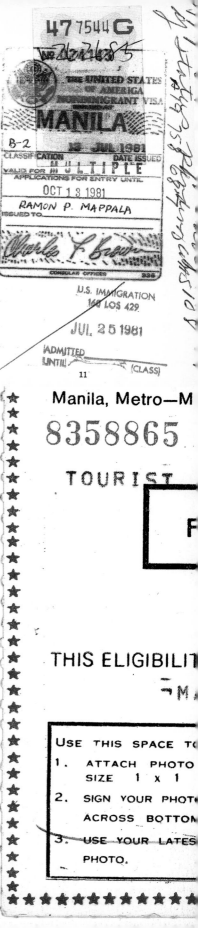

on a farm in Iowa. I was the only person of color in the school. I grew up in a middle-class family in Manila and we had servants. All of a sudden I'm living on a farm in this abundant country and I had to wake up early in the morning to feed the livestock and when I got home from school I plowed the fields. Before I came to Iowa, my picture of a farm was the TV show *Lassie*. My host family was so nice to me, they got me a puppy Collie that looked just like a little Lassie.

Even though Iowa was far away from the action in 1969 and 70, I was watching very closely what was happening in the country. Particularly the anti-war movement and rock 'n' roll. In those days you couldn't be a rocker without getting involved in politics. Woodstock, SDS, the Black Panthers. I'd be riding the tractor listening to tapes of the Woodstock festival blaring out into the fields.

give me an F!

My Iowa father would yell at me, "Ramon! Turn that thing down!"

PHOTOGRAPH OF BEARER

bears the signature and in a likeness of the person included in this passport.

I remember when I first got there I used to cry every evening. My Iowa family didn't understand the way I did things, like slurping while drinking soup. In the Philippines if you're loving the food, you make noise. By the time I left, I was feeling very American. When I came back to the Philippines, my own family couldn't understand me.

College was my baptism by fire. The more aware I became, the more vocal I became. I didn't know that expressing my opinion against the Yankee military bases and the unjust treatment of peasants meant that I would be branded as subversive and a Communist. I joined a youth organization that had rallies against Marcos getting paid millions of CIA dollars to send Philippine troops to Vietnam. I'd show up with my electric guitar and sing anti-war songs. We rallied against tuition increases and demanded the removal of Spanish as the mandatory foreign language. The Philippines had been a Spanish colony, so we hated all things Spanish. We won the language battle and I studied French instead. Now I regret not learning Spanish, because I really need it selling houses in Queens. *¿Donde esta la casa?*

Ramon became an organizer of the leading radical student organization. When martial law was declared, he was arrested, served six months in detention, and was then held under house arrest for two years.

In 1981, I got an invitation to go speak at the centennial celebration of the high school in Iowa. I found out later that my parents had contacted my U.S. exchange family to tell them I was in trouble. If I could have lived any kind of normal life in the Philippines, I'd still be there. I love my country and I love the people.

The guy in front of me at the American Consulate in Manila sang *America the Beautiful* at the top of his lungs. He didn't even know the lyrics. The woman behind the desk thought it was so funny, she gave him a visa. When it was my turn, I gave her the letter about the high school in Iowa. She says to me, "This letter could be written by anybody." I said, "I studied there and they're asking me to speak on the occasion of the school's centennial." I showed her my income tax returns and my bank book but she didn't want to give me a visa. I'd learned already that there are two ways to talk to an American. One is through humor and the other is through intimidation. The guy in front me already used humor so I thought I'd try intimidation. I threw up my hands and yelled, **"This is bullshit! If you don't want to give me a visa, tell me. But don't treat me like I'm stupid."** She said, "Okay sir. I'm sorry. Just sign here."

Ramon got a job with an investment house in the World Trade Center. When the stock market crashed in 1987, he and his wife bought a co-op with low maintenance and no elevator in Jackson Heights through Century 21 Realtors, where he now works.

A friend said, "Ramon, with your talent for people and networking, and the fact that you're the only person I know who never gets lost in Queens, you should go into real estate." And that's what I've been doing for the past seventeen years. Another friend called me up recently, "I hear you're a capitalist now, Ramon." I said, "No. I'm a real estate broker. A capitalist is someone who lays out money to make a profit. I just help people find housing. That's the American dream, right?" After fifteen years renting, I told Ninotchka, "You're just throwing your money away." I helped her and dozens of other Filipinos get good deals on co-ops.

It's easy for me to be in America. I love the people and in Queens I can get all the food I like from the Philippines. But now, with this whole war on terrorism thing — every time I open my computer, I'm nervous somebody is monitoring it. President [Bush] said he was sending troops to the Philippines to go after terrorists associated with Al-Qaeda. So the President of the Philippines [Arroyo] said, "Hey, let's include some other groups because they're our enemies too." Does it take 100 million dollars in military aid to go after 100 Abu Sayyaf guerrillas?

It's impossible for Filipinos to exist by themselves. We always have to set up kinship systems wherever we are. Almost all my Filipino friends have moved to Jackson Heights. I can't even be a hermit if I tried. Wherever I go in this world, there are X–Ds who will take me in. Wherever I sleep, I can't keep the door closed. Even in my own apartment, I sleep with open windows and open doors. Up until the last two years, I've had nightmares from October to April – the same period of time I was in detention. I'm just thankful I wasn't detained all year round.

A Philippine-U.S. women's solidarity organization, The Gabriela Network works against trafficking and abuse of women. The network got its name from the woman who led the longest uprising in the Philippines against the Spaniards in the 17th century. Gabriela Silang was captured by priests and hanged as a witch.

In 1989, I started Gabriela New York as a sister organization to Gabriela in the Philippines. Hours after Benigno Aquino was assassinated in 1983, the first people to pour onto the streets were women. Tens of thousands of upper class women brought their maids along to hold up umbrellas and to hold their water bottles. Except the maids didn't just come because they had to. All women were enraged. And out of that came the Gabriela Network talking about the social costs of the U.S. military bases, the prostitution, and the exploitations of our women for manual and sexual labor. You have a listing of so many pounds of coconut exported and so many pounds of pineapple, and at the very top you have so many pounds of female flesh. Twenty thousand women are exported every year from the Philippines, not just as sexual labor but as domestics and menial workers, and very often their employers require sexual service. That's why we have all these women who kill their employers when they are raped. They think we Filipinos look so unthreatening. We are small women. We speak very mildly. We are always charming, as they say. But they forget we've been at war for 400 years, and if you push us too hard against the wall – we'll bounce back and kill you.

RAMON

It's scary thinking that tax dollars from my pocket might be spent to kill my own people. That's the irony of being an American. Every time I see **UNITED WE STAND!** It scares me. Does *United We Stand* mean if you are not united with what everyone is thinking, you're a terrorist? Having lived through martial law in the Philippines, I don't feel free to say what I believe. They're already going after foreign students here. In the Philippines, they can do whatever they want, put tanks in the streets, take away the rights of the people. But here in America there is always hope that the civil libertarians and the freedom-loving people will fight against rewriting the civil rights laws and turning the country into a military state.

IRA

I am not going to apply for citizenship in the United States, because there will be a point in my life that I am going back to my own country. The government is not going to care because I will be an old lady. What's an old lady going to do? There is a small piece of land that I'm going to live on. I'm going to do organic gardening and I'm going to keep some wild animals that are becoming extinct. We have a lot in common, me and those animals.

JUST
PROTEC
OF WOMEN's
RIGHT!

FILIPINO
MFORT WOMEN

AMONITA BALAJAI
14 YEARS OLD

NSATION TO
IPINO COM-
WOMEN.
OSE JAPAN BID
S PERMANENT
ROF UN-SEC-
COUNCIL

 victo

uan

p

20.46

ROSITA NACINO
14 YEARS OLD
TASK FORCE
FILIPINO COMFORT
WOMEN   TFFCN

From a quilt in Ninotchka Rosca's apartment, made in commemoration of comfort women from the Philippines, for the 4th World Conference on Women. Filipina women were used by the Japanese military as "comfort women" [sex slaves] when the Philippines was occupied by Japan during World War II.

Ana Maria Asuncion was married at 16 and had two children. When they were three and five, she left the Philippines looking for work and began sending money home to her parents so they could take care of her kids. She worked for wealthy Iranians in Iran, in Paris, and in Switzerland before coming to the United States in 1986. In 1994, Ana hired a lawyer to help her with her immigration papers. We interviewed her in the summer of 2001 just after her 50th birthday. She chose not to have her image portrayed.

ANA

It was 1994 when the incident happened. I found the lawyer from an advertisement in the Filipino paper. Abrams. I went to his office at the Federal Building, downtown Manhattan. He started this thing with me, "You look so good. Do you always look like that?" I just answered right away, "Of course. I'm going to work and I have to look proper." He stopped writing. Me, sitting there not recognizing what he has in his mind. I thought we were through, so I started to leave. He said, "No, we're not done yet." I sat back down. He starts taking off his shoes. I'm thinking, maybe he wants to be comfortable, but in the back of my head I'm wondering, *why is he taking his shoes off?* He comes from behind his desk and sits next to me. I move away. Now I'm thinking, why is he sitting here instead of at his desk. He starts stroking my arm and... and kissing me. I tried to shove him away but he's a big tall man. He struck me down onto the sofa and started to unzip himself. He put his hand over my face, pulled his pants down, and oh shoot, he pulled my face and made me do the thing he wanted me to do. I was choking and crying but there was no voice coming out. When he tried to grab my blouse I ran out of the office and into the elevator.

I was crying, buttoning up my blouse. My face was red. Why did this thing happen to me? I paid that lawyer. I was telling myself I'm going to go home and shower and go to work. I thought that's it, I will not be able to do the papers, because, I was thinking the lawyers know each other and they will say, "Don't help this girl." This is the way I was thinking in the elevator when another lawyer, Mr. Goldman, another Jewish man, got on the elevator and he asked, "Excuse me, miss. What happened to you?" I couldn't help myself. I started crying to him. I told him what this lawyer Abrams did to me.

In the lobby, Mr. Goldman asked the doorman to call the police. He sat me down and waited with me. Soon there were sirens and yellow ribbon and a police van. The police talked to Mr. Goldman and then they took me to the ambulance and showed me through the window, Mr. Abrams in handcuffs. They ask me if that was the man. I nodded.

At Bellevue hospital they examined my mouth and everything. They took the swab. Then I sat down to sign the papers. I took a pen out of my bag and that's when I saw the tissue. I said, "This is the tissue!" When it happened, I saw a tissue box on Abram's desk. It was so disgusting what he made me do, I wiped my mouth and spit it out into the tissue. I didn't see a garbage can, and me, I cannot throw garbage on the floor just like that. I am too polite. So I put the tissue in my bag. I wasn't thinking DNA or court. I didn't know it was the biggest thing that could nail him.

They took me straight from the hospital to the police precinct to talk to the District Attorney. I said I cannot afford a lawyer because I'm working day by day and check to check. The police assured me I wouldn't have to pay. I didn't know what is a district attorney. Plus I didn't have my papers and I was scared I would get kicked out of the country. God bless that District Attorney, he told me, "It doesn't matter who you are. Paper or no paper, you're a victim here. You're a human being." I was so thankful for that. In the Philippines, if you are poor, you won't be able to have a case.

The day after the incident, I didn't go to work. I called
up the Filipino papers to tell them,

"This lawyer, Abrams, that you let advertise is not
a good person. He did something wrong to me.
This is the docket number and this is the District
Attorney. I'm a Filipino and you're a Filipino and
he's abusing Filipinos."

The reporter said to me,
"Have you told this to anybody else?"

I said, "No, I'm telling it to you because you are
having him advertise in your paper."

He said, "Okay, I'm going to come and
interview you because this is a really big scoop."

"A BIG SCOOP!
Throw this man out of the
advertising in your paper."

"We can't do that because he paid us already."

I said, "That's crap," and hung up the phone.

One of the Queens newspapers called me and I trusted them, but it
was just a big picture-taking thing. They didn't care. Then a woman
called me from the Gabriela Network. God bless them. She called
another Filipino paper and they wrote an article, and then she called
the National Organization of Women and the American Civil
Liberties Union and an activist group called the
Women's Action Coalition. Meanwhile, the
newspaper where I saw the advertisement for H.
Abrams, Immigration Lawyer kept saying that
he is a very good lawyer who helped a lot of
Filipinos become citizens. They were vilifying
me in the paper and it made my story a bigger
thing than it needed to be. Then Gabriela
Network made the story even bigger, criticizing

I. COMPENSATION T
THE FILIPINO COM-
FORT_WOMEN.
II. WE OPPOSE JAPAN
TO SITAS PERMAN
MEMBER OF UN-SEC
URITY COUNCIL

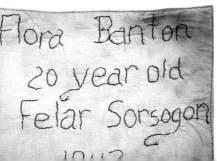

Flora Banton
20 year old
Felar Sorsogon

that paper for saying the victim was asking for it.
Every day there were letters to the editor about
my case. Some people were for me, some were
against me. On the Number Seven train one day,
I heard some Filipinos talking about me. They

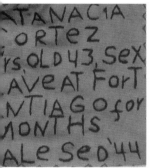

ANA

were looking at a photograph of me in the newspaper, and saying, "Is this the kind of face a prominent lawyer would attack?" I said, "Excuse me. That's me you're talking about." I felt so bad, I didn't want to be seen in public anymore.

The legal case took from 1994 to 1996. Almost the same time as the O.J. Simpson case. I said, "How come the O.J. Simpson case is over, and mine is not? It's too much for me, two years going to the psychiatrist, going to depositions and hearings. More than a dozen other Filipina women came forward after they saw the news — saying he did the same thing to them. Nurses, teachers. They came to the court and testified. We won and Abrams was sentenced seven to twelve years.

My life is right now back to normal. It helps to know that it didn't only happen to me. That I wasn't a bad person who brought this onto myself. My boss is also Jewish. He was so upset for me. I'm in love with Jewish people. He saw the pictures. He saw the articles. He even came with me to the court. I feel so bad because his textile business went bankrupt and I really did love my boss. Now I work for a magazine distributor. I just want to go on with my life. I don't want to be involved in another court case ever again.

a safety place

CAMILO PERDOMO
JUAN CARLOS VELOZA

We drive along Queens Boulevard into Maspeth, past the wide expanse of cemeteries, the new Staples Superstore, and blocks and blocks of chain-link fenced used-car lots, onto a quiet street dotted with small, one-family houses. Juan Carlos sits on the outside steps of his basement apartment, watching his beloved Carlota playing in the front yard. Once the second in command at Colombia's equivalent of the Federal Aviation Authority, Camilo rests his head on the grass, eyes closed, quietly identifying the model and make of each jet by the sound it makes taking off and arriving at nearby LaGuardia Airport.

VENEZUELA

Bogotá

COLOMBIA

MASPETH

BRAZIL

PERU

Always we are with the idea to bring Carlota to the United States because we miss her terribly and she was alone. She could be a model, our daughter. Gorgeous eyes. Maybe she could have a photo session for advertising. She likes it in Queens. All the trees. All the little animals. In our dreams we have a place big enough so Carlota can run around. A place she can have a room of her own, with plants.

We miss our families. We miss our country. We did not come here to have money to buy our first osterizer, because we had an osterizer and a car and a house and a garden in our country. We just can't live there anymore without being dead.

One year and one month we are here in New York and then we get our interview with INS. We couldn't apply as a couple because we don't have our relationship legally recognized, but we send together all our documents and insist on the interview the same day with same INS interviewer. This is the advice from our lawyers. It was a two hour interview for me, in the morning, and longer for Juan Carlos, all afternoon. For me it wasn't so bad because I just put the facts. Much harder for Juan Carlos. It was his job to verify everything I say. In between [interviews] I talk to Juan Carlos. The INS man walked into the hallway and saw us together.

Fewer than one out of four asylee applicants receive asylum in the United States — a fact that must weigh like the 225-ton Statue of Liberty on the shoulders of those who sit before an immigration judge or INS interviewer.

JUAN CARLOS

It was a regular desk, in a regular room, and a regular immigration official. It didn't matter how prepared we were. How many rehearsal interviews we had with our lawyers. Soon as I got there in front of that man, I became terrible nervous, like a shipwreck.

There you are in front of the United States government. You feel like they can just put you on a plane and throw you out. I kept worrying what they would ask me about specific details. When did the robberies happen? What kind of clothes did the guys on the motorcycles have? On what date did they threaten you? I don't keep dates like that in my memory. My head is filled always with many kinds of things. Like I'm working but at the same time I'm thinking about my sister, what is she doing. I have to call her just to say hi. At the same time I'm thinking I'm going to have a meeting on the fifth floor. At the same time I'm thinking about Carlota. But dates and names, I don't have room for.

CAMILO

The first practice interview we had, we are
peaceful and relaxed. We have truth on our
side and the Virgin Mary. But our lawyers said,
"No, this is not a good strategy to be so calm.
You need to look afraid, with problems in your
minds." After a year of being in New York we
don't feel afraid. So we thought about being
sent back to Colombia and that makes us
scared again. Each practice interview we go
over the death threats and the slurs.
How do you prove calls you get on your
cell phone from men who call you by your
name, saying "Maricón de mierda" [Faggot
piece of shit], and all these things I don't
even want to repeat? What can we show?
We have no police report. I reported the
breakins but never the slurs or the threats.
To tell the Colombian police that people
are trying to kill you because you are gay,
is like telling wolf you are a chicken coop.
How do you prove the guns in your face?
We do not walk around with videotapes
in our heads.

In the real interview, there was too much questions about our gay
conditions. "You ever have sex with a woman?"
I tell him, "No. I love woman, but never for sex."
"You never have dates with ladies in your life?"
"Of course. All my life I have dates who are women who have bad
marriage in their background and terrible guys around. With me

the woman says, 'This guy never said me to go to bed with him. This guy says my dresses are beautiful. This guy sings me boleros.'" The INS officer looks at me, "And never once did you. . . ?" "No, it's the system push me to be with woman to keep my lawyer image to the society." He writes notes in his pad.

"When I was a child, my grandmother didn't greet her brother Jose because he was a man who went with other men. Whenever he came to visit, my family put all children in a separate room, we shouldn't catch his homosexuality. Even when my grandmother was dying of cancer, and her brother came to visit, they lock us all in the bathroom till he leaves. My great uncle, he love opera and he was a lawyer and he love men. Here I am now, a lawyer, a lover of opera and a lover of men. Jose was the youngest of nine brothers and sisters and he die of AIDS absolutely alone at 74. I was the last person who saw him. I don't like that destiny for me."

The INS man wasn't so much interested in my family. He wants to know am I really gay. Here I am, a guy with a tie, absolutely clean, with no mannerisms, no purple shirt, no earrings, no yellow hair, and no buttons on my shoes. He must've thought, *is this guy gay or not?* "When did you first know you were gay?"

"Since before I can remember I was always different. I never used my hands to eat. My brothers – gobble gobble gobble. My youngest brother used to come home with frogs in his pockets. Terrible. My mother would tell me, 'Your brothers come home dirty, crashing into walls. You come just like you left in the morn-ing, perfect and clean.' I was her favorite. When I need to eat ice cream with red berries on it, I always change into something for ice-cream eating, then change again for the rest of the day. Six years old, I love Strauss, I love Mozart, I love adult conversation. Only by the time I was 12, 13 years old did my mother start to worry about me. All the boys my age, showing off for girls playing in the street, and I'm inside with my head in a book or playing my guitar. Mother said, 'Why you don't have a girlfriend? You need to practice about ladies.' I tell her every kind of excuse. I have to finish my studies. I'm practicing for the concert."

With me the INS officer kept asking, "How can you prove you are gay? Because you don't look like gay." I said, "I don't know, I'm just gay." "Did you go to bars? What is it like in there? When was the first time you kiss a boy?"

Each month the United States Justice Department makes a big declaration about what's going on in different countries. At one of those, the Attorney General made a press conference saying in Colombia they have a big problem because many people are getting killed when they belong to specific social groups. Our lawyers (it was their first immigration case) knew nothing in the beginning about our country. They just got the idea that as gays we are from social group suffering very bad violence in Colombia, and that's what they put down on our papers.

On the advice of their lawyers, Camilo and Juan Carlos applied for asylum based on their sexual orientation. The legal brief in support of Juan Carlos' application began frankly, "Juan Carlos Veloza should be granted asylum in the United States because he is gay." Camilo's brief began much the same way.

When we left Bogotá we did not think, oh we will live forever in United States. After we are here, we find out you have only one year to apply for asylum or they deport you. We cannot stay and work legally, and we cannot go back. It was eight months already before we look for a lawyer to help us. We did find a lawyer but he wanted $6,000 just to process our case.

CAMILO

The trouble really started when I move my travel agency and law office to exclusive area of Bogotá called La Cabrera. I never hang out a sign saying:

Little by little we develop a reputation for promoting gay tour packages. Some people in the neighborhood didn't like to see my clients coming and going. After 28 years living in the closet, always thinking it was a sin to be gay, I take both things I love – airplanes and my new life, being proud of my gay condition, and put them together into my business. It brings me success. And also terrible harassments.

Ever since I was a little boy I love airplanes and everything related to the sky. I grew up on a farm in a small town near to the Magdalena river. My father had a small airplane to fly to cotton farm meetings in different cities. He used to say to me, "If you don't have good grades, you don't fly." Always I study and every Saturday he would take me flying.

When I became a lawyer I specialize in aviation law. In time I became director of internal affairs at Civil Aviation Authority, running 500 people's operation. The new head of government management said, "When you leave your position in a public enterprise, it's like leaving a bathroom. If you find a bathroom dirty, and you leave it that way, you are the owner of the dirty." After I heard that, it becomes a trauma for me every time I go to a bathroom. I always clean everything. After cleaning up so many corruptions and so many bathrooms, I quit Civil Aviation Authority and open my own office, thinking now I have life the way I want it, doing travel agency on first floor and law office on top.

The first harassing phone call I got, a man says, "Afeminado inmundo" [Filthy effeminate] and hangs up. I didn't worry so much the first few calls – it is just something that comes with my condition. All different times, all different voices. Things like, "Tu no naciste de la matriz de tu madre si no de su culo" [You weren't born from your mother's womb, you were born out of her ass]. Or, "Aviseles a los suyos que si aparece con su jeta de puerco llena de moscas en una calle fue que lo mataron por marica para limpiar la humanidad" [Advise your friends that if they find you on the street with your pig's snout full of flies, it is because we killed you for being a faggot and to clean humanity of people like you]. The killing part is what really make me scared. Especially after three times my office was broken into, not so much because of the $13,000 they took, or the equipment, but the dirty toilet paper they spread around, and the words they scrawl all over the walls – ¡MARICAS MUERANSE [DIE FAGGOTS]!

JUAN CARLOS

I don't remember the exact date I met Camilo. What's it matter if it's two years or three? What's important is we love each other. You can see we are totally different. Camilo is ten years older than me. We both are raised Catholic, but I never had a problem about who I am. I know some places in the Bible it says you shouldn't be gay, but I really think God gave me this way of being. I never lie who I was. Except with my family and with the police of course I lie. Just walking in the street with a friend, the police will stop you and ask whether you are gay. I always tell them no. When police raid the bars, it's not so easy to make up a story. They turn up the lights. **"Everybody against the wall."** They pat you down and up into your crotch shouting, **"Perros degenerados"** [Degenerate dogs]. They force the bar owner to pay bribes so he can keep his business. Where do you go for protection?

I have the stark memory of this marriage. The moment I saw Juan Carlos and he saw me we were automatically in love. We start this relation two years next June 6th. It's a good complement the two of us. I'm absolutely romantic and he knows everything about responsibility. We go outside the office and I say, **"Oh the sky is beautiful! I offer you the color of the sky."** He says, "Tomorrow is the day for the rent." It's a balance combination. It's a permanent thing about the romantic and the practical sides drawing together.

JUAN CARLOS

In 1998, I was Colombian marketing manager
for a famous weekly international magazine. We
co-sponsored the Semana de Diversidad Sexual
[Week of Sexual Diversity] in Bogotá. All week
I sat at the booth giving away magazines, my
name and phone number listed as contact person.

The next week, I got phone calls at the office,
every kind of slurs and threats. A few weeks after
the campaign, my supervisor calls me in and fires
me. It was a total shock because the director from
New York had just visited saying how pleased
he was with my job performance.

CAMILO

Juan Carlos came to work with me at the travel
agency. For a year we receive three, sometimes
four, five menace calls a day. Not only in the
office, but on my private cell phone and at Juan
Carlos' mother's house. Everywhere there were
eyes on us. So I went to the new director of the
Civil Aviation Authority to see about getting a
job with the government again. He offers me
the position directly under him. I fill out all the
forms, take the medical examination, and go on
the scheduled day to be sworn in. When I get
there they tell me to wait. I wait the entire day
and then they tell me to go away. No one returned my phone calls. I didn't know what was
going on, until a friend tells me that my name
is blacklisted from all government jobs because
I am homosexual.

Juan Carlos said we must leave the country right
away. I couldn't imagine living any place but
Colombia. I couldn't imagine living without Juan
Carlos. I convince him we will figure out a way
to live a normal life.

One night in November, 1998, we finish locking the office when two men on motorcycles, in long black trenchcoats and dark helmets, pull up in front of us. It happened in just one minute. But a lot can happen in a minute. I could see under their coats, they both had big guns. I thought for sure they were going to kill us in one shot.

CAMILO

Everybody knows these trenchcoat motorcycle guys are paid assassins who kill the ministers in our country. They killed my teacher! They kill the most important lawyers and judges who say yes yes to extradition, and no to narcotics, and no to paramilitary groups and guerrillas. The judges wear hoods to hide who they are and still they are murdered. If you don't do what they want, you are the next body washing up on the river. And they are right in front us, yelling obscenities. Then they drive away on their motorcycles.

If you don't get killed by paramilitary groups who are paid War-on-Drug money from United States to clean up undesirables, then you get killed by guerrillas. If you don't get killed by either of those, you get killed by the police or one of their vigilante groups. There's a million different reasons you end up dead in Colombia. Because you have money. Because you don't have money and you live in the street or in the wrong village. Because you write an article. Only one thing all social cleansing squads have in common — if you are gay, they all want you washed away.

Homicide is the leading cause of death in Colombia. Despite the prevailing myth that these deaths are primarily drug-related, Amnesty International and other human rights groups have found that many of these killings are part of what is called "social cleansing." An average of five people daily fall victim to social cleansing.

I tell Camilo I can't live like this anymore.
We have to leave Colombia.

I wasn't ready to leave my country, but I love Juan Carlos and maybe life suddenly change my mind. I think don't be so near to your material things. We leave Carlota with my mother. I pack a few change of clothes, my Baby Jesus and a few other saints and that's it. I come to United States with my rosaries in one pocket, $80 in the other.

Soon as we arrive we start getting gifts from the Virgin Mary.

First gift was a room to rent from a Colombian woman and her mother in Flushing, Queens. They cook horrible things, those ladies. One day we said, "Oh, please let us cook. We love to cook." They said, "Oh, it's delicious." Next day they ask us to cook again for their whole family. All sons and daughters came to eat our food. The ladies were so happy because their family never came to visit and now that we cook, they come all the time.

Second gift, one of the sons gives us an old car. We got a job delivering food for different restaurant. It's a new thing for me – lawyer working as driver of food delivery service. First I think it's below me. Then I think we are together – driving in our car with road map of New York and a lantern, talking, eating. It become like we are carrying sacred things – food for people to eat.

We drive five hours in a row without a break and we're smelling the food in our hungry noses. One time Juan Carlos looks inside. "Hmmm, chicken wings, french fries. You want just one or two french fries?"
"Yeah."
"And maybe one small chicken wing?" We become experts to open and close again the food like nobody was there. I feel sorry about that. Really.

REINA DE LA PAZ
Ruega por nosotros

JUAN CARLOS

People on the streets see we are foreigners. They come up to us. "Social kit, sir?" For $200 they sell you a Social Security card. We didn't do that. Every job we do here is under the table. All kinds of things we've done already. We stand on the street in a costume in the shape of a bean for a promotional campaign, giving fliers away at Internet show for a new website — beenz.com. We work cleaning after fancy parties. One party for a vocal coach at Metropolitan Opera, the man says, "Throw out all these things." I look at Camilo. For a week we ate salmon, smoked ham, European cheeses.

We look at these jobs like an adventure. Whether we are a bean or a Santa Claus or just standing around in bow tie at a fancy party, we try to make people feel good. We know other Colombians they also have jobs like servant or maid, but that sounds ugly, so they say, "We are in catering business." If you clean a kitchen in Manhattan, you do catering. Same job in Queens – you are a maid. Ask us, we'll tell you – Yes we are a maid. Yes we are Colombians.

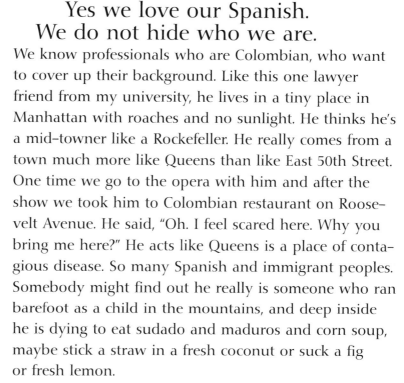

CAMILO

Yes we love our Spanish. We do not hide who we are.

We know professionals who are Colombian, who want to cover up their background. Like this one lawyer friend from my university, he lives in a tiny place in Manhattan with roaches and no sunlight. He thinks he's a mid-towner like a Rockefeller. He really comes from a town much more like Queens than like East 50th Street. One time we go to the opera with him and after the show we took him to Colombian restaurant on Roosevelt Avenue. He said, "Oh. I feel scared here. Why you bring me here?" He acts like Queens is a place of contagious disease. So many Spanish and immigrant peoples. Somebody might find out he really is someone who ran barefoot as a child in the mountains, and deep inside he is dying to eat sudado and maduros and corn soup, maybe stick a straw in a fresh coconut or suck a fig or fresh lemon.

I send pictures to my mother. She says, **"You work in a flea market selling jewelry like a hippie! This is the life you escape to?"** I tell her, "We didn't want to go away, Mama." She wants to know what kind of furniture did I buy? My apartment in Bogotá, everything was designer this, designer that. Here, everything we have is from the street. Chairs. Microwave. We clean it off and it works. Virgin Mary again. My mother says, "What kind of bed did you buy? What kind of suits?" It's hard to explain to her, everything I wear is secondhand. I am the same person. Better person. I have nothing, but I have love with somebody. I have life. I'm new in front of the life. Close a door, a window flies open.

Only thing I feel little bit lost without is my guitar. A guitar is like a toothbrush. Since I'm twelve years old I play and sing. In Bogotá I belong to rondalla, eleven guys group with guitars and one contrabajo. They call

me on my birthday, singing over the phone and crying.
I miss the music very much. Now I sing to Carlota.
She loves my singing. Don't you Carlota?

Isn't she beautiful?

A few months after we are here,
my mother helped arrange for a friend to bring us
Carlota. Mama had to send her executive class to keep her
apart from the other dogs. Some people use dogs to put
cocaine inside. I don't know if they poop it out or they use
surgery or what.

The poor dogs.

So we have Carlota. We have my sister who lives here in Woodside. And we have gay community. We were feeling good and relax, and working always. We forget about the time. A month and a half before our one year will be up to file for asylum, we get very nervous — What are we going to do? We're selling jewelry at a flea market in Kew Gardens and this African lady comes by our table, tells us about an organization, the Lawyers Committee, that help people about human rights. We went there and talked to a woman whose job is to listen to everybody's trauma stories. We filled out forms and dropped them in a box. Two weeks later we get a call from a lawyer.

Under the 1996 Illegal Immigration Reform and Immigrant Responsibility Act, asylum seekers must file their application within one year of their arrival to the U.S or they can be automatically deported.

CAMILO

We thought it would be just one lawyer in an old office with papers to the ceiling and a cigarette always hanging in his lips. It was 50 floors building on 55th Street and 7th Avenue. They have 239 lawyers and offices in 25 countries. Their clients are the country of Saudi Arabia, London Lloyd insurance company – and us. Only we didn't pay because we are social service case for them. They pay everything – breakfast, photocopies, translations, and four first–year associates straight out of law school.

They said, "Okay, we need to reconstruct your whole story into one file in less than a month. Ask everyone you know to send us affidavits, who you are and what happened." They deliver 300 pages file to the INS on the anniversary of our coming to America. A month later we went together for our interview.

Camilo says I shouldn't worry so much, we have our integrity story. "Just tell the truth." All while Camilo was being interviewed I'm going over every date in my mind. When it's my turn, I go inside the room and very quickly the INS man goes through my affidavit. All the most horrible, most dangerous things, he looks at me like okay, I'm agree with that. No problem. It was the personal things he kept pressing. For two hours he asks me questions about gay this, gay that. The final question was, "What happens if I give your boyfriend asylum and I'm gonna say to you no?" I told him, "No sir. If you deny asylum to me, I just take Camilo and Carlota and we go to another country. But we're not going back to Colombia to live in a permanent scare."

Not once did he ask me what day did this happen or what month. I lost three pounds in that interview.

Camilo received asylum on April 10, 2000. Juan Carlos, not being his legal spouse, was processed separately. Three very long days later, his asylum was granted.

For Camilo and Juan Carlos, the United States remains a "safety place." All their lives they had to conceal their sexual identity to keep from being killed. From their rather unique vantage point, the United States is a place where you must prove you are gay — really truly gay, always were gay, and always will be gay — in order to stay in the country.

Now that we are legal residents, my mother came to visit and she brought with her my guitar. It was a beautiful reunion. Also very wonderful to see my mother. I decide to tell her why we left Colombia, because still she doesn't understand. I think, in her mind it was safety problems, narcotics dealers probably, because I am a lawyer and I get involve with different clients. I take out my 300 pages asylum application and open it to explain her everything. "You see Mama,

I am...

Juan Carlos and I. . . ."

Then I think about this Irish friend of ours who won the green-card lottery. He goes to visit his family in Ireland. The mom says, "We are so happy for you, you finally have your green card. Let me see your green card." He opens his wallet and the mother is very upset. "Oh my little baby, your green card is pink! Your green card is pink because you are gay." Our friend says, "No, Ma. Everybody's green card is pink." She doesn't believe him.

I look at my mom – she is a simple woman. Why bother her with all the details? She suffer enormously that I am not in Colombia. If she knows I have problems because I am gay, that will make her suffer even more. She doesn't have to know every little thing.

JUAN CARLOS

Always mothers love their sons. Even if you are a million miles away. Even if you're weird. Even if you're in jail. Even if you're dead. They always love us. My father says,

"As long as you have a mother, there will always be flowers on your tombstone."

out of kabul

SHEKAIBA WAKILI
SULTANA WAKILI

Often, Americans discover the world by way of war. When we were kids, Vietnam was a war, not a country. Now we order "Vietnamese" to go. After the attack on the World Trade Towers, another part of the world was introduced to Americans. ABC anchorman Peter Jennings stood in a room-sized map of "The Islamic World." When he got to Central Asia, he crouched down, his left foot covering Tajikistan, and explained the things we ought to know about Afghanistan.

We meet Shekaiba at an asphalt park near her mom's apartment off of Queens Boulevard in Forest Hills. There's no grass, but quite a few trees, a playground, and benches where grand-mothers from all over the world watch their American grandchildren play on the swings. Shekaiba's mom, Sultana, sits on a bench with elderly women, some ten to twenty years older than she. Although there are three Iranian women (one Jewish, one Christian, one Muslim), as well as a Russian, an Armenian, and an Afghan, they all speak Farsi. When other Rus-sians come by, the Russian woman translates. Even a Filipina manages to participate in the conversation. Mime, photographs, and the occa-sional common word facilitate communication.

Shekaiba visits her mom on way home from teaching photography in a high school on Long Island. Years earlier, she moved to Queens with her father after the Soviets invaded Kabul. Shekaiba is an outspoken feminist, photographer, and Muslim, married to a half-Jewish "spiritual atheist." She translates for her mom, who escaped the carnage of a more recent war in Kabul.

SHEKAIBA

I've had people assume that I'm anything from Greek to Italian to Spanish or Native American. Maybe Hindu. But very few people ever guess that I'm an Afghan. So I can pretty much sit there like a chameleon and hear what people have to say. The worst thing I heard, I was in an environment where somebody said, "We should go and just nuke Afghanistan. They blew up the Twin Towers, so let's just get rid of them." I sit there thinking, *well, we didn't do it.* Those 19 hijackers weren't Afghan at all.

The day the U.S. started bombing Afghanistan, my husband called me at work. I cried all day. The American part of me said, "Go to war." That's what we do as a superpower. But the Afghan part of me was devastated. My father's brother, his wife and six kids live in Kabul. My mother's youngest brother was there too. Luckily, he made it to Pakistan before the bombing. What are we going to war with? Peasant people who've lived through 24 years of war. There's no social structure, no government, no army. Who are we fighting? A few Arabs hiding out in caves!

Once people know I'm Afghan, the first question is, "Are you Muslim?" The second question, "Where is your veil?" I never felt like I had to wear a veil. I see myself as Shekaiba the photographer, Muslim, contemporary woman. So I started a series of self-portraits looking at the different ways I can be perceived, and I perceive myself. The next question usually is, "Why are women so oppressed?" Then I feel like I have to explain the religion. That is probably going to happen for the rest of my life. So I'm studying Islam now with Imam Feisal to see for myself what it's all about.

Imam Feisal Abdul Rauf has been the Imam of al-Farah Mosque in New York for nearly two decades. He founded the American Sufi Muslim Association, and sits on the boards of the Islamic Center and the Interfaith Center of New York.

I was raised, like many Afghans in Kabul of my generation, as a cultural Muslim. Once a year my father would go to the mosque just because he was embarrassed not to be seen since he knew his friends would be there.

My parents were divorced when I was three years old. My father got custody of my older sister and me. My younger sister, who was a baby, went with my mother. Islamic law says that in any type of divorce, the wife should get two thirds of the husband's wealth. But in most "Islamic" countries, including Afghanistan, laws are tipped in favor of the man, and interpreted by the village mullahs who may not necessarily be scholars of Islamic law. You would think the mother would have the right to see her children! All my mother got was a piece of paper saying you're divorced.

When my father got remarried, there was a lot of tension in the house. Then the Soviets invaded and the tension was in the whole country. My father went to his village for a weekend. On the way back to Kabul he had to weave in and out of hundreds of tanks coming down from the north. That night there was a family meeting. Everybody was up in arms. "Who needs to get out of the country first?" My father was working for UNICEF, and as far as the Soviets were concerned, he was working for America. About a month later, the Afghan Communist Secret Service came knocking on our door at one o'clock in the morning. My father thought it was for him. My uncle Abdullah opened the door. They said, "Come with us. We're taking you in for questioning." Everybody was crying. My grandmother was hysterical. My father tried to pay them off. They took my uncle to a notorious prison called Pol-e-Charkhi, which means revolving bridge, as in, once you're on it, you can't get off. That was the last time anybody saw my uncle. Convinced he was next, my father managed to get a plane to India and then took a flight to America. That was 1979.

In 1980, when I was eleven years old, my stepmother, my older sister, my half sisters and I got visas to join him in America. All flights went through Moscow because Afghanistan was occupied by the Soviets. Soon as we landed in Moscow, there was total silence in the plane. Everyone had heard of people being taken off of planes in Moscow. When all the adults around you are panicking and crying, it affects you as a child. When the plane landed in Germany, the Afghan pilot said, "We're safe. We're in Germany!" Everybody in the plane started applauding. I remember thinking, *oh okay, this is safe now.*

From a series of photographs Shekaiba took for an exhibit at the Museum of Natural History in New York City. © Shekaiba Wakili, 2001
I took these photographs right after the U.S. started bombing Afghanistan. Each woman is from a different ethnic group. This is my neighbor. She's Pashtun. She left Afghanistan when the Taliban had just taken over Kabul. Two of the women came here when they were very little. Two are recent immigrants. It's basically about the lifting of the veil after the fall of the Taliban. I kept hearing people say, "Well, now that the Taliban are gone, women can go without the burqa." But I don't think it's true. There's still a lot of other social issues that need to be taken care of before women can really walk around freely.

We ended up living in a tiny apartment in a house owned by an Indian couple in Flushing, Queens. My stepmother cried the whole first night. We've come to America, and look at this apartment! It was one of those Archie Bunker neighborhoods. You know when you watch *All in the Family*, that first aerial shot with all those tiny homes right next to each other? That's exactly where we lived.

The pioneering TV sitcom "All in the Family" (1971–1983) depicts a blue-collar household in Queens, headed by a bigoted but oddly likeable guy named Archie Bunker. The show was the first of its kind on American television, tackling controversial issues like feminism, homosexuality, race, and the "onslaught" of immigrants.

I got left back a year at the local public school because I didn't know English. I didn't know how to say, "May I go to the bathroom?" or "I don't know what you're saying." My desk was right in front of the teacher's desk and I would sit there all day and not go to the bathroom until I went home. Then

I got a little picture book and I would point to a picture of a toilet, and the teacher would know, okay, it's time to go to the bathroom. My teacher told my stepmother at a parent-teacher conference that I wasn't learning English fast enough. When I came home, my father was extremely upset with me. He told me, in Farsi, that I must be stupid. I had

© *Shekaiba Wakili, 2001*
This woman is a Tajik like me. I also photographed a Hazara from central Afghanistan, but I can't let you show that picture. At one time the Hazaras were all Buddhists. So when the Taliban blew up the Buddhist monuments, it was not only a cultural genocide, it was an ethnic genocide as well. Like we are going to get rid of your heritage once and for all. Afghanistan may be a Muslim country, but we incorporate our pre-Islamic heritage into our daily lives.

the hardest time trying to tell the cafeteria lady that I couldn't eat pork. My father taught me how to say, "No pig! No pig!" It took about a month for the cafeteria lady to realize I couldn't eat pork. Whenever they were having pork products, she would make me a peanut butter and jelly sandwich, which was horrible because I hated peanut butter and jelly! So I didn't eat anything. Then my father told me to say chicken, but I would say, "kitchen" instead of chicken. It took me so long to differentiate between the two. Imagine me. "Kitchen. No pig!"

Our neighborhood was mostly Spanish and Russian and on my way to school, there was a man living in one of those Archie Bunker houses who would always say, "Good morning" to me, and I would say, "Good morning" to him and hurry past, because he was a stranger and we're not supposed to talk to strangers.

© *Shekaiba Wakili, 2001*
This woman is Turkmen. I had a hard time finding burqas in New York, so I sent money to my uncle who's a refugee in Peshawar, Pakistan. I asked him to send me four burqas. He sent me three. I asked him for colorful ones. He sent me a white one. That's all he could find in the stores there.

One day he asked me, "Where are you from?" I was a little scared but I told him. And he told me where he was from, which didn't make any sense, since I was a kid and I didn't know about every place in the world. I was like, "Okay," and kept walking. Then one day he stopped me and he gave me a little booklet. He said, "I want you to read this." I said, "Okay." He said, "This is very valuable. Every American should know this." I opened it up and it was the U.S. Constitution, and a copy of the Bill of Rights, and then little biographies of all the presidents from George Washington up to Jimmy Carter. From then on, this man was my friend. I remember he told me he was Jewish, but I didn't know about other religions or the

Jewish-Muslim history or what was going on in the Middle East. I just
knew this nice man said he was Jewish, and from reading the book he
gave me and going through all that I went through, I became very interested in history and politics and looking at things from a global perspective.
Twenty-four years later I see how my father and the rest of my family
became staunch Republicans. Because of their experience in Afghanistan,
they loved Ronald Reagan. He was such an anti-Communist! My father was

*Ronald Reagan began his anti-Communist
crusade during his five years as president
of the Screen Actors Guild. His testimony
before the House Un-American Activities
Committee in the 1950s contributed to the
blacklisting of over 300 people in the
entertainment industry. As a two-term
President of the United States in the
1980s, Reagan spared no expense trying to
purge the entire world of Communism. His
peacetime buildup of the U.S. military
was unprecedented, exceeding even the
peak years of the Vietnam war.*

liberal when he came here but I guess
America brought out the patriarchal
Afghan in him. I couldn't date. I couldn't
wear skirts or make-up. Couldn't go out
on my own. They wanted to find a boy
for me to get married to and I didn't
want that. In my second year of college,
I couldn't take the cultural conflict anymore. I switched from a political science
major to art and announced that I was
moving out. My father said, "If you move out, then I'm not going to talk
to you." I ended up being disowned by my father and haven't spoken to
him since. That was twelve years ago.

All these years I never communicated with my mother. I have no memory
of her. My older sister Nahid was also disowned by my father and she
started writing letters to Afghanistan to try and track down our mother
and her side of the family. In 1992, Nahid got a letter from our mother (in
Farsi) saying her house got bombed and she lost everything and fled to
Kabul with our younger sister, our aunt and uncle, and our grandparents.
Nahid and I made an agreement to send a hundred dollars a month to help
out the family. Then in '94 we got a letter saying, "The war is getting really
bad. It looks like the city is going to be destroyed. We need to get out of
here!" So we sent enough money for them to escape to Pakistan and live.
They got out right before the Taliban took control.

*The Taliban (masculine plural word for student
in Pashto) captured Kabul in 1996 and ruled
the country until they were run out by U.S. and
allied forces in 2001. The Taliban's extreme
interpretations of Islamic law resulted in public
executions, a strict social code, and severe
restrictions on the activities of women.*

In order to bring my family here, I first had to prove to the INS that we were related. They wanted a lot of documents that we couldn't provide. My mother had no papers. When the rocket destroyed her house, what was she going to do – run and get her birth certificate? I had to be able to write their story in a narrative document, so I decided to go to Pakistan to get the information firsthand and meet my elderly grandparents before it was too late. I packed my tape recorder, a camera, and some notebooks, and flew to Peshawar in 1995.

Peshawar is like the backwater, hick part of Pakistan. I'm at the airport and I look around. Not a woman to be found! As I'm walking to get my luggage, I realize I forgot to bring a veil. Every single man in the aiport is looking at me like they had never seen a woman before. It felt like I had landed in a male colony and I wasn't supposed to be there. Suddenly I see a group of people standing there, waiting. My uncle comes up to me and says, "Shekaiba?" What do I do? Total American, I go, "OH, MY UNCLE," and give him a big hug and a kiss. Then my sister, who I'd never known, takes out this veil, which she brought to the airport for me. That stupid veil, I wore it the whole time I was there.

I hadn't seen my mother in 22 years. I just stood there, like, okay, so you're my mother. She's very quiet and shows very little emotion. It was like meeting a stranger. I didn't know what to do. When she started crying, I started crying. I was devastated to see how my family and other Afghan refugees were living. There were open sewers in the streets. They had an apartment with no windows, no sunlight. This was the best my $300 dollars a month could get them. In one week I met over 60 different people who were related to me from both sides of my family. Within a few days I was so emotionally and physically drained, I got sick and had to come back to New York.

I had four different jobs and was a full-time graduate student but I started calling and e-mailing INS everyday. I finally had to pay $1,000 for a DNA test to prove my mother was my mother.

I was born in Khodaman, a large village just outside Kabul, surrounded by very tall mountains. It was a very beautiful, paradise type of place. Extremely color–ful. Green grapes, red apples, dark orange apricots, cherries, flowers, all kinds of birds. And we weren't that far from other towns that were also very lively and colorful. My father was the village leader, a Han, which means religious leader. He was very religious. Muslim.

I read and write a little Farsi, up to a third grade level. And I'm trying my English. Unfortunately, I did not go to school. In those days school had just started for girls and my father did not want his eldest daughter to be led in the wrong path. Of course my brothers went to school, and so did my younger sister who was was born ten years after me. By that time, most people let their daughters attend school. I stayed home with my mom cooking and cleaning, helping around the house. When I was 13 years old, I got married to my aunt's nephew. My husband was a bright, progressive man. But his father was very close-minded.

Was I happy?

When I think back, I was happy.

I don't know. I was just a child.

One day I was living in my parent's home and then I was married off to live with another family in Kabul. That's just the way it was. In Kabul, I had the opportunity to go to classes, so I took a sewing class. My first daughter Nahid was born when I was 16. I gave birth at Kabul Hospital and nobody was there. They wouldn't allow family members. Shekaiba was born when I was 19.

At the time, King Zahir Shah was in power. I was walking around without a veil, wearing short sleeves, short skirts and high heels. Nobody said, "Why are you wearing this?" Kabul was very cosmopolitan! We'd go to the cinema to see Bollywood movies, French movies, and some American movies. My biggest memory was a documentary on JFK. When JFK Jr. died, I cried, because I remember seeing him as a little boy in that movie.

As a mother, I wanted my daughters to get the highest education that I missed. But after my third daughter was born, I was separated from my two older ones. The plainest explanation is my husband wanted someone who was more sophisticated, because he had finished University of Kabul, got his Master's and was working for the Peace Corps. He traded me for a newer model. We had a home divorce because my father didn't want my name to be dragged through civil court and my name ruined forever. My husband got Nahid and Shekaiba, and the baby came with me back to my father's house. After the divorce, I worked as a seamstress, making suits and pants and all kinds of clothes for people. As a tailor I did well. As a mother my heart was broken being separated from my children. Always worrying how they're growing up.

In the early '80s, the war with the Soviets was slowly coming towards Khodaman. First we'd hear reports like a Mujahideen fighter is hiding in this or that house. Then the government soldiers and the Communists would come and raid that house. Then the young people would get scared. They'd leave home and hide in other homes or in schools. When the fighting got bad in your neighborhood, you'd pack up and move someplace safe. A lot of people went missing. Especially sons. In my family, it was my older brother. He went out one day to go shopping and the Communists picked him up and recruited him into the army. Then he got captured by the Muja-hideens and was forced to joined them, until he got stopped again by the Afghan Communists. We haven't heard from him since.

Backed by the U.S., the Mujahideen — an unlikely coalition of Islamic Pashtun and Tajik guerrilla fighters — eventually overturned the Soviet occupation. Forty to fifty thousand Soviets and about a million Afghans lost their lives during the ten years of fighting.

SHEKAIBA

To this day, she thinks he escaped and is living in Kuwait or Egypt. That's what she wants to tell herself, but we've told her many times, "He's not around, Mom." But she still doesn't believe it.

In the beginning we had no idea what Mujahideen were, except they were very religious. So we would cover ourselves up with the chador [headscarf] or put on the burqa [head-to-toe dress], just in case. Once the Russians left, and we lived under the government of President Najibullah,

we were living in Kabul and we dressed like normal people again. Then with President Rabbani, we wore a long dress with chador, because he had an Islamic government, but we didn't have to cover from head to toe. That was in the early '90s. My youngest daughter was a teenager going to an excellent government run school, and we could still go about our daily life pretty easily even though there were outbreaks of fight-ing. Then the fighting escalated.

SULTANA

We knew the Taliban were coming because we used to get fliers in our neighborhood saying, "We're going to capture the city." We knew the Taliban were very religious and their leader was Mullah Omar. And when they took over, like they did already in Kandahar, you did not leave the house show-ing anything from head to toe. We heard they took women out of their houses and beat and raped them and killed sons in front of the mothers. They started to hit Kabul with rockets and bombs and we huddled in the basement at one point for fifteen days straight. When our house was shelled, we grabbed a few pieces of china, some blankets and a rug, and the whole family left. We paid 1,000 Afghanis [Afghan dollars] each to drive through a lot of treacherous mountain roads from Kabul to Jalalabad. Then to get over the boarder into Pakistan we paid another 25,000 Afghanis. All the money we had. When we got to Peshawar, there were two million Afghans there!

SHEKAIBA

We knew more about the Taliban than many people in Afghanistan did. Some found out after it was too late. By now everyone knows that the Taliban decreed that women could not work or go to school. Almost overnight the women and the children of Afghan-istan were turned into beggars.

I'll never forget the day I got a phone call from my daughter in America. It was the first time I heard Shekaiba's voice since she was a little girl. It felt like the light of my heart was turned on. She and her sister kept sending us money, in Kabul, in Peshawar. Then for four years, Shekaiba tried very hard to get me to America. Finally the American Embassy in Peshawar did a DNA test with cotton swabs in my mouth. I was hoping they were doing the test correctly so I would be her mother, because I am her moth-er, and this way I can get up and go to America. And that's what I did. I came to America.

On the plane, I didn't feel scared, I didn't think anything except I'm going to America to be with my daughters. I'm going to be their mother again. Nineteen hours in the air, I couldn't sleep. When I got through customs, the young man handed me over to my daughters. They said, "We're so happy to see you, Mom," and I said the same thing.

SHEKAIBA

My relationship with my mother is one of discoveries. We are from two different cultures and two different generations. She's been a refugee for so long I had to teach her how to live again – how to shop, how to cross Queens Boulevard so she doesn't get hit by a car. We don't have much common ground but she's my mom and someone has to take care of her.

When I did the paperwork for my mom, I petitioned to bring my sister here too. By the time her papers went through the system, my sister was no longer under the age of 21, which meant, according to the INS, my sister was no longer my sister. She fell into a new category of "relative." I was told it would take nine more years for the paperwork to go through. I couldn't wait that long, so I contacted the Feminist Majority Foundation. They just started their Afghan Relief Gender Apartheid Campaign. I said, "You want to help somebody? Help her." She was the first recipient of their Afghan college scholarship. On the eve of the Feminist Expo – April 1st, year 2000, she came from Pakistan. I picked her up at JFK Airport, we got a connecting flight to Baltimore, put our bags in the hotel room, and within 20 minutes she was giving a speech in front of 2,000 people. For two years she was the poster child for the Feminist Majority, but she has no interest in activism, which is kind of disappointing to me.

Every day, if it's not raining, I meet my friends in the park. When I tell them I live by myself, they get upset. Many of them live with their sons and daughters. They see I'm always sewing, so they ask me to hem their pants or shorten their jackets. Then I started getting jobs from the Italian tailor.

Detail of baby booties hand-knit by Sultana Wakili

SHEKAIBA

My husband's father is Jewish. They came from Russia and believed in Socialism. They settled in a community of Russian Jews in New Jersey – nudists, artists, and Socialists. Derek's father really couldn't complain that his son was marrying a Mulsim because *he* married a German Lutheran. He told Derek one time, "When you date their women, you better be careful, because they might come and kill you." Derek said, "Don't be ridiculous!" His mom was really upset. Since she was German, I guess I was too close to being Turkish. She told him, "I want you to date somebody who is North European." He said, "How about somebody who is South European?" She said, "No. You can't go below the Alps." She eventually grew to tolerate me.

SULTANA

I'm happy for my daughter. I don't complain. Anything is better than what I experienced in Kabul. The only thing I worry about is the rest of my family who are stuck in Pakistan, and the fate of my country. We are poor people. If we could just get out all the people who are fighting in Afghanistan, I think Afghanistan would be okay.

His dad suggested we get a rabbi to marry us, but we really wanted someone spiritual like Imam Faisel, so he married us using elements of our different faiths. He made references to the Jewish family members, to our Christian Lutheran family, and my Muslim family. I'm grateful that our friends and family saw an Islamic marriage, not in the traditional sense, but an Islamic marriage nevertheless, before 9-11. You should see my father-in-law now. He's always talking to people about Islam. From dealing with my family, he knows we're not all fanatics.

After seven years working on her case, I was able to get my aunt a visa as a full refugee. Her flight was on September 11th, 2001. She took a bus from Peshawar to Islamabad, took a plane to Karachi, then on the flight from Karachi to Dubai, the plane was told to turn around because America had been bombed. The INS told them, "Go back to wherever you came from. Everything to America has been stopped." Some people sold everything and had no place to go. My aunt went back to Preshawar and every week they'd tell her, "Whenever we're ready, we'll let you know." That day I was so overwhelmed by what was happening, all those people dying in those towers. I wasn't even thinking about my aunt until I heard that all flights had been suspended. I thought, *oh my God, seven years of paperwork out the window.* I finally was able to get her here in March 2002.

I'm starting to photograph the Muslim families who lost loved ones in the Twin Towers. I have to give them time because like anybody else, it's been very tragic. You have to deal with the fact that this horrible thing was done in the name of your culture and your religion, and your son is dead because of that.

SULTANA

My Iranian friend called and said the two buildings were hit and I shouldn't leave the apartment. Shekaiba called and said the same thing. So naturally I went outside to see for myself. I said, "Oh, nothing is happening in Queens." So I came in and turned on the TV. I cried most of the day for all those innocent people. I knew Afghanistan was involved because they kept showing pictures of Osama bin Laden. When I left Afghanistan I didn't even know the name Osama bin Laden. Then when we were refugees in Pakistan, all of us would listen to the BBC radio, Farsi channel. That's how we got our information.

I have a dream that I want to visit Afghanistan. The Afghanistan of my childhood. I don't want to see the Afghanistan that's broken, ripped apart, and destroyed. I want to go to the village my father came from and make a documentary. That one little village tells the story of what has happened to Afghanistan. Every single house has lost someone either through violence, killing or war, or people have emigrated out. I *will* go back, but first I'm learning about Islam, because I want to know why this religion has been so misinterpreted and used for political gain. Why so many people who say they are Muslim, who know the language, have not done justice interpreting it. I know some people say bin Laden is the product of the CIA. That's too easy because he's also a product of the Islamic culture and the political system of where he grew up. In Saudi Arabia, they passed a law that said women can't drive, because somehow they found a passage in the Qur'an that said women can't drive. It's barbaric! It doesn't say anything

MSNBC's International Editor, Michael Moran, writes that "Osama bin Laden, our new public enemy number 1, is the personification of blowback." A CIA code name, blowback is used to describe a former agent or operative who has turned against the U.S. Moran and others question the wisdom of the CIA's support of a multi-national coalition of Islamic extremists to fight the Soviets in Afghanistan. The agency [during the Reagan administration] reasoned that "Arab zealots were easier to 'read' than the rivalry-ridden [Afghan] natives." Considering the heir to his family's Saudi construction company a "reliable" partner, the CIA aided bin Laden's organization, which funneled money, arms, and fighters to the Mujahideen. When the Soviets were defeated, the CIA packed its bags and bin Laden returned to Saudi Arabia to form Al-Qaeda. He's now regarded as the mastermind of 9-11 and other devastating attacks on America.

in the Qur'an about driving! Mohammed was very pro-woman. The mentality that led to the Taliban and Al-Qaeda is not Afghan. It's unusual for Afghan culture to tell its women to not be productive members of society.

I'm Tajik and the Tajiks are Persian, and before Islam we were part of the Zoroastrian culture, which is from the north where Rumi is from. I love Rumi's poetry and feel very connected to that whole mystical tradition, but how I am approaching life now is as a Muslim. I will always be a Muslim and I will die a Muslim. Especially since 9-11, I want to know about things that I did not learn growing up. I want to know what does it say in the Qur'an about the role of women? What does it say in the Qur'an about jihad? What does it say about how to be with your neighbor? I want to know these things because I want to have a constructive conversation when I come across people who question me as a quote-unquote Muslim. But then I also want to have a dialogue with people who are Muslim, but think very differently than I do. That's where I am right now. Am I practicing? No. But I want to learn about the hadith, which is the oral interpretation of the Qur'an. I want to learn about the shari'a, which is the law interpretation of the Qur'an. I know I'm not going to find anything that says you can go blow up people, but I want to empower myself with the knowledge. My kids are going to be quarter-Jewish, quarter-Christian, and half Muslim. When they come to me, "Oh, mommy, somebody said Islam is a violent religion," I've got to be able to fully explain Islam to them, because I don't want my children to learn Islam from somebody else.

Right now I'm trying to bring over my mom's brother. As challenging as it is, you can get Afghan women out. But to get an Afghan man out after 9-11 who fits the typical U.S. profile of a Muslim terrorist, a single man like my uncle in his 30s with no assets, no nothing – that's the holy grail of challenges!

SULTANA

Sultana lived for four years as a refugee in Pakistan, then she came to Queens. Now, four years later, the rents are too high, so she's leaving to live near Shekaiba's younger sister in a suburb of Baltimore, Maryland.

I'm going to miss all my friends I made in New York. I'm afraid everyone in Maryland speaks English. Hopefully I will run into people and they'll ask me, "How are you?" And I'll say, "I'm doing okay. How are you?" And I'll learn English. Maybe they'll ask me where I'm from and I'll say I'm from Afghanistan. Maybe they'll know where that is.

ties that bind
- the brothers rahman/el sayed
- the other side of the road
- goat songs and demon elks
- if there is no dance there is no life
- the christmas card
- a world of difference

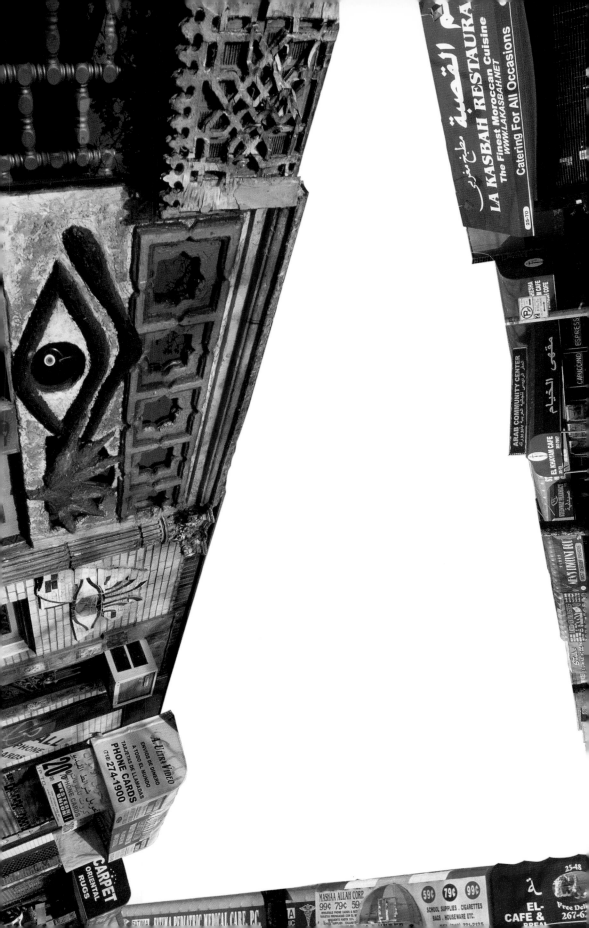

ALI EL SAYED
MOUSTAFA RAHMAN

the
brothers
rahman/el sayed

We hear a lot of complaints about how "new immigrants" are different than immigrants of the past. "They don't want to assimilate... They don't want to learn English," etc. For the most part, we do not see that to be the case. One difference we do see is the connection to back home. While most immigrants of the past knew they were never going back to their "old world," post–'65 immigrants have a much more fluid connection to their heritage. The Internet, telephone, satellite TV, importation of food, music, and clothing, and access to air travel make it easier to remain rooted to one's family and culture.

Two brothers, Ali and Moustafa, own and operate a café and restaurant a few doors down from each other on Steinway Street in Astoria. Ali was the first Egyptian to open an eatery on the street that has now become a Middle Eastern mecca. He dishes up as much tantalizingly delicious philosophy, humor and commentary as he does food at his seven-table café. Ali's soft-spoken brother Moustafa, spent seven years crafting his fabulous, densely-mosaiced, hand-painted, and collaged restaurant before opening to the public. Inspired by their mother's home cooking, both brothers build on authentic Egyptian cuisine as they artfully compose new dishes of their own invention. Today, Kebab Café and Mombar are hot spots for the many artists and musicians that have flocked to the village of Astoria. Like a lot of us who moved to Queens some time ago, Ali and Moustafa face the benefits and pitfalls of gentrification with mixed feelings.

ASTORIA

MEDITERRANEAN SEA

ISRAEL

Alexandria ●Cairo

Nile

EGYPT

SUDAN

Four kids from the neighborhood come in. They say, "Ali, we have $37. We want to eat, but that's all we have." I give them food and drinks, at least $100 worth. When you come from the background we come from, money isn't everything. An old man stops by. "I don't have money tonight, but I'm hungry. I pay you tomorrow." I'm not going to tell him no. You give him the food. Even the best that you have. He was honest enough to tell you his situation. But when you are rich, filthy rich, and you are cheap, and you are rude, then you really don't deserve to be in my place.

KABAB CAFE أبو درش FALAFEL
25-12 STEINWAY ST. 728-9858

VEGETARIAN

Ali, on the left, and Moustafa, on the right, hold court outside their respective restaurants.

MOUSTAFA

*A lot of people pass by. Even when
they look in, they wonder what is
it. "Do you have a mosque here?"
I don't put a sign up that says
Mombar or Restaurant or what the
hours are. All the years I spent
designing and making all the art-
work by hand, it was a secret place.
People thought,* what is this guy
doing? He rents this place to spend
all his time fussing around in there.

Tabletop by Moustafa Rahman

MOUSTAFA

The New York Times *wrote, "Michaelangelo did the Sistine Chapel in four years. It took Moustafa Rahman seven years to do his restaurant." They forgot to say Michaelangelo didn't do it himself; he had a lot of people helping him. The day I opened, I felt good to show everybody what I was doing all these years. But also that day, I had to move my studio into the basement, and give up my workshop for fixing copy machines and office computers.*

ALI

A man comes with four people. They have appetizers, main course, couple of drinks. They're talking about their summer homes, the money they made in the stock market. The bill is $80. He says,

> *"That's too much."*

I say, "How much do you have?"

> *"We have $50."*

I say, "Give me the $50 and don't come here anymore please."

Sometimes I wonder what am I doing this for. I put my heart into a dish. A guy comes into the café, he's just going gobble, gobble. He's not even looking at the plate. I cook to feed people. My mom, when she cooked, she cooked more than enough food, just in case somebody is going to stop by. She's our inspiration.

Look at Moustafa. He worked so long on his restaurant. Is he crazy or something? That's what I wonder. **Are we nuts just to work for the sake of working?** He's still doing computers to support his restaurant! We are so lucky to have a landlord like ours. A lot of months we can't pay the rent. God lives inside our landlord. I see him almost every day. If it wasn't for him we'd have to move from Astoria and find somewhere else. Maybe one morning if he wakes up on the wrong side of the bed, I'll be kicked out.

I was the first one to start a café on the block. Now they're calling the neighborhood Little Egypt. Other people I know, artists and musicians who come to my place, have been here for a while too. What we do, we make the area nice. We don't have much, so we create a state of mind to enjoy ourselves. We want to listen to good music. We want to clean the place. We want a beautiful view, so we make the place beautiful. Then other artists and musicians come here, and that's wonderful. We get together and talk about literature and art. We eat. We smoke shisha. And now comes the real estate people. Now comes the money. They say, "Oh, this is beautiful area." They buy the buildings and triple the rent. And for you – as an artist or a person who just wants to feed and entertain people, and have a roof over your head – you can't afford to do that in this area anymore. You have to move out. You really killed yourself with the atmosphere you created. The people who have money, they wait for the bees to build their hives, then they exterminate and move in. They change the gallery to a boutique, because that's what they need – a boutique. This is the natural flow of life.

Door with stained and painted glass by Moustafa Rahman

MOUSTAFA

Art was always something that I did for the love of it, but in college I went for electric engineering. My uncle was an engineer, my brother, my sister, we're all engineers. It was either that or math. Those were the choices. I thought with engineering I could build things with my hands and invent things. It ended up mostly I fixed things.

My son is six years old. He wants to go to McDonald's for dinner.
Not because of the food. He wants the toy that he can get there.
The toy that goes with the video game that goes with the movie.

That's what I should do. Make a toy.
A Falafel Toy!

A lady stopped by today. She said, "Why don't you put up the
article from *New York Magazine?* It was so positive about your place."
I'm not going to put up the article. I'm going to put a sign:

Won't sell anything else. Just come to Kabab Café for a toy. It's
time to get out of this financial hole. When I came to this country, I
moved right away to Greenwich Village. You couldn't mention Queens
to me. I really did hate Queens, especially Astoria. I thought it's a
stupid village, Astoria. I went to the clubs in Manhattan. I listened to
music in Manhattan. Everything was Manhattan, Manhattan, Manhattan. Then I lost my restaurant on the Upper West Side because of

the rents. So I came to Queens where
the rents were low. I said okay, instead
of facing the same dilemma, let me be
a real estate broker. Maybe I can have
a house. Then I can have a restaurant.
Have a couple of good chefs working
for me and some artists paying rent
in the building I own with a view of
Manhattan. This is what I was thinking
18 years ago.

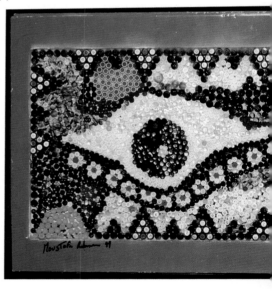

I got my broker's license. The Greeks,
the Italians, the Jewish, the Egyptians
came to me to sell their house. Great!
They say, "My house is worth a million dollars." It's a two-bedroom
house with dropped ceilings. I'm not going to show it. Someone comes
to the office. I'm not going to take them to a house unless it's good

enough for me to buy. I did bad as a real estate agent. I bought nothing. I sold nothing.

But I fell in love with Astoria, with Queens. It's a neighborhood. People know you by name. A customer of mine, a beautiful kid who plays jazz guitar wrote a piece of music and named it after me. To show me some respect he did that. All these hard working artists and musicians and kids in computers who come to my place, just meeting them is unbelievable. Every night I go home and I think about the conversations I had that night. It gives me hope that we might have a better universe. Like Picasso was Spanish and Braque was French and Gertrude Stein was American, but they met in the cafés in Paris. It was a place to exchange ideas. Astoria is becoming a place like that.

Now where we going to go? Maybe we can find a place in a high crime area with crackheads. The question is, can we turn crackheads into artists? Our next mission: turning crackheads' neighborhood into beautiful, mellow place, so real estate people can come and kick us out of there too.

MOUSTAFA

For the restaurant, I decided to mix the old civilizations with the modern art. Outside I put the Greek columns and the Islamic window with a lotus flower and the pyramid from the Pharoahs' time, and the eye of Horus and the eye of the dragon. In the Middle East, the eye takes the evil away. All around you see the eye as God watching over everybody. Ladies wear a necklace with a blue eye to protect them from the evil eye. For me it's more that I like to draw eyes all over. It's what I'm used to.

Some people think these are just abstract designs. For me, I like the abstract too, but almost everything has a meaning to it. The pigeons around the hands symbolize peace. The eight pointed star you see on all Islamic architecture. You're not allowed to draw a human image, so they use the star as a symbol of holy life and it repeats like a flower repeats in a garden.

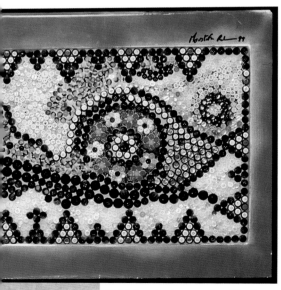

Tabletop design made of buttons
by Moustafa Rahman

ALI

MOUSTAFA

The half sun with the rays coming out symbolizes God. That is a very Egyptian thing. The sun with the water stands for the Nile. The lotus flower is not just a flower, it's a sacred plant. The mosaic on the floor is like a wine cellar. First, the grain of the marble made me think of flowing water. So I cut the marble to make it look like water. Then I cut jugs on top of the columns, and the water turned to wine flowing out of the jugs like a river.

When you're in Egypt you never meet a friend for a drink in a bar, because drinking is forbidden. You meet your friend in the café and smoke a shisha, play backgammon, talk about your social problem, political problem, talk about women, and the nonsense in life. But majority of people here associate this pipe with drugs. You take a picture of me smoking shisha pipe, people don't understand.

I remember when the Oklahoma building exploded, they thought right away it's an Arab who has done it. So people in Oklahoma went to the Arab area and they start to attack them. Later on they came to know it's not a damn foreigner – it's a white boy nobody ever expected. When they crashed those planes into the World Trade Towers, you see the terror in people's eyes, maybe you're one of the guys that planned it. It's easy to point to people and start to name them. It happened in Germany with Jewish people. You never get over the way people look at you. It can really hurt. The way we point to each other. You are Warren. You are Judith. You start to think, what kind of name is that? Jewish. Jewish is this and that. I am Ali. Oh, Arab. Every day we should change our names. Today I'm not Ali, I'm Eli. I'm Alay. Tomorrow I want to be Margarita. It's a cool drink. Day after that I'll be David. David Ben Gurion. It's illogical even to have names. We should have numbers. Yes! Or dots maybe.

Many times I have an idea in my head of what I want to do. Then I start making it and it turns into something else. That's half the fun of it, not knowing what will happen next. With the marble, I can't afford to get all one kind. So I buy leftover pieces, which forces me not to make the same pattern over and over. Instead of a symmetrical design, which is fine, I prefer the asymmetric.

No more Ali. I am ● ● ● ●. You are ● ● ● ●. What is race? What is color? Stay in the sun, your skin gets darker. Religions. We should get over this stuff already. We can't exist without each other. We don't live in countries anymore. We live in a very small village. We are the human race. That's the only race I see.

I went back to Alexandria this summer. It's very fashionable for Egyptian boys now to marry Israeli girls. Both sets of parents go bananas. Not only the parents – the Egyptian government is saying no, you cannot marry these Israeli girls. The Israelis aren't happy either. You think a nice Jewish mama wants her daughter to marry an Egyptian guy? They should just leave the kids alone. They're going to change the world one day.

In the Middle East, religion is not just something you do one day a week. It's a way of LIVING. Even the Western religions didn't come from France or England or Alaska. They all came from one triangle:

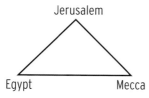

Or maybe it's a square. Start with Buddha in India, then Abraham, then Mohammed and Christ.

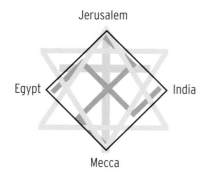

For me, religion was never the thing. I grew up in the sixties with the ideas of international student movement. We didn't believe in organized religion. We didn't believe in countries.

Tabletop design by Moustafa made with slices of colored glass bottles

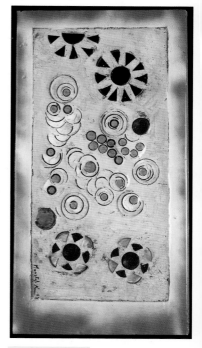

MOUSTAFA

You can make almost anything from anything else. I made chandeliers out of blue bottles. Hung the bottles upside down from a round metal pipe. Then I hung crystal so it dropped like tears coming down from the center. I have so many eyes around, I thought, let me have some tears coming down.

The whole system of dictatorship in Egypt was annoying me. Colleges and universities, especially in third world countries are the hotbed of rebellious thinking. That's where the educated minds are and the young people who have time on their hands and no responsibilities except to think about the way the world should be a better place. That's why to control a country, you always have to keep the people ignorant.

Detail above of collaged and painted wall by Moustafa

My degree was in agriculture with a specialty in chemical pesticides. After I graduated I got a job working for the Egyptian government inspecting pesticides. But my ideas got in the way. When you study pesticides you understand what is the chemical effect of the pesticide on the insect. But you also study the residual effect on the human being and the animals and the earth. At that time it was just coming out that DDT would give you cancer, not only you, but your second and third generation. So they banned DDT in the United States. But countries in the third world, we get the pesticides they don't allow over here. Who cares about the people in Egypt, the people in Bangladesh or Bopal or China? We are not human beings in the eyes of Dow Chemical or Union Carbide or Ciba Gigy.

I started talking like this to my bosses. So they put me to a back room job with no decision making. I could have fought harder but I took the easy path and left the country. It's not good for the third world countries for everyone like me with contrary opinions to go to Europe or America. We should stay in our country and go to jail and be killed. I should be DEAD by today. A guy like me. Instead I'm free to speak my mind here in United States where nobody cares what I say. Free to raise the value of real estate so I can't live here anymore. Free to work my pants off seven days a week to start again a new week.

Nobody works as hard as people do in New York. An enzyme
that changes one chemical compound into another chemical
compound – that is New York City. It turns slow into fast, rich
into poor, poor into rich, lazy into son-of-a-gun. I came here,
I was a chemist and a Communist. Now I'm a chef and a miserable capitalist. It didn't matter I had a college degree, I was
an immigrant so I got a job as a dishwasher. By the end of the
year I was a chef. I knew I was never going to be a rich man,
so I said,

> Let me do something that I really like.

I went to the Chef's Program at the Culinary Arts Institute.
I was so happy to do something very far from the disastrous
business of killing insects and animals and people. I love
people! I don't want to kill them. I want to *feed* them.

All that I've learned in schools and books and travelling to
different parts of the world – nothing compares to what my
mother taught me. She was a great chef. My grandmother was
an even greater chef. The way they made things from nothing.
The creation of food comes from the hardship, from the sea-
sonal fruits and vegetables, from a frugal way of preserving
things when they're not in season, from the jarring and can-
ning and drying. You're a kid growing up in the kitchen with
your mother. She never taught you how to cook, but you saw
her grow her own chickens and squabs and rabbits on the roof
of the house. You saw the breadmaking, the peppers pickling,
the preparation of sauces with a dozen different hand-ground
spices, having just a little olive oil in the jar and cooking with
it all year round. You never ate out. Even if you're back home
at two o'clock in the morning, your dinner will be on the table.
I don't know if it's good or bad, but that's how it was. Making
something wonderful out of nothing – it's a way of living.

Until recently, Egypt was a country occupied by other powers.
The last king in the '50s was Albanian! The Italians, the Greeks,
the Persians, the Turkish, the English – all occupied Egypt for
a very long time. They left a lot of political problems with us,
but they also left their cuisines. Instead of one mass cuisine,

*Mosaic marble
floor designed,
cut, and laid
by Moustafa*

every home, every little village has their own way of cooking. Take fava beans. Go into a store that sells fava beans, you will get one thing. Go to Egypt and you will eat it 50 different ways in 50 different homes.

What Moustafa and I are trying to get here is the origin of the Egyptian cuisine. But to nail it to the original Egyptian cuisine you'd have to go back to the time of the Pharaohs. Egypt was always the road of spices from India to Europe until they got tired of going through Egypt. **That's how they came to discover America. Columbus was looking for another way to get to the spices and he took a wrong turn.**

Detail of Moustafa's kitchen counter wall

A lot of immigrants think America is what they see in the movies. I know some Middle Eastern guys, they live four together in a small place and just last week they got a BMW. They're thinking James Dean and Elvis Presley car. Soon as they get here, they're walking with the cell phone, "Hi, how are you? You know where I'm calling from? Downstairs. I'm walking in the door." I go buy vegetables at night and I see mostly foreigners like me, but younger, on the phone with their wives. Spanish guys. Middle Eastern guys. Russian guys. "Okay, now I'm going to the tomatoes, three dollars per pound." He's talking to his wife three o'clock in the morning. "This is orange, 79 cents. Eggplant, 83 cents." I see this, I think I will never buy a cell phone because I don't want to look like that.

If I see garbage on the street, that might give me an idea. Like the U.S. mail chutes I saw lying around a construction site one day. I painted the glass, put a bulb in there and turned them into light fixtures. In the kitchen, I hung clay pots upside down as lamps. On the wall I made a tile mosaic out of broken ceramic. Not only Egyptian ceramic, I use Mexican, Greek, and Japanese, and in the middle I put an American turkey plate.

Tin trays I cut in half for shelves like shelf mush-rooms. A coffee grinder can be a bird with a tail. A door from an old book cabinet I use as Arabesque around a window. I got a lot of eyes from an old doll factory that went out of business. Made a tabletop that looks like Manhattan. Some of the buildings have eyes looking out at Queens. Hammers from of an old piano, gourds, pieces of earth from Mount Sinai, where they say Moses talked to God and saw a burning bush — all these things I make part of the restaurant.

ALI

Everybody comes to my place. Palestinians, Israelis, they all come here. Even they were in the military, they're tired of fighting. It's not like what they tell you on the news. The Middle East is a problem you think will never be solved because you think that's their nature to always be killing each other. It's not true. Has nothing to do with Jewish. Has nothing to do with Muslims. Has only to do with,

THE
OIL
IS THERE.

Start a war.
Create an oil shortage.

Queens is my home now. No matter what, this is my heaven. We've got everybody here and people aren't killing each other.

Okay, what would you like today? I have a whole mackerel wrapped in aluminum foil with vegetables, potatoes, peas, and lemon, cooked on the grill. Or maybe you want to start with a meze plate? Has everything: hummus, falafel, baba ghanoush. It has fava beans on there, swiss chard, dandelion. Excellent, excellent. You want mint tea with that? You have a cold. I'll make you a licorice tea. You'll feel better. Maybe you want hibiscus tea? It's nice. Or you can have Coke or Pepsi? We made some Pepsi this morning. Fresh. Actually it's from 1997. Excellent year for Pepsi, '97. Bottled right here in Astoria.

Bathroom tile to die for, by Moustafa

MOUSTAFA

I tried to make a place I feel comfortable to work in, a place people want to come and stay.

Tabletop by Moustafa made with matchbooks, shells, paint, etc.

Photograph taken between 1935–40, of Moustafa's and Ali's great uncle and uncle.

the
other side
of the road

*Seven days a week — early mornings
to mid-afternoons — men from south
of the border, mostly from Mexico,
hang out in work lines on Queens
Boulevard or Roosevelt Avenue. They
wait for cars, vans, or trucks belonging
to small business owners, contractors,
and construction companies who are
looking for cheap day-labor. It took
six years for Miguel to graduate from
being one of the guys on the line to
being one of the guys with the boss
in the vehicle, picking who works
and who doesn't. In between caring
for their three kids, Miguel's wife,
Marianna, practices aroma and herbal
cleansings. They shared their story
of forbidden love, migration, and survival as undocumented "aliens" from
their one room basement apartment
next to the Grand Central Expressway.*

UNITED STATES
OF AMERICA

GRAND CENTRAL PARKWAY

PARKING
FIELD

Shea
Stadium

MEXICO

AV

N.Y.C.T.A.   **CORONA**

Mexico City ●
Puebla
○ Oaxaca
BELIZE

GUATEMALA

When we first met, I was Marcelo, the soldier who kills Christ, and she was the Virgin Mary. She denounced Rome and tried to interfere with the crucifixion, so I had to get her out of the way at any cost.

It's a piece of theater called *La Pasion de Cristo [The Passion of Christ]* they do every year in my town. Thirty thousand people come from all over to see the celebrations of Good Friday. Everyone dresses in robes like the people of Israel, playing different parts, riding horses. The man who plays Christ has to wear the crown of thorns and carry a 200–pound cross on his back for hours and hours while soldiers hit him with whips. It's supposed to be a religious experience to play the part of Christ, but whoever plays it is usually sick with a fever for a week. After the processional, they tie him up on the cross and he has to stay there under the sun for three hours. That's where he speaks all the words of Christ.

I pushed him and then he lashed me five or six times. I liked the way he used the whip.

It's a hard job being Christ. There was one guy who did it for ten years. He was only 46 years old but he almost died from all the lashings. The soldiers don't hit the Virgin that hard because she's a woman. People used to ask me how I got myself to cry real tears. I told them, "He hit me. How am I not going to cry?"

After the play I started a conversation with Marianna. We were friends for a year before it got serious. I was 15, she was 18. Because of where we live, it's never been easy for us to be together.
I come from Tilapa, Puebla Mexico.

I come from Colon, Puebla Mexico.
Our towns are separated by one road split straight down the middle.

The Tilapa side is paved and the Colon side is unpaved. The people from Colon have more money but they never spend it. They are very stingy and would rather save their money than progress into the future. Tilapa is poor, but we needed a good road to sell our farm products.

Uh oh.
She is mad because I am talking bad about her town.

I can't be listening to this for too long.
My town buys all our food from Tilapa. Miguel's family had a carníceria [a butcher shop]. That's why people over there think that people from Colon have a lot of money. Because we're always giving it to them! People in Colon are more educated than those in Tilapa. We have more fun too. Our doors are always open and we sing and play music a lot. In his town all the doors are locked and everyone always crosses themselves.

MIGUEL

There is always competition between the two town. Especially in soccer. And the kids box against each other from an early age. We are one piece of land, but because the road divides it, everything is different. We have huertas [small pieces of land] that we farm, and *they* are large property owners. Her grandfather was a big cacique [indigenous word referring to overseer or proprietor]. We work hard growing mangos, avocados, and sugar cane. *We* cultivate the sugar and *they* buy it and make most of the money.

MARIANNA

One more minute of this and he's sleeping on the floor tonight. Yes. We have a sugar cannery in Colon. The fabrication of sugar from canes is the only thing people of my town dedicate themselves to. They work very hard at it.

They make a lot money selling sugar, but we always have plenty to eat. There's a saying in my town that the people from Colon, when in Tilapa, look up to see if a mango will fall from a tree, and the people from my town go through Colon looking down to see if they can find any coins.

The problem really comes from the older folks. If you are from Colon, they tell you people from Tilapa are inferior. And vice versa. **TO THIS DAY,** my family never accepted I married a man from Tilapa. And his parents don't like my face. Everyone says I have a face of few friends [cara de pocos amigos].

One of my cousins told me, "You can't live with a face like that for more than six months." When we first got married, we couldn't even spend Christmas together. Marianna would be with her mother and I'd be with my mother, and at midnight we'd meet at the church to give each other a hug. Then we'd go back, each to their side of the road.

As long as he loves me, it doesn't matter what his family thinks. They'd say, "You two are like oil and water." We're married eight years. We have three kids and another on the way.

For a long time I worked as a secretary for a clinic that helped disabled children and I was going to school to become a nurse. But when we got married, Miguel wouldn't let me work. He was crazy back then. He wouldn't let me peek outside the door. He was jealous of any-thing that moved. His mother wanted us to live with them in their house. She's a metiche [slang for someone who meddles]. She likes to order him around. She tried to order me too. Instead of living with them, we rented a small apartment in Tilapa where we had our first baby. I would cook in our little room and when he got home, instead of eating with me and the baby, he would go eat with his mother. I was always left with the food gone to waste.

Before we got married I was going to high school and selling water bottles. I dreamed of becoming a lawyer but I quit school to be a father instead. After our first baby, I got a job cutting sugar cane. It was the hardest work of my life, but you get paid more to cut cane than to be a teacher in Tilapa. At noon the sun is so hot, the juice of the cane heats up. When you chop it with the machete, the boiling sugar sticks to your skin. You can hear it burning your cheeks and arms like *sssshhhhh.* By the time you come home you're as dark as an African and your hair is matted with honey. That's why I was excited when a cousin in Tijuana called asking me to come work with him. He said he got paid in dollars and spent pesos and lived in a gigantic house. I told him I'm coming. That's the way I am. If someone tells me about an opportunity, I go for it. Right away, I sold our donkey. It was the only capital we had.

MARIANNA

Back then, one donkey went for 500 pesos. **And he sold our donkey and a baby donkey for 200 pesos!**

MIGUEL

Marianna and the baby came with me. She wasn't going to stay with *my* family, and I was afraid her family would do something to the baby because I was the father.

We arrive at the Tijuana airport and we can't find my cousin. He never came to pick us up. So we found a taxi and told him the address. I said, *"It's a mansion. You can't miss it."* The taxi drives towards the tall mountains beyond the city. We go up a steep hill, forty, fifty meters, and there's the mansion right near the top. A man answers the door. I ask him, "Is Moisés here?" The man says, "Moisés lives there." He points to a tiny shack made of cardboard on the other side of the road.

After I got past the urge to kill my cousin, I worked with him in a car mechanic shop for ten days and he gave me $30. Then I wanted to kill him again.

In the day, I stayed with the baby at the shack. At night, the three of us slept on a small mattress. I was already pregnant with our second child. Miguel would wake up in the middle of the night, smoke a cigarette and cry. I would watch the horizon and think, *oh, my Lord — I want to return home.*

I thought the same thing, but if I came back too soon to Tilapa, my family would say that I was a quitter.

We went to Tijuana to get away from our mothers — but we ended up with his crazy cousin. A 28-year-old man married to a 68-year-old woman. Nothing but a liar and a thief, his cousin. I kept saying, "Miguel, let's go north, to New York. We can stay with my father. Make enough to live good and send money home to our families." But Miguel was so macho about the United States.

MIGUEL

I always thought, why would I go to the United States? Just so they could humiliate me for cheap labor. *Never!* My great grandfather fought alongside Zapata. The high school I went to was a Socialist school. Always in my mind the United States was an evil place. If I ever crossed to anywhere, it would be Russia or Cuba – Socialist lands! Marianna and I kept fighting and one day I slapped her. That was the first time I hit her. She said, "I'm leaving." I pleaded with her not to go. A tragedy could happen crossing alone just her and the baby.

Miguel called a cousin who gave him the name of a coyote who could take them across the border.

We go with the baby to a bar in a neighborhood mostly of prostitution and drugs. I ask for El Sabrás [a knick-name that literally means, *He Would Know*]. They send us upstairs. A man asks, "Why you looking for El Sabrás?" "I'm a cousin of El Flaco" [the Skinny One]. Three hours later El Sabrás arrives. Normally he charges $2,000 per person to get across. We only had to pay $1,000 for all three of us.

He takes us to a town closer to the border where he has other people waiting to cross. At one o'clock in the morning we leave in a Camaro with California plates. We were three men in a trunk big enough for only one man. There were two big speakers covering us, like the kind Dominicans blast out the back of their cars. I was curled up sideways in the trunk. Another guy was curled up the other way. The third one went across the two of us. It was incredibly hot to begin with. If any one had farted, we'd probably all be dead.

Handmade shrine to Emiliano Zapata, the revered Mexican revolutionary

MARIANNA

I was in the backseat with the baby, three other women and two other little girls — all squashed together and a big cloth over everything. I was worried my baby was going to suffocate under the blanket. El Sabrás finally said, "Okay, you can uncover the baby, but don't let him look up."

MIGUEL

If you look up, the search beam of the immigration helicopters can light up your eyes and then they call the patrol car and everything is over.

Right before we got to the crossing point my baby started crying. El Sabrás tells me to shut him up. I put the baby on my breast. There was no milk in me because I was really thin and I hadn't eaten in days. I don't know whether it was the heat or a miracle, but the baby was suddenly still. One of the women starts whispering a prayer called "The Magnificent" to the Virgin Mary. I'm so worried what's going to happen to my baby. I start saying it too.

El Sabrás stopped the car and waited till the customs officers changed shifts. I don't know if he had a deal with the second officer, but as soon as they switched he pulled up to the border. We're all holding our breath. We hear, "Where you heading?"
"Over the border."
I'm wondering, *are they going to put us in a Mexican jail or an American jail?*

I think the immigration guy heard the baby crying. He starts hitting the car with a stick. I was trembling. No matter how hard he hit the car, the baby was suddenly silent.

They let us cross, but we still had to hide because of the helicopters. The baby was pooping and the stink was really bad under the blanket. I didn't have a change of clothes for him or Pampers, so I took out some toilet paper just to keep him dry and to keep the smell down.

The car stops and the trunk door opens. I say, *"It's immigration!"* The speakers come off us. We look up and El Sabrás is waving us out of the car. Two hours in the trunk and we could barely stand. Even if your whole body is numb, you have to make sure not to look suspicious because INS knows the look of people walking out of trunks.

MARIANNA

The day we crossed the border was the baby's first birthday. He didn't understand it, but the United States was his gift.

We spent whatever money we had left flying from L.A. to New York so Marianna could be near her father and sister. Everyone else in the airplane was white. They were staring at us with our nerves all at an end. Probably they were thinking, look, they are mojaditos [slang for Mexicans who cross; literally the wet ones]. My father-in-law forgot he was supposed to pick us up at JFK Airport. We're waiting in the cold for a long time, putting quarters in phone booths.

My father always used to be so happy to see his little girl. Now that I had a husband from Tilapa, it was like he didn't want to see me at all. Even my sister didn't hug me or the baby.

We stayed with Marianna's father and sister in the attic they were renting in Corona, Queens. Even though her father had only been five years in the United States, he called us *the Mexicans*. Like that is a dirty thing to be. To this day, he doesn't speak a word of English, but he will always be the American and we are the immigrants. We have a saying:

IF YOU HAVE MONEY,
SI TIENES DINERO,
YOUR FAMILY WANTS TO BE WITH YOU.
TU FAMILIA TE CONOCE.
IF YOU DON'T,
SI NO,
THEN THEY DON'T KNOW WHO YOU ARE.
NO TE CONOCE.

Before my second girl was born, my sister and her husband asked if they could baptize the

MARIANNA

girl so they could be the padrinos [godparents]. We said sure, but after Miguel had the accident, they changed their minds. In the Mexican tradition, to be a padrino means you have to take care of the baby in case the parent dies.

MIGUEL

We met a white man named George who had a house he was willing to rent for $500 a month. We moved there with our two kids, Marianna's father, her sister and her sister's husband. Everything started good with the house. But then we saw the water was getting more and more yellow. We couldn't even give our kids a bath. I asked George, "Why is the water yellow?" He didn't fix it. Next time he came for the rent, I said, "What about the yellow water?" That's when he called me a *damn Mexcian*.

He said he could get me in trouble because he knew that we were undocumented.

I told him I *was* documented.

He told me I wasn't.

I told him, "Every month I pay the rent. What's the difference who...." That's when the gringo pushed me. I told him, "I'm not going to hit you because you're an old man, otherwise, le parto su madre!" [I'd kick your ass!]

He said, "Do it! I dare you."

He picks up the phone to call the police. I run out of the house thinking, why is this man so cruel to me? In Tilapa we get a lot of immigrants from Honduras and we always help them out. I ran one block to Queens Boulevard past the deli on 69th Street. When the light turned green, I dashed across the Boulevard and a car hit me. I went flying five, ten meters into the air and landed right on top of the car. The driver ran a red light and he's screaming at me, I'm going to pay for his broken windshield. I'm lying on the ground, all these people around me. Sounds of sirens are getting closer and closer. I'm petrified that George called the police. I'm sure they're going to send me back to Mexico.

207

I didn't understand that in this country the police and the ambulance both show up for an accident. I told the policeman, "Please not to call my wife. She's not feeling well." But the real reason I didn't want him to call, we have a belief where I'm from, if a woman receives bad news while she is breastfeeding, it can scare her, and the baby could die. I told the policeman to call my brother-in-law. At the hospital they ask me for my Social Security number. I shook my head no. They took me anyway because it was an accident. I am grateful for that.

MARIANNA

Miguel was urinating blood and he couldn't move his legs. That's when my sister changed her mind about being the godmother of our baby. I was upset but a friend told me not to worry. "I will baptize your baby girl and be her madrina no matter what happens."

It took a long time for Miguel to learn how to walk again. For the sake of the children I got a job in a factory stamp-ing T-shirts. Every day I stamped thousands of shirts. You put a shirt on the stamping machine,
flatten it out,
press down on the iron
so the picture or the slogan is
stamped on the shirt.
Then you take out
another shirt,
put it on the
stamping machine.
Like that. Every hour they placed 12 to 17 boxes next to me. Each box had 12 dozen shirts.

I only made $200 a week as a stamper, so I put a flier on my door and at church to do healings. The priest got mad, saying I was doing the Devil's work. But people started showing up. Ladies. If they have pain in their feet, three cleansings and the pain will go away. Or if she is depressed maybe it's because her husband hurt her or she is sad because of her mother. Depending on what the person has, I have various lotions; ammonia with lemon or lime, different things I get from the botanica.

I pass one egg with my hand over the body of the person. I start to pray, Our Holy Father, Ave Maria, and a credo. Never out loud. It is a prayer you have to have within you always. After you cleanse the body with the egg, you break the egg into a glass of water, and you can see what's going on with the person by the bubbles that are formed and the shapes the egg takes.

I started the healings to feed my family. But I never charge the people. If they want they leave me five to ten dollars for fifteen minutes. For longer cleansings like the one with seven eggs for seven days, they usually leave more money. I feel bad breaking so many perfectly good eggs, but many people are really sick and one egg isn't enough. Of course they bring their own eggs. Otherwise I would have to really charge them!

When I was nine years old, my mother took me to the town of Atlixco because I suffered from headaches. They trained me to heal by praying. Praying a lot. They would put me to sleep and when I woke up, it was late and I didn't know what happened.

From the time I was very young, my mother told me that I had two spirits:

one bad and one good, and that I had to develop the good one because the bad one was finishing me off. That's why I was having the headaches. I would see images as a little girl. At night my sister would sleepwalk and I would follow her. Next to us where we lived there was a woman swinging on a makeshift swing. The woman was not real. She would call me, but I wouldn't follow her. I would follow my sister because she was sleepwalking toward the river. I would grab her and on the way home, the spirit-woman would always say to me, "Come, I want to speak to you."

I told my father, but he said I was crazy. I told my mother and she said it was possibly the spirit of Dona Marguarita, the woman who used to live next door. My visions were almost always at night. After a while I became known as the "spiritualist girl." People from all over would come to see me. People I didn't even know from Colon and from Veracruz, which is very far away. They said that only I had the gift to cure them.

MIGUEL

Yeah. Doing some kind of witchcraft that is not real. Lying to the people.

Many people think that the things I see are the fantasies of a crazy girl. But it has given results my whole life. If I was a charlatan, people would stop coming to see me. Miguel says if I'm such a good healer, why can't I fix our daughter? I can do the cleansings for other people but to do it with my own family, in my own home, is not permitted.

The paint on the walls of our house was crumbling. Any part of the wall you would touch would come right off. I called George and told him he had to paint the house. He refused. My second girl wasn't looking good, so we took her to the doctor for tests. Marianna came crying to the house saying the baby had been poisoned by lead paint. She was nine months old when it started. Now she has a three–year retardation and her sight and her hearing are affected too. She's five years old and it's as if she were two.

I tell George about my little girl. He shrugged his shoulders, like what's that got to do with him. That's when I painted the whole inside of the house. When George saw his house was painted, instead of thanking me, he sued me for $5,000 for damaging his property.

In housing court, we tell the judge about the lead paint and what happened to our little girl. George starts shouting that I am an undocumented Mexican pig immigrant who does not have a right even to be in this country. The judge said that is not something we are here to discuss today. Instead of ruling against us, the judge told George he had to pay me $2,000 for *improving* his property.

In my country I would have lost the case for sure, because Mexican justice is cuanto tienes cuanto valez [how much you have is how much you're worth]. If a poor man wins a case in Mexico, they take the judge away from his position or kill him.

MARIANNA

I'm watching Spanish language TV and I see an advertisement for a lawyer:

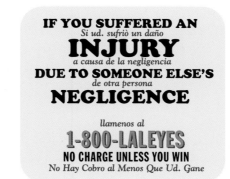

IF YOU SUFFERED AN
Si ud. sufrió un daño
INJURY
a causa de la negligencia
DUE TO SOMEONE ELSE'S
de otra persona
NEGLIGENCE

llamenos al
1-800-LALEYES
NO CHARGE UNLESS YOU WIN
No Hay Cobro al Menos Que Ud. Gane

The lawyer had the house tested and found out that it was full of lead. Then she lent us the money to move and told us it was one of the best cases she ever had.

Marianna, Miguel, and family moved to a one-room studio in the basement of a large apartment building in the shadow of Shea Stadium. They paid their rent in cash to the superintendent for six months without getting receipts. A knock on the door and they're evicted by a city marshall for nonpayment of rent. After being homeless for months, the superintendent got caught pocketing the rents of other tenants. Marianna, Miguel, and family moved back into their basement apartment, resuming a more normal existence. The case against George is still pending.

Most of the jobs I've had here I got from the workline on Roosevelt Avenue. In the beginning they were day jobs, doing yardwork, washing cars, passing out fliers, installing air conditioners. Sometimes the jobs are more steady: busboy, dishwasher, mechanic's assistant, selling carpets.

Worklines are like survival. The one who runs the fastest gets the job. We could be six or seven of us standing around, talking. When a van pulls up, you stop what you're doing and run. If they need two painters, you say you're a painter. If they need a mover, you're a mover. The guy working

for the boss looking for people is an instant employment
agency. *"You, you, and you come with me."* I'm that guy now.
I'm working for a guy who's Turkish and it's easier for him
to have me do it, because a lot of Mexican guys don't
want to go with an Arab or a Chinese or a Greek.

We ask, "After everything you've been through,
was it worth it, coming to the United States?

MARIANNA

With the problem our girl has, it would be very hard
to find a school for her in Mexico. We could find one,
but it would be very expensive. As for Miguel, he
still doesn't want me to work out of the apartment.
In Mexico I was an outgoing young woman. I worked
where I wanted and dressed the way I wanted. Then
I got married and started to bear and bear children
and now I'm feeling a little bitter.

One advantage of being stuck at home — they can't
catch me on the job with no papers. I make more
money than him doing the cleansings, but now that
I'm pregnant again I have to stop. Some people
come with an immense heaviness like they are carrying a corpse. After seeing me, they feel better but
I am left with their heaviness. With the baby inside,
I can't risk taking in any bad spirits.

I pray that my husband will get a job with better
pay and that my children have a chance to study and
have a good head so they don't become little bums.
That's what they learn over here. Children are out
by themselves without their parents' permission.
Many of them are in gangs. They should be in their
homes studying or with their family. Even if they
are drawing on the walls, at least they're in their
homes. More than anything I want my son, Lalo, to
have the opportunity to study. It is better for him
here in the U.S., even if it is not better for us.

MARTA GHEZZO
DINU GHEZZO
CHRISTINE GHEZZO

goat
songs
and
demon elks

Working as professors of music, but fed up with living under a totalitarian government, Dinu and Marta Ghezzo fled Romania in the late sixties. In 1976, they settled in Queens and had a daughter, Christine. Today, the Ghezzos are a family of musicians: the parents, steeped in contemporary composition and theory; the daughter, studying ancient Romanian folk music. The Ghezzos are also a family of deep religious faith. The parents, Greek Orthodox and Roman Catholic; the daughter, a practicing pagan.

We meet the three of them at Dinu and Marta's house in the half-industrial, half-residential neighborhood of Hollis. From the outside, the brick two-story house, situated on a suburban-looking block, is fairly unre-markable. Once inside, we've entered a shrine filled with religious and musical icons from Romania, Hungary, and Greece.

UKRAINE

ROMANIA

Bucharest ●

Black Sea

BULGARIA

At first Marta is reluctant to talk about her past. Once she gets going, the people and the memories come alive in her eyes.

Knock on our villa in Transylvania, it was like Greta Garbo opened the door. That's how beautiful my mother was.

My father was very proud of what he could offer to her and our family. He did not inherit his wealth. He made it with his own hands. A whole lifetime for that and just from one day to the other to lose everything. It was a terrible, terrible experience.

They were a group of Communist soldiers who came to the house, and father was not there. My mother opened the door. I was four–and–a–half years old and I remem–ber so clearly. One of the men looked right past my mom like she wasn't there. She was surrounded with her children, we were five kids in the family. The soldier said, "This is *our* residence now. You have to move down to the basement." We used to keep potatoes there during the winter. It was that muddy kind of a cellar. "Pack up immediately your children. We don't want to see

MARTA

you on this level of the
house." My mom said, "I
don't think I'm going to do
that because my husband,
he is not here." The man
looks at the huge mirror
we had from the ceiling
down to the floor. He takes
his rifle and starts shooting
in the mirror from the top
to the bottom. Everything
shattered in front of us.
That is a frightening picture
in my head I will never
ever forget. My mom was
strong on her feet. She
looked at these people like
– *you jerks*. She didn't say
one word or make a scene
out of it. She was holding
our hands and she told
her mother, my grand–
mother, "Let's pick up the
children and go down."

217

When my father returned home he went crazy.
"Where is my family?" He saw these strangers
in his house. They told him, "Your family is in the basement." He came down and said, "Everything will
be all right. Just keep your calm."

Us crazy kids. For us something new was happening.
We took potatoes and were hitting each other like it was
a game. It was a long time, the whole winter we stayed
there. With huge pillows and blankets on the floor so
we wouldn't catch cold. Then one day, my father came
home and said, "We are going. We are moving to another
part of the country." We moved about four
hours by train to the border of Hungary and
Romania where nobody knew about us. He
started working like a worker. Just like that he
lost his home, his name. But mostly he lost his
focus… his spirit. He just sat looking neither
up or down, saying nothing, eating nothing.
This is how he died, with a broken heart. That's
why whenever I hear about the Communists, I can't be
sympathetic. I don't care where and how – for me the experience was so traumatic. I cannot bring back my parents.

HUNGARY

ROMANIA

Years later my father moved back to the villa and he got
back one room and then another room. And then he called
for the rest of the family. And now my sister lives there and
when we go to visit, every second year, every third year, we
sometimes have the whole family there. We are five very
different people in my family. But you reach some maturity
and the resemblances come out. No matter what else.
That's the way I feel with my sisters. It is a closeness
I cannot explain.

Dinu is philosophical and very animated. He talks with his whole body.

D I N U

I could tell you I'm from Romania, but that just covers up the whole mess of what my family represents. My mother was born on a Greek boat in Turkish waters, kept a secret until they reached Romania. The Romanians didn't care where you were from in those days. My father — Ghezzo is a Venetian name. His father came to Romania as part of the big buildup, working on the Austro-Hungarian railroads. He married a lady who was half Austrian.

C H R I S T I N E

Wasn't she an orphan?

That's another reason I can't tell you exactly where my family is from. I come to this country a Romanian, but I am also Greek, Italian, Austrian — God knows what else. Ask me again what I am, I'll tell I am composer. It's easier to say.

I was born in 1941, the son of an officer in the Royal Navy. He was about to become an admiral when the communists took over. They made a very brutal regime in Romania. Just because of political status or class, they would liquidate people. We always looked suspicious, our family. They'd say, "You are Ghezzo. You are what? You are Jew. You are Greek. You are something. You are not Romanian." I was six when they came and arrested my father. I saw them beat

I'm sure we have Gypsy blood in our family. I'm the lightest one on both sides. On my mother's side, her brothers and sisters are quite dark, and the photos of my grandfather, he definitely had Gypsy features. But you know in Hungary, in Romania, you're not supposed to say you have Gypsy in you or you're immediately ostracized. I've asked about Gypsies

Rooted in the tradition of the avant garde, Dinu composes electronic music. Born in America, Christine is a singer specializing in Eastern European and Gypsy folk songs. Father and daughter have been performing together for a little over a year.

DINU

him bloody at our house. I will never forget. We were waiting the next day to be thrown into the labor camp with him, and then suddenly my father was released. I thought it was a miracle. Really it was because my father, when he was a commander in the Second World War, there were many deserters from the Russian front who were supposed to be killed. But my father never sent them to the military tribunal like he was supposed to. He saved a lot of men that way. And one of those men was now a commander in the new army and when he saw my father — he let him go.

The fifties were terrible years. Constantly there were shootings, people disappearing. We had lots of relatives that were sent to Siberia. When Ceausescu came to power, things got better and worse at the same time. Ceausescu was a total idiot – a shoemaker who couldn't read or write. The Russians chose him because he was the least educated guy of them all. But things were beginning to change at that time. A couple of countries were trying, how they were calling it,

on both sides of my family and it's always, "Well, Uncle So-and-So was Gypsy but only by marriage and he was killed in a labor camp." There's something going on with that in my family, but I'm not sure what. I'm trying to find out.

Performing and recording with my father is an opportunity of discovering new ways of making music. He's the experimental one and I'm more like a folk person and the combination of the two is really interesting. It's a role reversal in a way because with us, the father is the one who says anything is possible, all sounds can be music, and the child is saying, what about the roots and the power of the song and what do the lyrics mean. Then I realized, we were building a bridge between the two of us because we were always so different. And through the music and the costumes we are becoming partners.

At first it was all very intuitive. I was listening to a CD of Andean music and I started making this mask out of papier maché. I painted it yellow and orange and red like a sun. It was a sun mask with almond-shaped eyes, very Andean features. Then I made another mask from the same mold, with blues and purples, kind of like a moon. Dad started using masks in his concerts at about the same time as I started making them.

"Communism with a human face." The Russians didn't like it, but after Czechoslovakia and Hungary, they didn't want another war. So Ceausescu opened things up for us enough to get passports.

Seen by the West as a "reformer," Nicholae Ceausescu was eventually toppled and murdered by a popular revolt in 1989. Among other crimes, he was accused of embezzling hundreds of millions of dollars from state coffers and overseeing the murder of thousands of his countrymen.

Marta and I met as music students and we both ended up assistant professors at the conservatory in Bucharest. After first semester, I said to Marta, "If we ever get a passport, I want to get out." And she said, "Yes." We were both bonkers to go. So we bit our tongues and joined the Communist Party to get our passports, but we still couldn't go anywhere other than Bulgaria, Hungary or Russia. Until one day in 1968, I saw

CHRISTINE

I thought hmm, what an interesting parallel. I'd put on a mask and all of a sudden borderline aspects of my personality would come out. Then I started researching what masks were all about — Venetian and Japanese and then the Romanian masks. Put on the old man mask or the goat or the demon elk and it's like we're reclaiming all the characters from Romanian folk heritage. And when we perform, each mask is tied into the songs. There are so many songs about goats and sheep and all the other mountain gods. I'm interested in how through these songs, ancient practices can be carried into the present. My father respects all my digging around in a scholarly way, but when it comes to actually putting it into practice, that's another thing. Looking at it as myths is fine — looking at it as an alternative reality is something very difficult for him because he is Greek Orthodox and my mom is Roman Catholic. Their religions are ritualistic, but in a very different way.

CHRISTINE

When I was a little kid, I always saw spirits. Somehow I knew that they were communicating with me, but none of the religious structures I grew up with would tolerate or acknowledge that in any way. So in high school I searched for something that fit my reality. That's when I became Wiccan.

DINU

a former colleague of mine who was working for the touristic police. All tourism was done by the police. He called out to me from across the street, "Hey Ghezzo! You are Greek aren't you? Now you can travel." Marta and I made arrangements to go to Greece for two week vacation. We didn't say to anybody that we were leaving other than my brother and my father.

Even before high school I would gravitate to the occult section of the library. I remember coming upon this white magic book, reading the whole book and wanting to do everything it said in there, but at the same time feeling that it was the work of Satan. I was very excited about it, but I was also very Catholic when I was a little girl. So I ran back to the library and checked the book back in. It's a very difficult topic with my parents because for so much of their lives they had to hide the fact that they were religious, and here they are in America, free to practice their religion and their daughter comes home from school one afternoon and tells them she's a pagan. "My God. Our little baby is a witch!"

MARTA

Nobody on my side of the family knew we were leaving. If I told my mother, she would cry and people would say, "Why do you cry?" You couldn't say anything, even to your best friend. Not that the best friend would go and tell, but the secret police knew who were the best friends and they would go to them to find out about you. They were very, very, how can I say, not tricky...

Suspicious. It was a suspicious system of terror and control.

223

Dinu and I came off the boat into Greece with our suitcase and no money and went straight to the police station asking for political asylum. We stayed six months in a refugee camp for them to check if we were spies. This was not a fun thing at all. This was a very hard step to take, to leave my family and my entire life. If we should discuss it now, would we do it at this age? I don't think so. At the time, we had no fear. We were sure everything will be nice and we'll be musicians and have a child someday and a house. We were dreamers! But then the soldiers came with their guns and took us into a room, completely isolated. Suddenly you whisper into your pillow, "Boy, why did I do this?" That first night at the refugee camp, I put a little picture of Saint Mary by our bed, and the next day and all the rest of our time there we were completely fine.

DINU

They asked us where we want to go. First choice was Australia. Romantic idea maybe. Nice water. New fresh country. Then we read the president of Australia was eaten by sharks.

They started making our forms for Australia and we said, **"Stop. No Australia!"** They said, "Why? They need musicians in Melbourne. They are waiting for you." I said, "I want to swim. I'm not going to where even the president gets eaten by sharks." They laughed like we were making a joke. But you know what is the very funny thing – that we were serious about what we said.

The *Jaws* movie was not yet out, but we knew enough not to mess with sharks. The next choice was Canada, but then we received a letter of invitation from a cousin who married an American pilot that got shot down in Romania during Second World War. She was living in California since 1946.

MARTA

We arrive in Los Angeles, two refugees coming from the refugee camp. I had one skirt, one pair of shoe. Dinu's cousin came to the airport with her child Jackie. Little Jackie says, "Let's go home." Okay, home, I thought, home would be nice. She had a house like a museum! The most expensive, exquisite paintings and furnishings. I thought, we came here to build our life, not to live in fancy place. We had our first Thanksgiving dinner. I never saw such a gigantic turkey on a table. Twenty-two people. We didn't know there were so many unhappy rich people. After a month, we left. Eight o'clock in the morning we took off on foot and eight hours later we ended up in North Hollywood.

DINU

We found an apartment that was a converted washroom. Forty dollars a month. If you wanted to write on the table, you either sit on the bed, which is not at the right level, or you open the door and put your tuchus outside and write from there.

We got jobs as a stock boy and stock lady in a fabric shop in Hollywood. Marta was in the notions department and I was in wools. When we first got to this country we don't have friends. And in one month we had so many people inviting us, "Come for dinner. Come for lunch." The whole universe opened to us. Our bell would ring, "Here is an iron for you. Here is a television." In six months our apartment was completely full. This is the fabric of American people we found extraordinary. Willing to help. We met a woman who was a musician for Hollywood films. She was applying to be a flute teacher at California Institute for the Arts. And she wrote a postscript in her letter saying, "I know a woman who is musician from Eastern Europe and she is very well-qualified for assistant professor, and she is looking

for job too." They answered, "We are not interested in you, but please send the musician from Europe." And this woman remained a friend! Which says a lot. Marta went from notions to the professorship. The same woman commissioned me to write a piece. I had a concert and fortunately I got a good review. I met Aaron Copland and was invited to UCLA to tell something about myself. They ask me what was my life like in Romania. I said, "Well, I was assistant professor, but now I work in fabric store."

In 1976, I received an offer from Queens College all the way in New York where they had an interest in microtonal music. This is how we came to live in Queens, because of microtonal music! Soon after we got here, the city collapsed from debt and I lost my job because it was university of the city.

MARTA

We had Chrissy and now 24 years later she and I are becoming friends. When I was a child, relations between parents and children were very different. My mother and I were not always a hugging, kissing relation. But we knew we are always there for each other. Even after we left the country my mother gave me her blessing. My older sister was the only one who sent a very bad letter to the refugee camp, "You are going to a strange country and this is a shame for the family." I wrote back, "This is my choice and I'm going for it."

Now I'm full-time professor at NYU and Marta is at Kingsborough College. And Chrissy and I, we are finishing our first CD of music together. We went to Odessa to perform in a music festival. We met a lady out on the street, with a little black scarf selling ceramics. We found out she was one of the very important doctors in the Second World War.

DINU

Is this the life somebody deserves after all she did? She said, "You should put a scarf around you. You'll be sick and if you'll be sick where will you go here. There are no good hospitals here."

MARTA

In this country too it's not easy to be an old person, or a young person either. In between you work, you have money, a car. When you are very young, it isn't easy to know what to select out of this so-called freedom. You are surrounded by your friends, everybody's taking drugs. If you are the one person not going along, isn't it hard? To make a life that is meaningful -- this is very hard. Then to get old and your health fails or financially you cannot afford anymore.

Both systems are hard. In Russia, an ugly system comes down and what comes in its place? An uglier one! Right or left is the same. There was an article in the paper the other day, that many American businessmen prefer the former Communists because they know business ways better and how the world works. All these countries, it's the same system – whoever is trained to do international business. Romania was the worst. They were masters of control.

I am always telling to my students our beginnings. I never hide it. I tell the immigrant ones, "Get assimilated and learn English." If Marta and I have people to pay tribute to in our life, we have a long list in Romania, but we have a longer list here in America. Now it's our turn to help.

I dream of the forests in Romania.

When I was eighteen I went to study at the conservatory in Cluj and I became friends with this one family. The mother was dying of rheumatoid arthritis. I didn't know you could die of rheumatoid arthritis, but that's what they told me. Her husband was a real mountain man, a mushroom picker. He looked exactly like an elf. He was short and dark with fluffy black hair and pointy ears. He took me into the woods and showed me how to pick mushrooms. We're going through this wild, thick forest with pine trees and oak and birch and wildflowers and he's picking poison ivy because in Romania, they're a big meat-eating, dairy society. And the ivy, once the leaves are dry, it doesn't have poison in it anymore. You can make tea with it and it reduces the uric acid in the blood. It's called Ceai de Urzici.

So I'm in the woods with this elf man and I keep seeing these claw marks on the trees. He says, "Oh, that's from the bears." I'm like, "Oh my God." Then we came to a big mud pit and I could see the mud was moving. He said, "Oh, those are the wild boars." I'm getting pretty scared and he's hopping around like it's no big deal. Then we come to an opening in the forest and we see these shepherds in the grazing land calling out to the sheep. And the sheep are calling back to the shepherds, back and forth and back and forth. If I close my eyes I can hear it.

It's strange being in Romania, because I feel so much a part of it, especially in the forest and the mountains. But then when I start to interact with people, they make it clear to me that I'm not part of them. I will always be the American. I have money and so I have the ability to leave. They are stuck there with skyrocketing prices and a lot of unemployment and pension rates the same as when it was Communist. What the hell are they supposed to do? There are reforms that are happening but they are taking forever to have an effect.

CHRISTINE

When I come back to New York, I'm not the American any longer. I'm not sure who I am. Queens can be an ugly place. Concrete and warehouses and big boulevards. It can be beautiful too. Concrete and warehouses and big boulevards. Whenever I can, I walk to Kissena Park to watch the hazy orange sun set between the trees, listen for the echoes inside my soul.

I dream about marionettes

if
there is
no dance
there is
no life

ARTHUR GULKAROV
MALIKA KALONTAROVA
ISKHAK GULKAROV

The Gulkarovs are descendants of a Jewish tribe who migrated to the ancient city of Bukhara 3,000 years ago. While most Jews felt liberated leaving the former Soviet Union, this family of performing artists fared very well under Communism. Living in the Central Asian state of Tajikistan, Malika was re-nowned throughout the Soviet Union for her mesmerizing performances of classical and traditional dance. Iskhak, an accomplished percussionist in his own right, was Malika's principal accompanist. In 1993, they left a war-torn Tajikistan with their two teenage sons, Mark and Arthur, and settled in Queens.

We visit Malika, Iskhak and Arthur in their one bedroom apartment/dance studio in Rego Park. Once inside the brick six-story apartment building — the lobby with its marble floors and mirrored walls, the incredibly slow-moving brown elevator with its too-heavy door and unmistakable stale odor — sends me [Warren] back to the days of visiting my grandparents, who lived in an identical building two blocks away. The most apparent difference: instead of speaking Yiddish, the Gulkarovs and most of their neighbors speak Russian.

REGO PARK

QUEENS

CHINA

TAJIKISTAN

Dushanbe

GHANISTAN

PAKISTAN

From 1990 to 1994, 51,000 Jews from the former Soviet republics emigrated to New York City. Seventy percent of Bukharan Jews settled in Queens, most of them in the Rego Park, Forest Hills section. When the Gulkarovs came to New York, Arthur was 14 years old. At 21, he lives with his parents while pursuing a career as a dancer and actor.

ARTHUR

I live to dance. To dance, to dance, to dance. I will dance even on a downtown roof for no money. Anything to dance.

When I was a kid, I copied exactly what my mother did. Guys used to say to me, "Oh, you dancing like a girl." I couldn't understand why. Now when I see tapes from when I'm young, I see I'm dancing just like my mother. I did her face, her eyes, her hips, everything. I did her singing. Announcing myself all the time my mother's name like, "HERE WE GO. Malika onstage doing classical Indian dance!" I do Afghani dance like her. Russian dance. Persian dance. Everything. There are old people here in Rego Park who were there in the parties in Russia. They see that I'm change now, doing jazz and hip–hop.

ARTHUR

They say, "You remember when you was young and announce your mother's name?" I say, "Yes, that's why God gave me this talent to continue in my mother's job." And when she is going to be older, she is going to look at me and still feel like she's on stage.

The Gulkarov's apartment is adorned with images of the nearly mythic Malika, woven into tapestries, glazed on cermamic vases, printed on posters and concert programs.

MALIKA

Four daughters my father taught to be hairdresser. First one Sveta. Second one Daniella. Third one Eira. Then he brought me to hair salon, thirteen years old. He tell me to take customer to dryer room like assistant. All women sitting there under dryer. I tell to the women, "I don't really want to be hairdresser." They said, "So, what you want to be?" I say, "Me want to be famous dancer." They say, "Why? Can you dance?" I say, "Yes, I can show you the concert now. I start dancing. **Roon taka tan toon. Raka tan toon. Taka tan toon.**" *Ladies in drying room start clapping. My father runs to see what is all the noise. I am bowing for customer. "What you doing here?" I said, "Nothing, I just showed them my show." He came home and yell at my mother.* **"Don't send that girl no more to the shop."** *Every day I come to salon and dance for customers. And one customer my father had says, "Please, Yasha, your daughter is very talented. No make her work beauty salon. She will bring you money in future." I dance on stage for first time, thirteen years old. The newspaper came out, it says my name is Mazol.*

Malika's father

Ceramic plate featuring Arthur at 9

ARTHUR

My mother's name is Mazol but the family always call her Margot. You know why she didn't like the name Mazol? It is Jewish name – **but in Russian it means blister!** If you walk and the shoe is small for you, you say, Oh, I got a *mazoil*. She always asked her mother, "Why you give me that stupid name?" Then in 1989 she went to Israel to tour. She see every wedding, every bar mitzvah they say, *Mazel Tov*. When she came back to Russia she say, "Thank you, Mama, for my Jewish name. Means good luck. Everything works out." In 1964, she passed a competition and was hired to popular dance group *Lola* and they give her the name Malika. She perform many years all over Russia, everywhere as Malika.

MALIKA

People ask what is your...
You Russian? You Jewish? You Tajik?
Most Jewish people say they Tajik or they Russian because Jewish get no good work. No good pay. But once I'm famous I'm not afraid. I say, "Me Jewish." Still they give me salary. Sixty-five countries tour. Even if I don't work for three months I still get salary.

When I was a little boy, I think Tajikistan is best place in the world to live. Best place until war: 1991, 1992, 1993. No more Soviet Union. Before war country was beautiful and clean. Very safe to go out and play. Everywhere flowers, fountains. Little

Tajikistan was decreed a state by the Soviet Union in 1924. Soon after the dissolution of the Soviet empire in 1991, the five Central Asian states including Tajikistan declared their independence. By 1992, power struggles between pro-Muscovite and "reformist" factions, along with ethnic, cultural, and religious tensions, culminated in a bloody civil war. Fifty thousand people died and one tenth of the population fled for their lives.

by little there's fighting here, fighting there. First war we got was Muslim fighting Muslim. Because some Muslim people they want everybody to be under religious law, you know like girls have to cover their face, everything. For two years the schools were closed just for safety. One of my friends, he went to throw out garbage and he never came home. Every day boys were kidnapped to be forced to fight in Afghanistan. And war over there was very big war. Very bad war.

Second war started because no food in stores, no money. Mafia. Our part of Dushanbe was where most of the fighting was happening. Sometimes we got no water for two weeks in a row. We took water from the fountain, dirty with stones and leaves and then boil it. Mix with dry milk. It was disgusting, but what can we do? All Jewish community got from America, food, like olive oil, candy, medicine, rice, everything. You go to the synagogue, show your passport. If it has JEW printed on it they give you a big bag of stuff. Some Jews like my mother said, "It's not fair. We can't take all this everything for ourselves if other people need it too." They decide to share with Muslim people too. War or no war, everybody love my mother, from the President to everyday person, and she love everybody.

Malika received the rare honor of being certified an official artist of the Soviet Union.

Thirteen years old I got kidnapped. After four o'clock nobody was supposed to go outside. How you call

there to visit and lost track of the time. I'm walking back home and nobody else is outside except one guy behind me screaming, "Hey you, come here!" I just keep walking. "Come here or I'm going to shoot." And this scares me. He starts shooting to the air. *Deduvz, deduvz, deduvz.* I couldn't move because I thought I was shot and it was the last second of my life. I see he has a big rifle in his hand. "I told you come here or the next one is going to go on you." He grabs hold of me and takes me inside a cafeteria with all these mafia men hanging around. He locks me into an ice-cream room in the back all by myself. I could hear him saying, "Let's wait for our boss and

then we going to see what we to do with him." I am screaming and crying my head off. I break a mirror and some glasses. They didn't even open the door to check what I'm doing. Finally the boss came and they said to him, "We have Malika's son in there." They knew it was me and that my mother was visiting in America. When the boss opens the door he says, "Arthur! What are you doing here?" Because that man, I danced for his wedding! His wife is a good friend with my mother.

I think to myself, oh my God, I can't believe he's leader of mafia. He punches the guy in his face for kidnapping a friend of his family. The guy says, "I didn't know. I thought we could get money for him." The boss says to me, "Go!" I start to walk but I couldn't move my legs. I was so scared I was in shock. He says, "I told you. Go!" I was screaming, "Open the door! Open the d

I'm screaming for him to let me out, but I'm already outside. He says, "What the hell are you screaming about? You are free to go." He gives me an ice cream and walks me home. When we came to neighborhood where I'm living, all neighbors are looking like why I'm walking with mafia guy with gun. Everybody runs inside. When my mother comes home she says, "We are going to live in America." Her worst nightmare, her sons would be kidnapped to war and die for nothing.

It seemed like forever the war kept getting worse and visa never came to go to America. One week we got President, next week they kill the President, my mother's friend. In newspaper they put he got heart attack, but he didn't have heart attack because he had on his neck, bruises. My mother kept calling, "Where is visa? Where is visa?" One year after the president got killed, Helen Schwartz from Jewish Immigration Center in United States, sent us emergency visas. Helen Schwartz is very famous lady in Russia. You ask any Jewish person from Russia, they'll tell you Helen Schwartz is most important person.

We sold our five-bedroom apartment with 95 percent everything in it. Now we live in one bedroom apartment. We fly here with seven cousins in big Boeing airplane. The flight attendant goes, "Whad'ya like to drink, tomato juice? We got Coke, we got Sprite, orange juice..." I said, "Please give me tomato juice, give me orange juice, give me Coke, Sprite. Give me everything!" After having nothing for so long, all of a sudden I can have everything. The lady says, "You will blow up with all those drinks." She gave us chicken to eat. I ate everything so quick I got really bad stomach ache. My one-year-old nephew got fever before we left Moscow. In the airplane he's sitting there with his mouth opened sideways. We thought he was going to die. His

r!"

mother, wear two sweaters on him, and underneath she wear him tights. When we got to New York my cousin starts screaming, *"Somebody call 911! Call 911 – or it's a lie!"* Because in Russia we have that cop emergency show *911*, they translate into Russian. She wants to see if it's truth or it's lying. We couldn't believe you just call 911 and in five minutes they're in front of your house. We called 911 and the police came and they yell at my cousin, "You don't dress your baby so hot in New York, especially in summertime." You know what they do to him? They took him to the hospital and throw him in the ice. My cousin screams in Russian, *"What are you doing to my baby?"* Only English she knows is 911. They tell her, "It's okay. It's okay." The kid was boiling up. Four o'clock they release him from the hospital. The baby's laughing. We find out it's true about 911, and summertime in America much hotter than in Russia.

We stayed first with a cousin here in Rego Park. Four families, one-bedroom apartment. Nineteen people, one bathroom. We slept one, two, three, four, all in a row, with blankets on the floor, pillows. I got job picking up cans from the street. They give you a nickel. Five cans, a quarter. Twenty cans, a dollar. For me a dollar was like, *Whoa! I have dollar in my hand.* I didn't have to pay rent. For my parents, they got very bad depression. Most people here don't know who Malika is, what she can do. Everything with her just stop.

We watch videotapes of Malika and Iskhak's performances in large Russian theaters. The concerts are high energy Bukharan, Indian, and Russian dance. Iskhak's powerful drumming sounds like an entire percussion ensemble. Malika's arms move like snakes. She commands the stage with precise but fluid movements of every part of her body. Iskhak watches with a mixture of pride and melancholy.

All the time my mother and father sitting at home, watching videotapes of their shows from all over the world. Sitting, watching, thinking – life is over. Always my mother is with problems in her mind which is why she almost got hit by car crossing Queens Boulevard. The light says WALK, and you step off to walk and halfway across it begin to flash DON'T WALK, DON'T WALK, DON'T WALK. The cars rush forward and many immigrants, they are thinking, what I'm going to do with my life here. Smack, they get hit by car. A cousin of ours from Tajikistan got killed on this corner. Two years

ARTHUR

later his niece got killed, exact same corner. There's always flowers left on that corner for the girl and her uncle. It's a miracle my parents haven't been killed crossing boulevard. In Russia, if somebody see your talent – you're working every time under Communism. In America, if you're not going to show them your talent, nobody will see your talent. Like me, I just play Spanish dancer in *Nutcracker*. Now that show is finish, I got to go to audition. My parents see after a while, nobody will send them money in envelope, so they say, "If we're sitting home, how we going to make money? We need to eat." So my mother start school for dance in our apartment.

ISKHAK

Soviet Union, we live good.
    Light, two cents.
    Rent, ten rubles, one year.
            America good country too.
                Different.
                America, go college, good.
                Anyone can go college here.
                Jewish, Russian, Chinese, Mexican.
                    All can go college.
                    Work in office is good.
                    If English good, work good.
                    Me English no good –
                    no work.
                    If you come here when young,
                    is good.
                    Is better.

SUBWAY

ARTHUR

In Russia I learn Russian, I learn Persian and start to learn English, but I think, what am I want to learn English? Nobody to talk to. Now here I am in U.S.A. In beginning I missed little bit my country, my friends. Over there, childhood was really friendly. We play outside. We play inside. You know what we did in our building in Dushanbe? First floor, we did this big room for wintertime, all neighbors can go downstairs, drink tea, watch TV, and each neighbor cook something. Summertime they did outside the same thing, make a special place. All neighbors friendly, but here is little bit boring and more alone. Now, I'm used to it. But before I was like, My God, where is everybody? C'mon everybody, come down! But this building now, everybody Russian, Bukharan now. That's why I can't improve my English better. I only hear Russian language here. I speak with Americans and they say, "Eight years you been here?" I say, "Yes." They say, "For eight years you speak English good." And I say, "I don't think so." Only parts I get cast in are foreigner parts.

MALIKA

My country is small competition. In America, one Broadway show, 200 boys show up, dance one role. Here is very difficult. I say, "Son, you get job, something else. Little bit you dance on the side." He say, "No, I dance, Mama. I show you."

ISKHAK

In Russia I teacher,
many student.

In U.S.A. I have one student.
No job to play music.

Three months I am here –
get job shoe repair.
Two years work for boss.
In Tajikistan, no boss.
Only play music, 35 years.
Then come here.

Malika DANCE SCHOOL 718/ 997-7005

THE MALIKA FUND FOR DANCE ART & E

ISKHAK

In America, you musician,
            famous artist nobody know,
            you shoe repair,
            you sell coats,
            you push broom,
            you homeless — all one person.

When sleep, I dream Tajikistan.
Always Tajikistan.

When Iskhak plays his large frame drum, he is transformed; drumming, smiling, singing prayerful, modal songs of love, loss, and friendship.

            Father buried there.
            Die 25 years ago, 63 years old.
            My mother die in Israel two years ago.
            My brother die here in October.
            We bury in ground 49 street cemetery.
            Soldier grave, soldier, soldier, soldier,
            then my brother.
            I die here too one day. Near my brother.

            America is free country, is working, working, working.
            Is money, money, money.
            After saving their money, money, money, they die.
            No good.
            Money is die.

We visit the Gulkarovs after not seeing them for over a year. Arthur is dancing in Las Vegas with Cirqe du Soleil, the contemporary circus that originated in Montreal. Iskhak is working in a jewelry store on weekdays and is performing in a Russian restaurant on as many Saturday nights as possible. Beaming with pride and excitement, Malika tells us she moved her dance school out of the apartment into a studio on Queens Boulevard, by the subway. When she takes us to see it, we are surprised to discover that it's not just near the subway, it's down in the subway. She's offering a full roster of classes and has a decent studio for her dance company. From performing in castles and gargantuan theaters to reigning over her subterranean school, Malika is Malika again.

            Yesterday is killed, 65 year old man, bank killed.
            Millionaire. International bank.
            Working money, money, money for America.
                        After working should go to restaurant.
                        Drink, I like you, you like me — enjoy!
                        After working, working, working,
                        you must kiss your husband, kiss your wife.
                            Okay.
                        Make music. Love family.
                        Then can die.

RALUCA ONCIOIU
IAN ONCIOIU
LIVUI ONCIOIU

the christmas card

We first met with Raluca Oncioiu to talk about her work as an immigration lawyer specializing in refugee and political asylum cases. Although we were thinking of featuring Raluca along with some of her asylum-seeking clients, her own family's story of migration captivated us even more. Meet here the Oncioius: Ian left Romania and came to Queens in 1982; Raluca came in 1983; and Liviu came in 1999. Ian and Livui live in Kew Gardens, which is where Raluca grew up since the age of 14. Named after the London botanical gardens at Kew, the Queens' Kew Gardens was founded in 1910 as an enclave of English and Tudor-style homes offered to "acceptable purchasers only." The neighborhood has since become a densely populated bastion for immigrants and refugees. A large community of Jewish refugees from Germany settled in Kew Gardens after the Second World War, then Chinese immigrants came after 1965, Iranians after the 1979 Iranian revolution, followed by large influxes of people from Colombia, Korea, Afghanistan, Israel, the Soviet Union, and other former Soviet satellites such as Romania.

KEW GARDENS

LEFFERTS BLVD

NGARY

UKRAINE

ROMANIA

Bucharest

Black Sea

BULGARIA

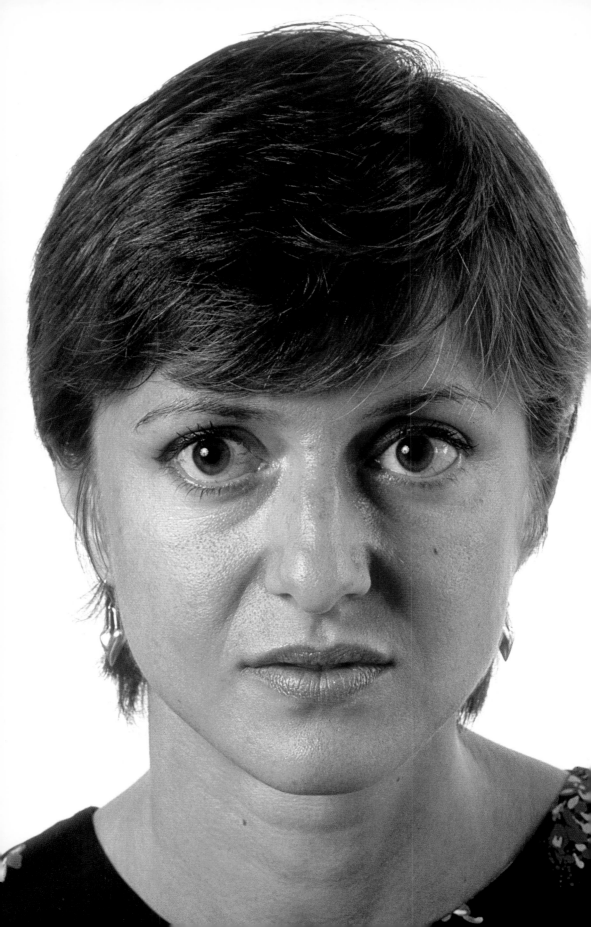

It was 1982 — the height of the cold war. Ceausescu was President and I was suddenly parentless and going through puberty. My parents didn't tell me they defected. I thought they were just on vacation. Knowing their letters would be read by the Romanian authorities, they wrote that my mom was pregnant. "With all the troubles she's had keeping a pregnancy, she'll be better off with medical care in the United States." I thought, forget it, they're going to have a kid over there. I'm never going to see my parents again. Stuck forever with the wrong grandparents in the wrong part of Bucharest.

After a year and a half, my name ended up on a list of bargaining chips Romania needed to trade with, so they could get *Most-Favored Nation Status* with the United States. October 1983, I'm put on an airplane and the next thing I know I'm living with my parents in Kew Gardens, Queens. I resented my mom and dad so much for abandoning me, I didn't speak to them for a year.

Senator Al D'Amato (known as "Senator Pothole" for his hands-on constituent service) used the Helsinki Accord and hardball trade negoiations to secure Raluca's entry to the United States. Although Raluca came to despise much of the Republican Senator's politics, she remains grateful to him for his help on her behalf and on behalf of some of her clients, who he helped before he lost his Senate seat in 1998.

Going to Forest Hills High School was like going to a different planet. You can flip though the yearbook — there's almost no Anglo-Saxon name in there. For the first time in my life I was surrounded by people from India and Africa and South America, and for some reason there was a huge anti-Communist feeling in the air. Maybe Ronald Reagan going around calling the Soviet Union an *Evil Empire* had something to do with it.

I remember kids calling me a Russian commie, which
was absurd because I wasn't Russian and I wasn't
a commie. I made sure never to wear red. I was so
embarrassed about my accent, I invented a different
identity for myself, seizing on the fact that my grandfather on my mother's side was French. I'd tell everybody I was half-French, half-Romanian, then study
like crazy in my English as a Second Language class.

In Bucharest we wore school uniforms that had to
be starched and ironed, and the skirts had to be just
the right length, and socks pulled over the knees.
Then I come here and it's the middle of the *Flash-
dance* era — all these girls with lots of makeup on
and T-shirts falling off their shoulders. I'd seen
images of Americans on TV programs like "Bewitched"
and "I Dream of Jeannie." Even though they were
witches and slept in bottles, they seemed normal to
me compared to the kids at Forest Hills High School.
It's supposed to be one of the best schools in New
York, but it looked to me like no one was listening to
their professors. If you actually wanted to learn, most
kids looked down on you. I wasn't the best student
in Romania, but at Forest Hills they skipped me two
grades, and except for English, I was at the top of
every class. Which is why I got to really like school.
The subjects they were teaching in tenth grade, I
learned already in fifth grade.

When I came home from school, I wasn't a pleasant
person to be around. Of course I didn't have a warm,
fuzzy relationship with my dad *before* he left Romania. He's a very dictatorial, military-type, my father.
I'd liken him to Rudolph Giuliani. He used to punish
me when I was a little girl if I didn't recognize a particular symphony or know who the composer was.
We spent a lot of time in museums — I think because
he never had anything like that growing up and he

*Heralded by
some and hated
by others for his
prosecutorial
style of govern-
ing, Rudolph
Giuliani was
the Mayor of
New York from
1993 to 2001.*

wanted to make up for it with his only kid. When
we came home from the museum, he'd test me with
reproductions of the paintings. "What's the name of
this painting? What style is it?" He'd have me read all
these books and then I had to write a report on them.
One time he caught me reading a book I found on
the shelf. It was an Italian book written by Giovanni
Boccaccio in the 1500s called *Decameron*, and some
of the stories in there are a little bawdy. My dad was
so upset, he confiscated the book. So I got another
copy from the library and read it cover to cover.

I don't have a very good sense of humor in English,
but in Romanian I'm very funny. Growing up, we
didn't go out to eat at restaurants. Our idea of en-
tertaining was to have people over on Sundays. My
mom would cook and everyone would gather around
the table, eat, play cards, and tell political jokes. If
Ceausescu was giving a speech, which he would do
for like two hours straight, we would turn on the TV
and laugh at him. We weren't allowed to have social
classes under Communism, so we distinguished ourselves according to education, which was very important in Romania. If people were uneducated, like
Ceausescu, we looked down on them. He was the
President of the country but he couldn't pronounce
words right at all. We thought he was hysterical.
I'd liken him to George W. Bush.

My dad always talked bad about the Communists.
He'd make these propaganda films for them and then
he'd come home and say, "This is ridiculous! They
want me to manufacture a history." I think he was
afraid that he couldn't keep his views out of the films
anymore. That's when he knew he had to get out.

*Even though he was
born in this country
and attended the most
elite schools, the 42nd
President of the United
States, George W. Bush,
has a reputation for
mangling the English
language, especially
when caught off script.
His defenders refer to
him as "plainspoken,"
while comedians take
pot shots at his mala-
propisms. "You teach a
child to read, and he or
her will be able to pass
a literacy test." —
President George W.
Bush, 2/21/2001*

247

After my sister defected to the United States I was obstructed in my
activity as a filmmaker in Bucharest. You could say I was blacklisted.
Eventually I wanted to get out. 1978 was considered the International
Year of the Children. I thought, there will be less restrictions applied
to my child. So I applied for Raluca to come to United States to visit
my sister. If she goes over there, she will stay and then I can go. That
was my thought. They called me from the Political Department.
"Are you insane? What are you doing?"

                                  I said, "Well, I have the right."
                        "You don't."
                              "Yes I do."
                        "You don't."
                                "I do."

I opened up the Bible — the military rulebook. I thought I had the right.
There was a line there that said you have to inform your superiors
about your relative's departure. I said,
                              "Okay, she didn't depart yet.
                              Let her go and I'll inform you."
We are reading the same line different ways. They said,
                        "No.
        First of all your application will
be denied. But if you want to maintain
  her application, then we don't think
      you can work for us anymore."
                              "From what point of view?"
                        "Ours."
                              "Yours or the rulebook?"
                        "Both."

I went to my office and wrote out my resignation. Then I went to the
special office handling those documents. The guy in charge was one
of my friends. He didn't look at what I gave him. I said,
                              "You need to sign and stamp this.
                              Not there. Stamp it over here."
                        "Okay."

He stamps the symbol of power without even reading the damn thing.

I smile. He looks down at the paper.

"No. I cannot do that for you."

"It's too late, guy."

"No, I'm serious, I can't."

"But you already did. Now you file that."

He filed it and a few days later I get a call from the Political Department. "Onchoiu, your resignation has been approved. You have ten days to finish the movie you're working on."

I finished with the army, finished with the Communist Party, and got a job at a movie studio as a stuntman, spinning cars out of control. Eventually I became a director for that studio. My first film for them won the local Academy Award. All the while I kept applying for visa to travel out of the country. All my applications they put in the garbage. I kept applying. They kept throwing. Application. Garbage. Application. Garbage. Then in 1983, a man from KGB called me in. "If you travel to the Western side, they will try to trap you. If we let you go, should we have full confidence that you will come back?" "Of course. I swear I will come back. Definitely." He must have thought this guy has his life as a film-maker, has military pension, has his daughter here.

My wife and I were approved to go to Rome. I kept secret my plans of defecting from my colleagues, my parents, my daughter, even my wife. Any information gets back to KGB, they grab you at the airport and your life is ruined. I shot three rolls of film of all my awards and newspaper articles proving I am well known movie maker. This would be my resume for getting movie job in America.

My wife and I go with vacation suitcases to the airport. They find the rolls of film in my bag. The guy ask me, "Is any of them used?"

"No. All the film is virgin."

"For sightseeing? Good."

Ian describes how he became a filmmaker:

I never thought I wanted to be in the army. My parents sent me to a military high school. After that I went to military superior school and decided to become a pilot. I was very much in love with stories about aviation heroes, especially from the Soviet era. I remember a book called *The Story of Real Men* about Alexander Meresiev who shot down, I think, 111 German planes. And Ivan Kojedub, the first pilot ever to fly a plane after having both legs blown off. Thirteen of us in school were going to train for aviation. First was a medical examination, which I failed because of an infection I got in my ear when I was a little boy. The other twelve guys went on to become pilots and I ended up on the ground as a military engineer working on tanks and trucks. When I became an officer, I found out one of the twelve guys (my best friend from the academy) crashed in a flight excercise. Then another guy crashed. By the time I left Romania, all twelve guys, one by one, had died in military excercises, flying these old Soviet-made planes.

As an officer, I had very good positions, except each unit always had one political appointee who knew just one thing — how to apply the red wire — which is the Communist line. One time I got into a terrible fist fight with one of these primitive guys and it turned out this guy was a cousin to the Minister of the Army. I received advice at that time from two great guys. One was a doctor friend who said, "Your only solution is to play insane. Otherwise you will end in the martial court." So I pleaded temporary insanity and went to a mental sanitorium for 45 days. The second good advice came from a General. "I know that you always have a lot to say about films. Why don't you go to the Army film studio to watch over movies made for training our troops? Because the last few years, we're just getting garbage from them. You can become a consultant." After a few months, I liked it so much, one of the directors said, "Why don't you make your own movies?" I was reading a little book about how to drive safely in all kinds of bad conditions written by one of the most famous car racers in Europe. I wrote a screenplay and that was the first of forty short documentary and training films I made for the Army.

I made a few secret movies under category, "Arms for Sale." Ceausescu was getting very good at buying second-rate arms from the Chinese, from the Soviets, putting the stuff together and selling them to Third-World countries that didn't have enough money to purchase from "real" arms makers. He was selling to Libya, Iran, Iraq, all kinds of dirty business, and I was a part of making commercials for that. We made one film about high-speed torpedo carriers. And to do this we had to launch two torpedoes and blow up a boat. The crew was making bets where the torpedo would actually land. I consider that film one of the best I ever made. It was really very nice.

IAN

In Rome we met my sister, who was working for Pan-American Airlines. She had free tickets for us to fly with her to New York. I couldn't wait to see America. In my mind it was a huge, modern place where poverty does not exist. Where everything starts out in the medium class and higher, and everything is precise and clean and fair. I was very well prepared because I was reading all American authors alphabetically. Dickenson. Emerson. Fitzgerald. And Hemingway — how he wrote of Americans taking first the fun from whatever they got a hold of. I'm ready for this fun. This was the bright easy feeling I had about America.

My first impact from the moment we landed at Kennedy Airport was very disturbing. After many attempts we were lucky to find a gypsy cab. One of the sloppiest guys you could imagine. A blonde guy. I could paint him for you if I had to. Holes in his jeans. No shoes. He had slippers, and they were filthy. There was a hole in the bottom of his oily trunk where I put our few belongings. The traffic on the highway was bumper to bumper. He switched to the service road, which looks a lot better now than it did in '82. I'm not prejudiced in any way, but you couldn't see a white face. All the kids playing basketball. Guys fixing cars on the street, smelly plastic garbage bags all over the place, and the traffic even on the service road barely moving. I'm telling you, I lost my voice, I was so shocked. When we got to my sister's place in Queens, I just said, "When can I start working?" My sister says, "But you're not legal."

"Legal?
I'm here!"

That's when I told my wife — ex-wife — about my plans to defect. She had a crisis. Crying, crying, crying. We left our daughter in Romania with my family. Everything in a marriage is supposed to be shared, but I did a terrible thing to her by not saying anything that was in my head. By the time I got to sleep I was quite sad and exhausted.

The next day I went with my broken English to a photo place to have the film developed of my awards and articles. "Do you process black and white Agfa film?" In those days very few people in United States knew about Agfa. "Of course we do." The next day I come back, "We're sorry, your film came out blank." They processed the film with wrong chemicals. It was one of the most terrible days of my life.

First job I get is auto mechanic. Walking to work on the street, I'm shocked by what I'm seeing. Nicely dressed ladies with sneakers. Okay. I understand you wear comfortable sneakers to reach your office. **But, to see a woman with beautiful outfit and sneakers. Nothing can be more awful than that!** Still I believe that women are the softer gender. I don't expect to see a nice lady chewing bubblegums like a frog. That is really disgusting. Or seeing a 20-year-old guy sitting on the subway and a 70-year-old lady standing over him, he's listening to his headphones instead of offering the seat to her. When I go back to Romania and I see a man hold a chair for a lady, I'm touched to tears to see that again.

When we left, the authorities tried to brainwash Raluca. "See what your parents did to you?" She became a child actress over there, starring in a TV show every Saturday, living with my side of the family where they let her be free to do what she wanted, compared to my very severe mentality. I leave and she starts to get her wings, and a year and a half later, we were able to send for her, and her wings by that time were very very large.

I didn't get close to my dad until he got divorced from my mom when I was in college. Once their marriage fell apart, he proved to be very fallible and I didn't have the same tolerance for him telling me what to do. We both changed and a different relationship emerged. I'd come back from Boston to visit for the holidays and we'd have actual conversations about things. It was very nice, mostly. Then in 1991, I was getting my Master's degree

in International Studies, and I was visiting him in his little house in Kew Gardens, and I was opening Christmas cards from Romania. In a very stereotypical, chauvinist, Romanian fashion, all the cards are always addressed to my dad, even though they're for the whole family. And I open this one card and inside it says, *Draguh Tata,* which means Dear Dad. I threw a temper tantrum and ripped up the card. When my dad came home, I said, "I have to talk to you. There was a card in the mail. I ripped it up and it's in the garbage. It was from your *son.* I want you to tell me who is this *son* of yours." He denied it. He said he doesn't know if it's his son or not. We didn't talk about it again.

In the U.S., Raluca was suddenly a nobody. She didn't speak English. I was her worst enemy. For almost a year she gave me the silent treatment. She wouldn't even walk next to me on the street. I lied to her, then I took her from her home. I am self-doomed father.

Raluca learned English very fast, started making friends, graduated at the top her class, and applied for seven universities, and all of them accepted her with scholarships. Now her mission is human rights, which she does in the immigration field as a lawyer. Doing a very correct job. She tries to be correct in everything that she does. This is number one attribute that maybe I have given her. I hope she got something good from me because there are lots of bad things about me. I'm a very stubborn person who sometimes, even in situations in which I fully knew that my position at the time wasn't the right one, I was still doing it.

I've changed a lot. My second ex-wife was very American. She helped me see things from the other side. Of course at the beginning I didn't agree there was anything for me to change. I had my way of looking at gays, for instance, or even races. I came to this huge ocean of races from a country where we are very chauvinist about our culture. Little by little, with her help, I started using different lenses, expanding my mind of what is normal. I didn't change entirely – otherwise she would still be my wife.

RALUCA

I'm taking this class on asylum law in graduate school and the professor starts talking about how difficult it was in the '70s and '80s for people from Africa and Latin America to get asylum. He's talking about women and children being terrorized and slaughtered by the U.S.-backed contras in Nicaragua, and the disappearances in Chile and Brazil; and no matter how textbook-perfect the asylum claims from those countries were, they couldn't get asylum here. Then he said, "It's people like Raluca and her family that were able to get asylum." I was so embarrassed. "They gave it to anybody if they were from a Soviet republic." I felt so bad, because it's true. When we got asylum we were so much less deserving. Waiting on food lines, not having free elections — it doesn't compare to being afraid that someone is going to kill or mutilate you. If we were from a military dictatorship that the U.S. supported, we'd still be there, or maybe we'd be dead. Still, my professor shouldn't have used me as an example. It was a rotten thing to do.

I went to NYU Law School on a special scholarship that makes you promise to do ten years of public interest law after you graduate. This is my third year working for

Raluca tells us about some of her clients, including Osadeba Eboigbe:

a Refugee Assistance program that supplies free legal aid to asylum seekers. Even if I didn't have to do public service law, it's what I'd be doing, because I love it. It's my job to screen the hundreds of people who contact our office seeking asylum, link up the claims that seem valid with volunteer attorneys, and then facilitate the relationship. Sometimes, if I really have a feeling for someone, I take the case myself. At the beginning I wanted to help anybody, whether or not I believed they had a real asylum claim. As time's gone by, it becomes clear whether or not they are telling the truth. Sometimes I find myself getting upset when I think someone is lying to me. You know, a guy says he's from Sierra Leone, and he doesn't even know the names of the neighboring countries. If I don't believe him, imagine what an INS judge is going to think. I can get really mad when someone is lying to me. But then I take a step back and think about where they're coming from and what situation they've escaped. Then I usually think, *any normal person would try to get away from a situation like that.*

I was interviewing a lot of people at the Wackenhut Detention Center and I decided to take one case for myself. It was my very first case. Osadeba Eboigbe was forced off his farm in Nigeria. There was oil on his property and the government wanted to lease the land to an oil company. The soldiers threatened to kill him if he came back to the land, and of course he came back, because he knew of no other way to survive. There was a shootout and the soldiers killed his brother, but Osadeba escaped and sold everything he had for a plane ticket and a passport. He asked for asylum at JFK, so INS shipped him over to Wackenhut. I made a very thorough case, but the judge denied asylum but gave him a *Withholding of Removal* Status, which means he gets a temporary green card and employment authorization until the conditions change in his country. But I didn't think that was good enough. According to the Geneva Convention, if there's a 10% chance going back to your home country will result in persecution, you're entitled to asylum in any signatory country. So INS was going to let him out of detention, but because I appealed the ruling, and the government appealed my appeal, they kept him locked up with no end in sight. The funny thing is, if you get snagged at JFK Airport, there's practically a 100% chance of being indefinitely detained, but then you could end up getting asylum because of a 10% chance of being indefinitely detained in your own country.

I come home from work one day and get a call from my aunt. She just came back from Romania, and while she was there, she met the boy who sent the Christmas card that said *Draguh Tata*. She brought him something from my dad, and sure enough "he looks exactly like your father." All these years I thought I was an only child. Then my dad had a DNA test and after he got the results, he told me that he does have a son and it's definitely *his son*, and then a couple of weeks later, he asks me, "What can we do to bring him over?"

So here's this guy who spent his entire life outside, stuck inside a windowless prison with no end in sight. One thing they give you in there is unlimited free calls to your volunteer lawyer, if you're lucky to have a volunteer lawyer. So Osadeba called me all the time. Sometimes I would be like, "What, Osadeba? I can't talk to you every five minutes." I felt so bad. One time he called to tell me he was going on a hunger strike. What if I said the wrong thing? Five months later, a different judge overturned the original ruling and granted him asylum. In the words of a wise old immigration lawyer I know who works for Catholic Charities, "There's three things that count in every case: The law. The facts. And the judge."

Osadeba didn't know anyone here so I went to pick him up. The subway took forever. When I finally got out there Osadeba had been waiting outside for hours in his clothes that had been crumpled up into a ball and thrown in a locker for months. I see him standing there all wrinkled from top to bottom. I'm in tears and he's all smiles. I look at him and think, *oh my god, you have nowhere to go. What am I to do with you?* He comes from a small village in Nigeria, how's he going to survive in New York City? He doesn't even know what the currency is like here. I really didn't know what to do. Finally I connected him with a Nigerian man who said Osadeba could live with him. We threw a 25th birthday party for him at the office. Now he has his G.E.D. and a job and he sent me an Easter card.

RALUCA

It turns out, while he was married to my mom back in Romania, my dad was having an affair with a married woman, and they had a son. His name is Livui and he's ten years younger than me.

When my dad asked me what we can do to bring him over, I didn't hesitate. I agreed to do the papers. Since Livui wasn't the child of a legal marriage, according to immigration law my father had to prove that they had an ongoing relationship. In order to prove that, he gave me all these letters to submit to the INS. When I read the letters, that's when I got really upset. I'd look at the date and remember what we were doing as a family and where we were, and then I'd think how, at the same time he had this whole other family. It was very odd reading these poetic letters my dad wrote to his secret son. All through the years, he talked to me often in that strict tone of voice dolling out punishiments, but to Livui he wrote loving, metaphorical letters that were very beautifully written.

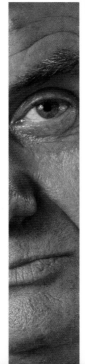

IAN

My son Livui was a hidden fact until my sister found out about him. She maniuplated the situation to make sure that Christmas card reached Raluca's hands. I told her half the truth: "Yes, I had an extramarital affair while I was married to your Mom. That lady had a baby, but I have no way of knowing he's mine." I knew the kid was mine. I took care of him the first three years. Seeing him every day like a father. When I came here I sent Livui all sorts of parcels until I couldn't afford it anymore. For many years I stopped all communication. Then my second wife started asking me about my son. I said, "You know I have nightmares about him."

In 1997 my sister ended up with a picture of Livui as a
seventeen year old. She said, "You know this picture?"
Immediately I call him. He hadn't heard my voice since
he was a little kid. He said, "If you are my Dad, stay
                              with me. Don't hang up."
  The connection was terrible.
   "Okay, I'm staying with you.
                  How are..."
                      "No."
        He interrupted me.
                      "I want to get your phone num-
                      ber and address from you."
  I said, "Livui, I will send you
       a letter with everything."
                      "No. I want you to give it now."

I could hear his desperation. He started emailing right
away. I wrote him a few long letters, trying to recover
parental guidance and such. I started talking with his mom.
"You find the best tutor for him. I want him to go to college." The competition in Romanian colleges, for one seat,
three hundred people apply. He applied to three different
colleges and was accepted the top in every single one.

LIVUI

For twenty years my name
was Livui Manolache. A year
ago I took my father's last
name, Oncioiu. Livui I kept
same. You pronounce it *Leave-
You*. I wonder, does my name
sound like *leave you*, because
I've left things in my life, like
my country and all my friends
and my mother? And people
have left me, like my father.
Or, is it just in my mind, this
thing about my name?

LIVUI

I was the youngest disc jockey in Romania. When I was sixteen years old, I was going through the dial and found this new radio station. I just called them up. They listened to tapes of the radio show I did at my high school and gave me my own show, 10 to midnight. Whatever I wanted to play. Mostly I played American and British stuff from the '50s, '60s, '70s and '80s. The Beatles. Simon and Garfunkel. Blondie. I started buying all the tapes I could find from that period. You'd call them bootleg tapes, but in Romania, there was no such thing as copyright law. I'd play a tape of Joe Cocker singing at Woodstock and I'd think, this is 30 years old and it's like, Wow! This guy sings great! It was an oldies show, but to me and my listeners it was all new. Growing up, all I ever heard was traditional Romanian folk music. That's what the Communists allowed on the radio and that's what my grandmother and mother listened to.

I never thought America is a place I'd like to live. I just looked at it as a place where great music came from and lots of interesting things happened, like Woodstock festival. I was very happy in Romania. I didn't care so much about long lines or the economy not working. I had friends, and ever since the Communists left I could listen to whatever music I liked.

The whole thing started on 17 December, 1989. I'm about to be ten years old on 19 December and there's a revolution going on outside. From our tenth-floor balcony in the middle of Bucharest, I could see huge crowds of people on the boulevards marching and chanting slogans. By the time it was my birthday, the soldiers were shooting at anything that moved. My mother wouldn't even allow me on the balcony. It was a ruined birthday.

I remember staring at the TV, thinking, *hey, this is new thing. After so many years hearing people complain how they hate the system, they're finally doing something about it.* So they killed Ceausescu and power went to his friend Illiescu. With him you didn't have to stay in long lines, but there wasn't money to buy. Today, it's almost as bad as it was under Communism. You can say whatever you want in the street or the newspaper, but what good does it do?

When you're a kid, revolution in the street and stuff like that, you just accept, okay, this is happening now. I think it was the same way with my father. After a while he just became a symbol to me. I have a father. He lives in America. Period. My mother always showed me letters and cards and a few photographs, so I would know that he really is an actual person. That's how she grew me. Sometimes he'd call on Christmas or my birthday, saying, "Hey, how are you?" I was always calling him Daddy. Until the revolution came. Then nothing. No more phone calls or cards. I don't know why.

One night in '97, the phone rang. I hear that same voice who used to say "Merry Christmas." I don't remember what he said, but when I heard him again, I had to sit down. After that he called more often. He told me I have a sister in America and she is a lawyer and she says if I ever want to come to the United States, I have only two weeks more to do it. Because my 21st birthday was coming up and United States law says only when you are under 21 can you apply for family reunion. I had a girlfriend who I'd like to marry and I was already one and a half years in college, but I thought this may be my only chance to see my father. So like a child, I thought, *oh, I can go to America.* A few weeks later I was having 21st birthday party with my second family in a Romanian restaurant in Queens.

I don't ask questions. If my father ever wants to tell me why we didn't hear from him all those years, or why he left my mother, that's fine. If he doesn't, that's fine again.

Raluca's reflections on Transylvania after a recent visit to Romania.

RALUCA

My dad used to make tourist films up in the mountains in Transylvania. It's so beautiful there. I miss the mountains very much. To me, Transylvania is this wonderful place where my favorite grandmother lived and tended her plum trees and apple trees and sour cherry trees and apricot trees and a big rasberry bush that had serpents in it, and she grew potatoes in the backyard and in her vineyard where she made this awesome white, thick wine that left a film all around the glass. Transylvania — it's a place with beautiful rolling hills and incredible forests and high-peaked mountains. But to Americans it's where vampires come from. I never heard of that till I came here. First time I saw a Dracula film, I was flabbergasted. It would be as if you went to another country and saw a movie where George Washington is a werewolf. Because Dracula was one of Romania's great heroes. He wasn't a count. He was a Prince. Prince Vlad Dracula of Wallachia was a very feared warrior who fought against the Turks and pretty much prevented the Ottoman Empire from spreading into the rest of Europe. He got the nickname "Vlad the Impaler" because of his method of execution. There's a great legend that one time there was a huge Turkish army coming, not just to invade the Romanian principalities but to go forward into the heart of Europe. The Turkish Sultan sent a large scouting detachment first, and Prince Vlad caught the detachment and had them impaled. So here comes the rest of the the Turkish army trotting along and one of them in the front says, "Look. There's a forest ahead, but there isn't any forest on our map." They came closer and closer till they saw it wasn't a forest. It was a field of tall wooden stakes on which thousands of Turkish

LIVUI

My dream is to make money and go home. I miss my friends. I miss my family. I miss my cat. I miss playing soccer. I can't get into playing soccer on my computer. I did play an actual half game the other day with real people, but my physical condition wasn't up to it. Since I came here, I'm sitting, sitting, sitting. That's what I do all day. I sit at home. Sit in the car. Sit at work. I don't know where my time goes. I miss having time. I miss spending a half hour in the morning to make lunch for myself, instead of grabbing a fast-food lunch.

RALUCA

When Livui came here, I didn't think I was going to have anything to do with him. Now Livui and I are friends. His mother pretty much raised him on her own. She did a great job. Livui lives in Queens. My father lives in Queens, and my grandmother on my father's side and my aunt are here. They all live in Queens. Myself, I got tired of Queens. I prefer Manhattan.

In Romania people are not concerned about making so much money. They may make some money but they enjoy their life also. They enjoy their friendships. More than we do here. Here I'm going to work, I'm coming back, and my day is over. What I really miss is talking to people in Romanian language. Not having to think of every word before I talk. I miss listening to my tape collection where American oldies are not so old.

soldiers were impaled — from their butts to the back of their necks, so they appeared to be standing. *What a way to go.* The Turks were so scared they retreated and never came back.

That's the legend. Bram Stoker was British, and he heard stories about Vlad from an Austrian who probably got it from some Hungarians around a campfire. You know Romanians and Hungarians don't like each other very much. That's probably how the whole vampire myth got started. I went back to Romania with my husband last year, and we visited my relatives in Transylvania, and I couldn't believe they have a big tourist trap there now called Dracula's Castle. Vlad Dracula never even lived there! He slept in a bed in that castle one night in 1460-something and now someone's making big bucks on the whole Dracula thing. *They're* the vampires if you ask me.

IAN

Livui and Raluca are like brother and sister, which is very much modeled by Raluca. Of course it helped Livui has such a nice character. He fixes all our computers. The three of us go hiking together. Sometimes with Raluca, a small amount of anger that is hidden, gets out. Not strong enough to be seen by outsiders. But I see it.

I'm happy for my kids we are in America. For myself, I don't know if I made the right choice. I made a few approaches to go back to my beloved field, moviemaking, but I had to go to my other direction – cars. If it's prostitution you're going to do, you might as well work for the best on the market. So I became a mechanic for Mercedes Benz. Now I own my limousine company driving millionaires and famous people. The wife of Francis Ford Coppola was one of my clients. She's a documentarian. She told me the real thing. "In documentaries, you have to have another field in which you make money." I have the other field, now I'm ready to make documentaries again. Next time I will tell you some of my ideas.

a
world of
difference

We met Vikas Gera through our friend Ed
O'Dowd, who sold him some Butthole Surfers
records on eBay. Usually, if you sell something
on the World Wide Web, you send it through
the mail, but it turns out Ed and Vikas were
neighbors. They made the exchange in person
and have been good friends ever since. Sometimes that's the kind of thing it takes to meet
your neighbor in a place like Queens. We're
packed in right next to each other on the
subway, crossing the street before the light
changes, on long lines at the supermarket.
Then we go home and turn on our computers
and surf the Net. Who do we meet online
but the guy down the block.

Vikas is a lovable, soft-spoken college student,
trying to balance the world of his parents and
his Indian culture with his own aspirations
and decade-long experience of living in
"the West."

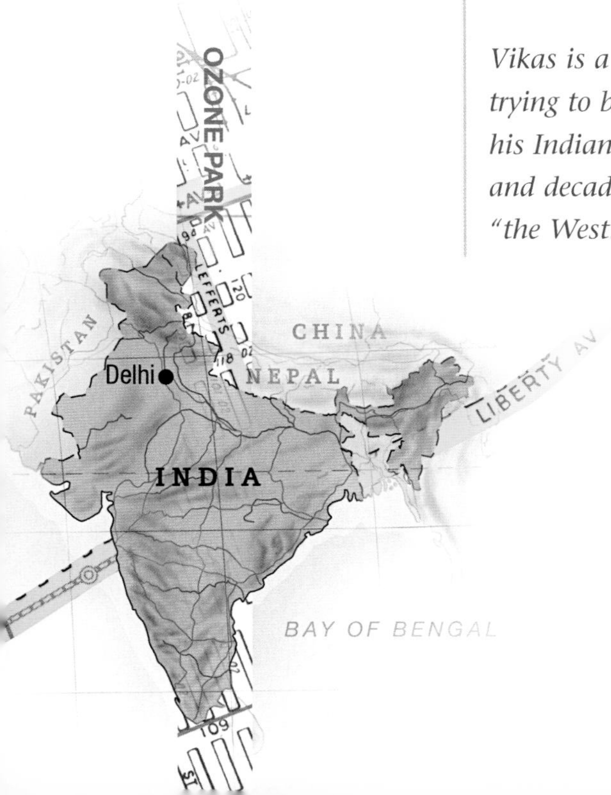

OZONE PARK

LEFFERTS

PAKISTAN

Delhi●

CHINA

NEPAL

LIBERTY AV

INDIA

BAY OF BENGAL

When it comes to the Butthole Surfers, I guess you could say I'm a collector. I collect everything and anything related to the Buttholes. Patches. Pins. Stickers. I'll buy CDs but I prefer records. Twelve inch. Singles. I like the sound of the crackle. It feels natural to me. CDs are very good and everything, but to me it sounds fake.

I used to only be into popular stuff. Whatever my cousin liked, I was like, "Oh yeah. I like that too." I was new to this country, so whatever he had, I absorbed. Run DMC and En Vogue. Early rap and hip-hop. Stuff like that.

Run DMC was the first hardcore rap group to earn gold and platinum albums and to be featured on MTV. All three members of the band are from Hollis, Queens. Founding DMC band member and pioneering turntable DJ Jam Master Jay was gunned down in his Jamaica, Queens studio in October 2002.

When my family first came here from India we lived with my father's brother in his house in Ozone Park. He lived there with his wife and two kids, and another sister and her three kids. So when my parents and me and my brother moved in, there were twelve of us living in that house. This is where the stereotype of Indians living 20 people in one house begins. I guess there's some truth to it. If it was up to my father and my uncle, the three families would live together forever. And if another one of their brothers came here from India, they'd want his family to move in. That's the idea — the whole extended family should live together.

There was only one kitchen in the house, so Mom and my two aunts all cooked together. At first. Then my mom and my uncle's wife started snapping at each other. After all, they weren't blood relatives. Then things got bad. Everybody started cooking and eating separately. Got to where you wouldn't go into the kitchen if you smelled someone else in there. And there was always someone else in there.

My uncle and my father were both happy as can be. But the wives kept turning up the heat. By the time we left, it was a very hostile environment. The kids mostly got along. Kids usually do. It was the adults that were acting like children.

We moved a few blocks away so my father and his brother could still see each other every day. There's no bad blood between them, ever. My uncle was a cab driver. So my father was a cab driver. I was ten years old when we moved here. My eleven-year-old cousin was into rap. So I was into rap. That's how it is. You come from another country, you just want to fit in. Everything was unfamiliar to me. In Delhi you flip a switch *down* to turn on the light. The driver's seat in a car is on the opposite side. Everything seemed backwards to me here. In Delhi you eat dinner at nine, ten at night. You play with all the other kids in the neighborhood. Here, you don't know your neighbors. Maybe the locals know their neighbors, but the immigrants speak different languages and everybody is like a stranger to everybody else. Fifth grade, I'm the new kid from India. Within days, Vikas became *Vik-ass*, and then *Vik-ass* mutated into *Virus*. You know, all the childish things kids come up with to make you feel welcome.

Miss Gutzman didn't make it any easier for me. The first day I was in her class she asked me to read a passage from the textbook. I stood up from my seat and started reading, and everybody in the class just burst out laughing. I'm wondering, *why are they laughing at me?* Instead of taking me aside and explaining — in this country you don't stand up to read aloud — Miss Gutzman just gave this disgusted look and told me to sit down. I sat down and read the passage, my heart beating like crazy. Then she started sending notes home to my parents. She said I was daydreaming in class, which I'm sure I probably was, because I still do sometimes. Daydream. And I'm a senior in college now!

At the end of the day, Miss Gutzman would put a letter in an envelope, seal it, and tell me to give it to my father. I could have held it up to the light and read it. I could have torn it up or thrown it away. But nothing like that ever occurred to me. In Indian culture you're trained to just follow the rules. Especially when it comes to elders, you do what you're told. There are Indians who break the rules. But I never have.

VIKAS

I discovered the Butthole Surfers after we moved into our own house. They had a hit song on the radio in '96 called *Pepper* and from there I started getting into their older stuff. You know, *Locus Abortion Technician* and *Rembrandt Pussyhorse*. *Cream Corn from the Socket of Davis*. All the early LPs. At first it repelled me, but the more I listened, the more I saw how cool they were. It's hard for me to describe why I dig them so much. It's not just your typical drug music, and it's not just the psychedelic sounds and the twisted lyrics. Or that they were the first band to use samples and loops, or that they're from Texas. I think it has a lot to do with Givy's intense personality. Givy's the lead singer. **I just love his attitude** — the image he projects and how it comes out into this music that is so completely distorted and weird and different from anything else.

My parents like Indian film music, which I despise. Not Indian classical music. That would be totally different. The stuff they like is what they were exposed to when they were young. My father doesn't like new Indian film music. He's not a movie person. In fact, he despises movies. He's not a TV person. He's not a book person. He's not particularly a religious person. He's just — a person who wants to go back to India. He dislikes the States. Once his kids get their Western education, I think they're going back. If my father sees a woman in a bikini on television, he gets angry that I'm watching it. He doesn't actually say anything. He just gives me this look like I'm doing something really evil.

I love my parents. Obviously. But we're not close. *We're family.* We all know that we love each other. But there's no physical affection. I think this is common among Indian families. If you see your mother after a month of being apart, you don't hug her. You don't kiss her. The way you show your respect is by doing what they ask. And by doing certain things that let them know that you respect them. In India, if you see an elder, you bow down and touch their feet.

There are a lot of taboos too. Sex. *God forbid.* You never talk about that with your parents. If a thing like that ever were to come up in conversation, it would be just terrible. It's out of the realm of possibility. I don't even date. I've never had a relationship with a girl. It

wouldn't be acceptable while I'm living in their house. They expect me to remain a virgin until marriage. They expect me to have an arranged marriage. Even then, they expect me to live at home with them until they're deceased or they move back to India. They expect a lot from me. And up to now I've given them what they expect. The thing that they don't realize is that I don't feel Indian. The idea of an arranged marriage is just wrong in my opinion. My parents had an arranged marriage and I truly believe that they love each other. But that's not for me. Whenever I do get married, it's going to be to someone I choose. For now I'm just playing the game, and then hopefully, soon as I graduate and find a job, I'm going to move out. Probably.

I'm such a good boy, it makes me sick. You know what I'm majoring in? Take a guess. What's the most stereotypical thing for an Indian guy to be taking in college?

Computer Information Systems. That's me. I don't even like computers. You know who I admire?

Salman Rushdie. I admire any Indian who's taken a different route.

The Ayatollah Khomeini of Iran was so incensed by a book he never read, he issued a 2.5 million dollar fatwa (bounty) on the head of its author, the Indian-born Salmon Rushdie. Instead of retracting The Satanic Verses *or any of the novel's passages on Islam, Rushdie went into hiding for over a decade. While the brilliant writer survived and has since migrated to New York City, his Japanese and Italian translators were assassinated.*

Earning money — that's the only gauge of success for the Indian mentality today. You know what I aspire to be one day? An historian. Or maybe a political scientist. A left-wing, anti-capitalist political scientist, with no money.

You know where I work? H&R Block. Yeah, I voted for Ralph Nader and I get paid to help people pay as few taxes as possible. As long as I'm living in my parents' house, I'll never be the person I want to be. But I feel like I have an obligation to my parents. I owe them at least… a graceful departure. I won't tell them I'm leaving. Whenever I bring it up, they get this look like I'm abandoning them. When I move out I'll still give them money. They won't ask, but I'll do it anyway.

When I first came here, I was the little Indian boy. Now I'm more Western than I am Eastern. I'm just used to it. When I see Indian people behaving in certain ways, sometimes I feel ashamed. Like when I see an Indian man on the street with his finger up his nose, digging stuff out, I want to hide, like I have nothing to do with these people. Hey, you don't do that in this country! In India, it's normal.

VIKAS

You have to clean your nose don't you? That's how Indians view it. Sometimes India seems so foreign to me. Other times it's like the most natural part of me. I wonder sometimes if all my memories of India are just things I dreamt or did they actually happen? Did we go every week to these ritualistic ceremonies at a coven in my uncle's house, sitting around a fire praying as he poured mustard oil on everyone to purify our thoughts? Did my father sell motor scooters in the scooter shop he ran with his two brothers in Delhi or did they just repair them? Did I have a crush on this girl Medha who lived across the street or were we just two close friends playing tag on the brick streets and in and out of the small herb gardens in front of the attached cement houses of our neighborhood? I guess nobody really knows what their childhood was *really* like, but when you move to the other end of the world at ten years old, all you have to go on is fragmented, distorted memories.

That's why I'm planning on going back to visit India after I graduate. I want to meet the rest of my family. I want to see what it's really like there. Track down my old friends. Maybe track down Medha. And when I come back, I'm going to move out of my parents' basement. I'm going to take my records and find a place I can play them as loud as I can without having to hear, "Oh that's not music, that noise!" And one day, I'm going to make a difference, you know. I don't mean I want to change the world. I don't care what it is. Just, I want to do something that will make *me* proud of myself. I'm not looking forward to that anytime soon.

Right now I'm dying to hear some new stuff from the Buttholes. They haven't come out with anything new in over five years. I already have all their legitimate records and a lot of the bootlegs. You know what I'm really into these days? These Asian underground groups like The Asian Dove Foundation. Ever hear of them? They're very political and they mix electronic scratch, you know DJing rock music with Indian music. It's not like I'm doing a get-back-to-my-Indian-roots kind of thing. I just like it! There's a world of difference between Indian music and these Asian underground groups. Believe me. A world of difference.

neighborhood stories

- no bull
- asthma alley
- we shook the bridge
- the latimer senior center
- labib's café

no
bull

LAZARRO NAVARRO
JUAN NAVARRO
HELEN ROCOS
LEO SANDEEP JAKHU
IRMA CALDERON
JORGE CALDERON

Neighborhoods, like people, have memories. Most experiences, individual and collective, fade into the fuzzy realm of the past. Some events live on in the mind, and a handful of others leap into the consciousness of those who were not even there — as legend. In another place and another time, a story of a runaway bull would not seem quite so remarkable. But a bull running down the middle of a boulevard in Queens on an unsuspecting Father's Day in 1999, well, that made for a sight and an eventuality that was incredibly strange, scary, and some would say, tragic. The path of the bull crossed through three neighborhoods, starting in Long Island City, into Astoria, ending up in the Ravenswood Housing Project. In these pages we bring you the perspectives of six people: two of the producers of the Mexican rodeo from which the bull sprung [who until now refused to go on record about the event] and four eyewitnesses from the Ravenswood apartments.

RAVENSWOOD

Punjab

INDIA

Tungarahua

ECUADOR   MEXICO

NORTHERN BOULEVARD

JACKSON AV

Puebla

TRANES 7-N QUEENS BORO PLAZA E-R-F-G QUEENS PLAZA

translated from Spanish JUAN

With the money we saved working in the factory and our restaurant, Selena, we decided to give the Mexican public something they never had in New York – rodeos with the very best musical groups and comedians and equestrian horses and, of course, riding bulls. We thought this would be a healthy business to make spectacles for the whole family, not just something for gangs or crazy people at night.

LAZARRO

When we grew up, we didn't know nothing about rodeo. But 80% of Mexicans in New York love rodeo because they are Pueblanos [people who come from the southern state of Puebla]. We're from Ciudad Serdán which is not an area for rodeos. It's like the difference between growing up in New York and growing up in Texas. Same country but different lifestyle.

Ever determined, the Navarro brothers tried their hand at producing rodeos after their first restaurant in Queens burned down and their second DJ competition party resulted in a gangland murder.

LAZARRO

Since I was six years old and I make gelatin cups and sold them on the street, I know what it means to make your own business working with the public. My father would give us a peso, "Here, go buy something and sell it for a profit."

Instead of booking mariachi bands, the standard fare at anything Mexican in New York, the Navarros booked Norteño groups, a popular music from Northern Mexico.

The first time I saw rodeo was in California. In 1990 my brothers and I formed a band there called NAVARRO SHOW. Everybody in California will drive two hours to watch a rodeo at ranches equipped for music and bull riding and every kind of thing. In New York City, you don't have space like that, but you do have many Pueblanos wanting something to do. Five thousand people came to our first rodeo in Queens. Some people on Long Island tried having a Mexican rodeo but they did not have the popular bands. They rely on the bull ride which is no good because the bulls here don't give the kind of excitement they give in Mexico. The Mexican bull riders use spurs on their boots to jab the bull. That's what makes them jump all over. You can't do that in United States because of animal rights laws. In Mexico, when the bull throws a rider, people say it was a good event. If he topples the rider and steps on him, even better. If he kills the rider, that drives the people crazy.

Our second rodeo was on Mother's Day in a parking lot at Queensboro Plaza. We got all our permits to serve food and the Humane Society came to make sure everything with the animals was by the book. We made a verbal deal for $2,000 a month to sublet the lot every weekend for ten years. When I asked for the sublease, the parking lot tenant said, "Don't worry, we'll sign when the owner comes back from vacation." I paid the $2,000 and we had a wonderful Mother's Day event.

JUAN

The next rodeo was on Father's Day. The bulls arrived the night before. We set up the bleachers and the stage and put the bulls in a corral so they could get a good night's sleep. Nine o'clock the next morning, the parking lot owner shows up saying the event cannot go on. We tell him we already invested $130,000 and there's nothing we could do to stop it. So he calls the police.

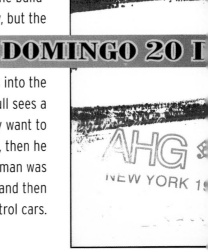

JUAN

A few minutes later, three patrol cars arrive. In front of the police, the owner says he wants $40,000 for the day. That's when we found out there was a problem between the parking lot guy and the building owner. We were willing to pay up to $10,000 for the day, but the owner wouldn't have it. He starts telling the sound people to pack up or they'll be arrested. He's bothering the bulls, so the bull handler starts to bring the bulls into the trailer. That's when the biggest bull got loose. When a bull sees a person they don't know coming at them, the first thing they want to do is charge. The bull runs around the entire parking lot, then he jumps the gate and escapes onto the street. One policeman was so scared he dropped his gun. Another one fell and then they all jumped into their patrol cars.

LAZARRO

The bull crossed Northern Boulevard and ran about a mile under the train tracks towards Astoria. At 36th Avenue, he turned left and went on the sidewalk.

Everybody is running after the bull. I'm running after the bull, the bull keepers, two animal control trucks with tranquilizer guns, a guy with a lasso who was coming to watch the rodeo – but nobody could catch up to him. It didn't take long before there were three helicopters following along telling the police on the ground where to go.

Finally the bull started getting tired. The guy with the lasso was just about to catch up to him when the police told everybody to stand clear and one of them shot the bull.

The police didn't know the bull can only run so far before it gets too tired. I think also the police wanted a victory to say they had killed the bull. I'm sure the guy with the lasso also wanted to be famous.

In Spanish, the Father's Day rodeo ticket boasts, "The Event That Will Make History."

The whole time I'm scared that the bull is going to kill somebody. Especially when it headed for the projects. What if it hit a kid playing in the street or ran into a grocery store?

I was just sitting down to enjoy my cup of coffee and the Sunday paper when I heard Bam Bam Bam. I jumped up and saw a bull coming down 36th Avenue at a pretty good clip, and cops chasing behind it in their cars shooting. They must have fired dozens of bullets into the street. People coming in and out of the supermarket, children, cars everywhere. I've heard bullet shots around here before. I mean these *are* the projects. It's one of the smaller, nicer public housings, but we have had some young people take a shot or two. But this was a non-stop shootout. Like all of a sudden I'm at the O.K. Corral.

The daughter of Greek immigrants, Helen Rocos grew up in several places including Panama. She is currently a resident of the Ravenswood complex. My business partner Leo comes running out of the bathroom. We were working on restoring some furniture for the business he and I have together that we run out of my apartment on the fourth floor. Leo lives with his parents on the fifth floor. Right away he grabs this cheap throwaway camera and starts taking pictures.

I'd seen bulls before but never in the city. And this was a really huge, bigger than your average bull, bull. The biggest wild thing we have running around here is seagulls. We're not even permitted to have dogs over 40 pounds in these buildings, and there's this big fat beautiful bull. It was not a wild bull like these images you see of *Running the Bull* in Spain. His horns were polished and his coat was so neat and clean. He glistened! Even his hoofs were perfectly manicured. He was clearly somebody's pampered pet. Somebody's show bull. He came at a slow pace into the parking lot right here between building 15 and 16 and he stood there in a daze. The poor bull was already stunned from being shot. The cops were sitting in their cars cross-shooting through the parking lot. They denied it later, but they lied.

Helen's business partner Leo lives in Ravenswood with his mom and dad.

The bull froze right in the middle of the parking lot like a frightened docile cow. I thought now they can just go in and rescue the thing. The bull was not menacing. He wasn't stamping his foot or charging or anything. It wasn't the bull that was frightening everyone. I just kept thinking, *what are these idiots shooting at?*

There were a bunch of Mexican men trying to get to the bull. One of them had ropes in his hands. I found out later they all worked for a rodeo that got shut down and the bull got loose. I'm pretty sure the bull was the pet of the guy with the ropes. The cops could have said, "Hey guys, jump on the car and let's go catch this bull." But the cops wouldn't allow them to do anything. They just kept shooting into the bull from every direction. After a while he started getting dizzy. I'm sure he was in terrible pain. For me it was excruciating. I kept thinking about this movie *Joselito*, I saw when I was a little kid in Panama. Joselito was a little boy who was raised with a pet bull that he loved, and when the bull got big, Joselito's father sent it off to become a bull fighting bull. Joselito runs away and eventually rescues the bull and brings him back home to be his pet. To be his best friend. I'm picturing this Mexican guy with the ropes as Joselito. He was holding his head in hands. I could see the look of devastation in his face all the way from my fourth-floor apartment.

Blam

In India you couldn't even hit a cow or a bull with a stick without getting into trouble. People are very religious over there. They believe in the holy cow! Rodeos they consider brutalization. On that point they're right. You know why the bull acts all crazy? They tie up their testicles. How would you feel, somebody takes a string and tie up your testicles?

Blam

Normally I don't go for any of that religious bullshit, but 15 cops shooting a helpless animal, there's no reason for that. The bull was just standing there looking around. In India we have animals all over. Parents send their little

After getting hit by a barrage of 40, 50 bullets, the bull sprung a leak. You could see the blood spurting out of him as though you had punctured a bag full of liquid. The bull moved a little to one side, his legs were twitching, and then he slowly laid down right by the handicapped parking space. At that point I fell to my knees, I was crying so hard. I don't ever pray. I guess you can say I'm an atheist. But I got down on my knees and I prayed for that animal to die fast. I remember the bull held his head up like he was smelling the breeze, like he was delusional or something, looking up at the sky. When he put his head back down, one of the policemen got up on his car with a shotgun, I suppose to blow the bull's brains out once and for all. That would be his final humane effort to put it out of its misery. But the bull wasn't moving at all, so thank God we were spared that sight. People were lining up all around the parking lot horrified and disgusted at how the police could just go on a shooting rampage against this animal with so many cars and so many people around. My friend Joey got a bullet through the back of his brand new car. He was lucky because he had a bag of charcoal briquettes that prevented the bullet from hitting his gas tank. The whole car could have blown.

kids out to get the cows and bulls to bring them back home. If you don't bother an animal, they don't bother you. Trust me — they have pretty good intelligence. They have instinct. They can feel things. But those cops didn't see that. All they saw was an easy target. BlamBlamBlam BlamBlam. Hey, if you want to kill an animal it only takes one bullet to the head.

By the time I came downstairs there were press people all over. I said, "Hey, I got some pictures here. Anybody want to buy some pictures?" The *New York Post* gave me $200. They blew it up and put it on the front page.

DEATH PLUNGE MYSTERY
Woman tosses cash, then leaps 29 floors
Suicide in Midtown: Page 12

Go KNICKS NEW YORK POST ONLY 50¢

MONDAY, JUNE 21, 1999 / Cloudy skies, chance of showers, 70s / Weather: Page 26 ★★   http://www.nypost.com/   · · · · 50¢

RAGING BULL

Bullets fly as beast runs amok on city streets

Camby

'IT AIN'T OVER'
Knicks star speaks out

SEE PAGES 3 & SPORTS

Stewart captures U.S. Open crown

SEE SPORTS

Cops take aim before gunning down loose bull. Full story, more photos: Pages 4 & 5.

The cops tied up the dead bull and dragged its bloody carcass onto a flatbed towtruck and carted it away.

A few weeks later, I read in the paper, somewhere in Japan a bull got loose and the people in the marketplace corralled him, tied him up, brought him to safety. They don't know from bulls, but they figured this is an animal — we can deal with it.

I've not been raised in New York, so I don't have any prejudice against the police myself. I've never had any run-ins with them, but now I'd take my chances against ten bulls before I'd take a chance with one New York cop shooting wildly.

A lot of my neighbors took it as a bad omen. They consider the spot bad luck. A lot of them remember the time three bodies were found burned to death in a car out there. Just this spring when they re-did the parking lot, I heard people say, "Maybe we can finally get rid of this bad-luck parking lot." Others just feel lucky it wasn't a human they shot up.

I grew up in a place [Punjab, Northern India] where you can't lift a finger to a bull, but people are killing each other left and right. Why are they killing each other? Over God! And in India there are just too many religions. Myself, I have a practical view of life. Instead of meditating, I practice martial arts. When I first came here I was thirteen years old. I got goofed on constantly. **"Hey, Gandhi-head!"** They didn't know Gandhi-head was a brown belt in Kung Fu. After a dozen fights I gained everyone's respect.

Now I'm going to computer technology school. Not just to learn a trade. My dream. I never told this to anyone. I don't even know what to call it. Way before there were people, this planet was ruled by dinosaurs for billions of years, until one day a comet collided with earth and killed all of them instantly. Now WE preside over the earth. If we got hit right now by a comet, there's no way we could survive. We've got all these missiles and anti-missile-missiles and nuclear weapons. Shoot any of that stuff at a comet, it won't do nothing. Because the comet is not coming in one big piece. It's going to come at us in a shower. So I'm thinking one day I'm going to invent a way to change the magnetic fields so we could change the direction of the comet. We don't have to destroy it. That's the old way of thinking that comes from the part of the brain that shoots bullets at bulls. I'm talking about a totally new technology that could change the force of gravity. Once we do that, we wouldn't have to worry about comets or meteorites anymore. We would just have to worry about killing each other.

JORGE

I was afraid for my daughter. She and my wife were coming out of the supermarket when I saw the bull running down 36th Avenue. In Ecuador you see bulls all the time, but it was strange

IRMA

My mom and dad made us stand behind the recycling containers just in case one of the shots came to us. They could have just given it something to make it sleep, but they used real bullets. I wanted to get closer so I could see, but my parents said no. When the police shot it, blood squirted out onto a white car. I felt so bad because it was an innocent animal that didn't do nothing bad to anybody. My mom said the bull escaped because it was scared and it didn't want to be in a rodeo anymore.

I remember it happening in slow motion. In my mind it took forever. Even before it died it seemed like the bull was crossing to the second point of life. I kept dreaming about it for weeks in a row — nightmares and dreams. I kept wondering, *where is the bull going? Is he going to Heaven?* Right now I think he's in Heaven not in Hell because I don't think he did nothing bad.

seeing one in Queens. My grandmother had bulls on her little farm. She would rent the bulls to make babies with her two cows. When I was 15, I was so cocky, me and my friend would climb over the plaza wall with a red cloth to where the bulls were and go *olé olé*. Even when the bulls threw us here and there, we weren't afraid.

The cops fired their guns, **tac tac tac tac tac**. My wife told me the Mexicans have a rodeo. It's prohibited you know, but I'm not going to blame the Mexicans. I'm not going to blame the cops either. If you grow up in a city, how you going to know about animals?

Daughter/father Calderon sought protection and a view behind a dumpster in the parking lot of their building.

HELEN

Some of the kids think the cops should have tranquilized the bull. I don't know what kind of tranquilizer you need for a 2,000-pound bull. A girlfriend of mine lived on the second floor and a squirrel jumped in her window. She got scared and called 911. The police stormed her apartment with shotguns and masks. "We're just going to tranquilize it." She went running out of the apartment. In the excitement, she forgot her husband was asleep in their bed. The cops come blazing into the bedroom. The husband wakes up, sees this squirrel jumping around and masked men chasing after it with shooting machines. When they finally shot the squirrel, the tranquilizer dart went right through the poor thing's neck and killed it. The police *do* respond. You just wonder if it's the kind of response you want. I would have just shooed it out the window or put out a trail of peanuts. The old people come down to get fresh air and feed them. A squirrel will walk right up to you and say, "It's feeding time!" The general consensus is, don't call the cops unless it's absolutely necessary. Like when the guy chopped his wife's head off and put it on the bed and then chopped his two kids up, you got to call the cops. But if it's anything to do with animals, you better handle it yourself.

You have to understand, I'm a real animal lover. I have nine cats, two turtles, two diamond doves, a bunch of little dwarf hamsters, and a shih tzu that nobody wants. He's a little blind, a little deaf. Any kind of animal my heart goes out to.

JORGE

My grandmother also had sheep, pigs, donkeys, horses. My parents only had a few chickens and a black dog named Asambita who gave birth to three puppies. When I was five years old, I was watching the puppies feeding from Asambita and I got the urge to feed too, so I curled up and started sucking.

I was a pretty wild kid. Maybe that had something to do with my parents letting my aunt take me to live with her in the city of Huayaquil when I was twelve years old. My aunt said she loved me like a son and could make sure I got a better education. Instead she put me to work selling soft drinks. I said, "No, I don't want to work for you." I met a shoemaker who taught me how to make shoes. My aunt wouldn't let me in at night unless I gave her the money I made, so I slept in wagon carts and covered myself with newspapers. At 16, I returned home a professional shoemaker. My whole village looked at me with respect. That's why my parents forced me to marry their friend's daughter. By the age of 24, I had four children and my own shoe factory with 15 employees.

The marriage didn't work out. And a huge volcano erupted in my city. That is why I don't go there, because the earth trembles and you have to wear a mask just to breathe. I divorced my wife and came here in agreement that I would always send money for our chil-

LAZARRO

The bull story came out on the first page of every newspaper comparing the bull to the guy they shot in the Bronx because the bull was black. Reporters from all over the world were calling me. I didn't talk to any of them. One paper said the bull hit an old lady. They said all kinds of things that weren't true, like we didn't have permits and the whole thing was *a clandestine Mexican rodeo*. It bothered us – the word *clandestine*. They invented things just to sell more newspapers. *La Prensa* had a picture of a cow instead of a bull right on the front page. This is the first time we ever speak what happened that day.

In the blink of an eye we lost $80,000. No more rodeos. It's too dangerous! We have four places now. A restaurant in Manhattan, and bakeries in Queens, Brooklyn and New Jersey. For eight years our customers in Manhattan were Mexican factory workers coming for lunch and dinner. After NAFTA, almost all the factories in the neighborhood went to Mexico and our customers lost their jobs. We had to shift the menu from *Mexican* Mexican to Tex–Mex, because that's what white people like. Whatever extra we make from the restaurant and bakery we put into producing things about Mexican culture. We don't give up. The men work all week and the women stay with the babies in the house. What do they do in the summer? Nothing! Just go in the park. So we're producing Mexican festivals and concerts now. It's what the people need.

In 1999, police officers shot 41 bullets at a Guinean man named Amadou Diallo after he stepped outside his Bronx apartment building to get something to eat. Diallo's death ignited protests about police violence and racial profiling.

JORGE

dren. Now I'm 59 years old with a second wife who is 38, the same age as my oldest boy. Together we have Irma here, who is the smartest girl in the world. I only made it to the fourth grade but she will go to college. I love my children very much but I didn't want any more because they're very expensive. When Irma was nine, my wife said, "I want to have a boy." I tell her no more children for me. "When our son would be ten, I will be an old man." I thought I won the argument but we had the boy anyway. Dear God, what is wrong with me?

Proponents of the North American Free Trade Agreement between the U.S., Canada, and Mexico speak of reducing tariff barriers and opening up markets. Opponents like the AFL-CIO and other trade unions point to the 2,000-plus U.S. establishments that have moved their operations from the States to Mexico (since NAFTA was enacted in '93) in pursuit of low wages and scant environmental or safety standards. According to the Washington Post, between the years 2000 and 2002, more than 500 foreign-owned assembly-line factories in Mexico moved to China in pursuit of even lower wages and standards.

FESTEJANDO PARA TI EN VIVO

asthma alley

TIM DU VAL
RAYMOND NORMANDEAU
RITA FRAZIER
MISS EILEEN
KATIJAH SABAN-PHILIPS
QUEEN
PASTOR BEA FUCHS

Western Queens, home to four power plants that supply 60% of the energy for the entire city of New York, has become known as "Asthma Alley" due to the high rates of asthma in the community. According to a 2000 Environmental Protection Agency study, residents of western Queens get more toxic chemicals pumped into their air than the four other boroughs of New York combined. Four new power plants proposed for the area have generated unexpected allies and enemies. Residents who fear for their health have joined forces with real estate investors and politicians who had other plans for the area. They organize poorly-attended rallies in opposition to the power companies who have teamed up with union workers who want to build and work in the power plants. Disempowered and immigrant populations living in the low-income housing adjacent to the power plants appear to be missing from the debate. As of now, the Power Authority is proceeding with its plans for expansion in the area. We focused on seven people who live and/or work in Asthma Alley — an activist, urban landscaper; two teachers with asthma; two tenant leaders from the Queens-bridge Houses (the largest public housing project in North America); an evangelist whose daughter nearly died from an asthma attack; and a pastor.

ILIPPINES
Manila ●

AUSTRALIA
● Sydney

QUEENSBRIDGE

NIGERIA   Manitoba
○ Lagos   CANADA

This plant has been up and running for a couple of weeks now and every few hours it lets off a very strong stench of natural gas straight into our building. Nobody ever told us, but it's amazingly loud, like a steam engine letting off steam at the highest possible pressure. I've called the city's noise complaint line and they say, "The noise has to be continuous and not intermittent." I guess intermittent industrial farts don't constitute noise pollution.

I thought we had made a pretty good life for ourselves here. Now I'm not sure what to do. My mother was a gardener. She might have planted something in me, but that was never the plan. I was meant to take over my grandfather's law firm in Australia. Luckily I kept failing the law exams. I asked my grandfather for a year off from the company. That was 1970. They're still waiting for me to come back.

TIM

Most Australians tend to go to London first to see our Queen. Being a contrarian, I came straightaway to New York. I got a job driving a truck delivering plants to penthouse apartments in Manhattan. I'd take an elevator to the top floor and suddenly I had access to the most fantastic places and the best views in the city. My wife was the girl who first inter-viewed me at the plant company. After we got together we started our own rooftop gardening business. We found a run-down building on 34th street and got six months free rent if we put on a new roof and rewired the building. When we finished renovating the place, the *Times* did an article in the Home Section called "Miracle on 34th Street." After the article came out our rent went from $2,500 a month to $10,000. That's when we started looking to buy something of our own.

We first met Tim Du Val at a protest rally in front of a new "temporary" natural gas power plant in Long Island City. The rally, like most rallies against the power plants in western Queens, had a turnout of only a few dozen activists and politicians, making speeches and chanting slogans like, "Hey Hey! Ho Ho! The Power Plants Have Got To Go!" Tim and his wife Dagny have an urban land-scape business directly across the street from the new power plant. Together they renovated a square block of old brick factory buildings where they employ 65 designers and gardeners and rent to half a dozen artisans and small businesses. We talked to Tim in his rooftop garden, which once had a magnificent panoramic view of the New York City skyline.

I didn't know anything about Queens. To me, it was just a place where they keep the airports. You know that cartoon in the *New Yorker*? A couple is going over the 59th Street Bridge in a taxi, and the woman says, "Oh, I've never been to Queens without luggage before." I was like that until we got a job working with the sculptor Isamu Noguchi, planting his garden museum here on Vernon Boulevard. He had me going all over the Northeast looking for oddball trees, like pine trees that had been blown over in a big storm twenty years ago. Everything he liked we had to dig out sideways. At the end of the day I'd get on my motorcycle with my shovel and my canvas bag full of pruning implements and zoom back to Manhattan.

One time I was heading back and I noticed this fantastic curve on the upper access ramp to the 59th Street Bridge. It was such a beautifully banked turn, I went back over the bridge just to feel that sensation again, only faster. Back at the access ramp I probably had it up to 35 miles an hour, which is kind of fast for that sort of a turn, and the throttle was pret-ty much flat, and the foot pegs hit the ground and caught the bottom of the bike frame. I was leaning into it too hard and I just went flying off into the guardrail. Your first instinct when you come off a motorbike is to jump

Tim on his rooftop deck, with the New Yo[r]

off the ground to see what kind of shape the bike is in. I checked out my bike and then I was looking around at everything and that's when I noticed what an amazing location it is here by the water in Queens. Now we live within spitting distance of where I took that fall.

We got a great price on a block of old paint factories. This whole area was the paint and varnish capital for the United States and our buildings are the only ones that haven't been destroyed. After the paint business dried up, one of the buildings was converted to a metal foundry and the other buildings were converted to an ice-cream factory.

This building used to have a 5,000-gallon tank of liquid chocolate and another one for sugar syrup. We had a hell of a time getting all the melted sugar off the floor. We put a lot of time into the neighborhood too, putting lights on the street, fixing sidewalks, planting street

Two views of Du Val's trees. You can ask the city to help you
rooftop garden plant trees, but by the time they get

around to it, you're better off doing it yourself. So we planted poplar trees around the block. In effect we donated the trees to the city. A few months ago, we were cutting dead branches off of one of the trees, and a city employee who calls himself the Tree Police gave us a summons for pruning a street tree without a permit. We tried telling the judge that we planted the trees ourselves, but he didn't want to hear about it.

There's less prostitution and less dumping mattresses on the sidewalks and fewer kids doing mischievous things, and the city has all these plans to develop the area and redo the waterfront, and then the state comes along and drops another power plant right where all that's supposed to happen. It makes no sense! Either it's a conspiracy or a lot of people are incredibly incompetent. We met with the Governor and he told us, "Don't worry." We met with the Power Authority and they told us they'll incorporate our thoughts into the program. That was less than a year ago. You really have to give them a lot of credit, to take a vacant piece of land and in nine months have a fully operational power plant running 24 hours a day.

While renovating his buildings, Tim came across a box of matches with the words Du Val French Ice Cream *printed on it. His last name is spelled exactly the same way. Du Val French Ice Cream was indeed made on the premises in the '50s. Tim reflects,* **"It seems funny that you'd buy a building and find that your family name was incurred in their manufacturing."** *Feeling somehow destined to find this place, Tim and his wife envisioned their complex of buildings and the inner courtyard it surrounds becoming the nexus of a revitalized commercial and residential neighborhood.*

The only good thing that came out of all of this is I got to meet my neighbors. Most of the community groups are run on the enthusiasm and perseverance of a handful of people. They organize all the meetings and all the rallies. They're terrific! But we didn't have the numbers of people, we didn't have the boisterous public actions, or that one person who becomes the champion needed to change the tide. Some of the little groups that are for windmill power, they're very well-meaning but they don't have a clue. They show up with windmills on their heads and gas masks. Then we've got so many people around here that all speak different languages, or they're undocumented and less likely to participate in civil disobedience. That keeps people from forming a solid opposition. That's probably why the Power Authority picks neighborhoods like this. So you end up with a lot of apathy in the area because the attitude is, What is the point of expressing our concerns, if the powers

that be are going to do whatever they want anyway? I hate to admit it, but that is in fact how it works. We demonstrated and wrote letters and then we took them to court and the judges in each case agreed with us. But the Court of Appeals said since it's already built, and the Power Authority says it's an emergency, they can go ahead and operate it. All our efforts didn't amount to squat. And now the apathy just builds up even more. Personally, I was surprised. I was one of those people who really believed that America was this democracy where the right thing always happens in the end.

What I can't figure out — if the power company is on the radio all the time saying, **"Don't use any extra lights or any extra appliances"** because there's such a big power emergency, why do they keep this power plant lit up like a Christmas tree 24 hours a day? There's lights on the bridges in the middle of the afternoon, lights on the empty baseball field at four in the morning. And now look at us. We never liked air conditioning. But now with the noise and the soot and the smell,

we keep all the vents and windows shut,

which creates more pollution!

so we have no choice but to run air conditioning,

which uses more energy,

Miss Eileen is a teacher at the PAL (Police Athletic League) Western Queens Nursery School, located at the heart of the 96-building Queensbridge Housing Project.

MISS EILEEN

My cousin, oh my, every time she had an asthma attack she had to go to the hospital. Then she moved to Texas and the asthma is all gone. So I said, "What about me? I immigrate in the U.S., my asthma will be gone for good." In the Philippines I live near the river, by a glassware factory. Also there's a place with a smoking chimney where they burn the garbage. And depending on the weather and the wind, I could have an attack just walking down the street. That was before I got married. When I had my kids, my asthma practically gone. Only just two or three times a year.

When I came here, it came back worse than it ever was. One day I was walking to work and I smell that incineration smell. I say, "Oh my God, I'm so nervous I don't want to smell that. Maybe it's only in my mind. I have to control it." I asked the director of my school, "Why every time when I come in here I have like this?" *[puts hand on chest, breathes hard]* Could it have anything to do with the Con Ed plant? Somebody came last year giving leaflets about the power plants being bad for you. I worry about that. But the smoke is white. I think, white smoke. It's good, white.

We always play in the yard and the kids ask, "What's that? Clouds?"
"No," I say, "That's the smoke."
Sometimes I wonder, *am I picking up the coughing from these kids or what?* Because they are always coughing. Out of twelve kids, four or five of them have trouble breathing. I ask them, "Do you have asthma?" They say no, but I say, "That's a sign of asthma." I am not a doctor so I can't say and I can't give medication.

If I feel an attack coming on when I'm teaching I try to make myself relax. I turn on the music. "Okay, kids, we're going to do some exercises. Breathe in, breathe out." Then we dance. It helps them too. They relax. They don't know that I'm having an asthma attack! Sometimes, when I have to use my inhaler, I turn around from them, because there is no one else to cover for me. "Okay, breathe in, breathe out. Okay, relax." Sometimes they say, "My mommy have that thing too." All of them, "My mommy has that!" I have to turn around. "Okay, inhale! Okay. Blow. Blow. Blow."

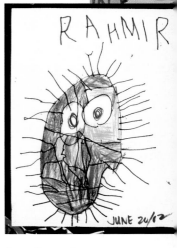

Now I have to use my inhaler four times a day. Two inhalers and a steroid too. The steroid I know is not good for me because it palpitates my heart, but when I stop it they have to take me to my clinic and inject me. The steroid also make me very hyper. My kids say, "Mommy, you're moving so fast." I tell them " Mommy cannot help. Sometimes Mommy have to move fast like that." What, am I supposed to live in a glass room?

Sometimes I wonder, is it from the stress? The children are more behaved in my country, and they listen. They respect their teachers and parents. Not here. In the beginning, I used to cry. "Oh, they don't listen." You learn to get used to a lot of things.

Katijah Saban-Philips, a.k.a. Miss Kathy, teaches at the same nursery school and suffers from severe asthma. Out of the 22 children she teaches, she says nine have asthma. Mostly males.

KATIJAH

Stefan definitely has asthma, because he carries the Preventol® with him every day. I have two Dayquans. They both definitely have it. Joshua Ray, he's out sick today. Christian and C.J. also carry Preventol.®

During outdoor play, you see all these fumes shooting out. And all of a sudden, I don't know if it's a mental thing or a head thing, but we all start coughing and itching. I'd say that happens a few times a week. Sometimes the kids'll ask, "Ooh, Miss Kathy, what's that?" I don't know all that much, so I just say, "Oh, smoke from Con Ed." They say, "What's Con Ed?" You know they try to drag it into a twenty questions kind of thing. I'll say, "Go play." I try to cut if off. If they really persist, I might say, "Oh you know, when you turn your light switch on or your TV, Con Ed is what makes it happen." And they giggle or they cough and go back to playing.

Cited by New York Newsday *as "notorious publishers," Raymond Normandeau and his wife Rita Frazier put out a muckraking desktop rag called the* Queensbridge Enquirer. *If you call them when they're not home, you get a voicemail message that says, "If this is not a political campaign call, press two." If you make it to the end of the message, you hear, "Faxes are only received by appointment."*

RAYMOND

Go ahead and build the power plants! That's all I wrote. We've already got five within choking distance. What's a few more? While they're at it, they should put up a waste transfer station here too. It's the best way to keep the real estate prices low and the yuppies out.

Hey. I'm not for pollution or ruining people's health. I actually think the closer you are to the power plants, the better off you are. Why do you think they build the stacks so high? The polluters don't want to be polluted themselves. The wind blows the smoke out to Manhattan and Long Island and places like that. Even if there's no wind, it's not going to come straight down. Most of the soot we get here is coming off the bridge. We're not called Queensbridge for nothing. That's where most of the asthma's coming from. I counted 288 steps from our building to the site of the new KeySpan plant. That's close, but we're even closer to the bridge.

All these politicians that come to the rallies making speeches and pontificating, you think they care about the health of poor people living in the projects? They never cared about us before. They want it stopped because the real estate interests who are giving them contributions want to put up all these luxury high-rises. I think they'd have trouble selling $500,000 co-ops with a view looking down the muzzle of a belching smokestack. If they don't build more power plants, we should put up some fake ones. You know, props. Fake smokestacks. Whatever it takes. Put up a huge sign that says,

NEW METHADONE CLINIC OPENING HERE

right across the street from City Lights *[the first high-rise luxury building in the area]*. The people who moved in there from Manhattan complain there's no amenities in the neighborhood. All there is is factories and warehouses. They knew they were moving into a factory town ahead of time. Now a lot of them are moving back to Manhattan.

Queensbridge Enquirer 25¢

Me personally,
I'd rather see a nice promenade out here

*Rita Frazier is the
Vice President of
the Queensbridge
Tenant Council.*

than have another one of these power plants.
Somewhere people can sit out, look at the river.

The Power Authority held a meeting here at Queensbridge and the KeySpan man said they'd be reducing the emissions at Big Alice so much, it would probably be healthy for us.

Big Alice is a big old belching mama of a power plant that would probably get shut down tomorrow were it not for it being exempt from many emissions regulations due to a grandfather clause.

Like we'd be getting therapeutic benefits, the emissions would be so clean. My goodness. Who do they take us for? If they lower the emissions at Big Alice, fine and dandy. I'm not against people having power for computers and air conditioners, but putting more power plants between the ones we already have and polluting us more, that's wrong. I know people who have asthma. Some of them have portable machines in their homes just so they can breathe. It's a very huge percentage of people with asthma here. Some families, multiple members have problems. The KeySpan man said, oh, their new power plants are nice and quiet. Quiet and clean. I'd like to ask if they'd give us a tour of one of their new power plants. We could see how quiet it is.

RAYMOND

If I wanted quiet and clean I'd go back to the midwest of Canada. That's where I came from. I was shoveling snow the day I made up my mind to move south. It was 88 below with the windchill, and as I shoveled from the front door to the city sidewalk, I turned around and the snow had fallen so furiously I had to go back and start again. That's how fast the snow was coming down. I asked myself, *What the hell did I do to be born in a place like this?*

Rita and I have lived in Queensbridge since 1973. It wasn't our first choice but we've gotten used to it. They put in a new subway station right here, which is handy because we're always going on auditions in the city. We're both members of AFTRA and SAG. You can see me in a video called *Light Sleeper.* They made it 20 years ago and I'm still getting residuals. I think I got $11 from them two years ago. You can see Rita giving an injection to Ellen Burstyn in the film *Requiem for a Dream*. Rita is prominent enough in the film where she should've been paid as a principal. There's a good five seconds she takes up the whole screen.

RITA

I was trained as an emergency medical technician. That's why my speciality in film and television is portraying medical-type people. The two of us were medical examiners on "America's Most Wanted." We have matching ambulance uniforms.

Before I got into acting I was a barker. Actually I was a talker. A barker is usually for games where the vocabulary is less. A talker gives a schpiel. My first talker jobs were with circuses and carnivals in Canada. After I moved here I got a job in Coney Island with the World in Wax. **COME INSIDE AND SEE THE TWO-HEADED BABY FROM PUERTO RICO. THE FIVE YEAR-OLD MOTHER FROM PERU. HURRY, HURRY, HURRY. YES COME ON INSIDE. IT'S A WORLD IN WAX.** Worked at the steel pier in Atlantic City where we had the world-famous high-diving horse, diving into the water from the height of a four-story building. Then I had some work in Times Square. **GIRLS, GIRLS, GIRLS, FROM THE FOUR CORNERS OF THE GLOBE WAITING TO PLEASE YOU IN A HUNDRED DIFFERENT WAYS. YOU'LL SEE TINA FROM HONG KONG, LOUISE FROM PARI, AND LONG, TALL, AND LEAN ERLINE FROM SEATTLE. ALL INSIDE, POSING FOR YOU RIGHT NOW.**

I was living in Brooklyn at the time and I needed to get a bottle of shampoo. So I go into A&S back when they still existed and I hear this loud voice that sure did carry. I thought it was some kind of special event going on, like a radio program. I follow the sound of the voice and there was this funny man doing a demonstration.

I met Rita on a demonstration job I had with the Denison Corporation. **THE DENISON BUTTONER ATTACHES BUTTONS WITHOUT SEWING. NOW WATCH CAREFULLY AS**

I ATTACH THIS BUTTON TO THIS SHIRT IN UNDER FIVE SECONDS. ONE, TWO, THREE, FOUR, FIVE. YES, LADIES, IT'S AS SIMPLE AS THAT. Through careful

bait and switch, Rita came in for a bottle of shampoo and wound up with me. Later on she became dissatisfied, but A&S wouldn't take me back.

If we're not out on an audition or on a call with the Queensbridge Volunteer Ambulance Corp, we're here working on our little newsletter making enemies. The *Queensbridge Enquirer* is a much-loathed broadside that has gotten us quite a number of death threats. That's the price you pay when you expose links between organized crime and the Housing Authority or the use of extortion to get free labor out of tenants or Nazis masquerading as a church a few blocks from here. I have tapes of some of the death threats. You want to hear some?

I was at the Housing Authority once, complaining about something, and I gave the guy a copy of the *Queensbridge Enquirer.* He scratched his head and said, "How often does this come out?" I said, "Whenever I get pissed off." *NY Daily News:*

CAT & MOUSE GAME

This is a Catch-22 with a twist. Tenant leaders at the 18,000-tenant Queensbridge Houses, alarmed by an upsurge in mice and rats, want to bring in cats to catch the mice. One trouble: Leases expressly state that no pets are allowed in Housing Authority projects. **Raymond B. Normandeau**, spokesman for the Queensbridge Houses Tenant Council, then asked why guide dogs are allowed. Authority lawyers answered: guide dogs are not pets, but essential animals. Cats are essential too, Normandeau wrote back. To which, **Ted Kwasnik** of the HA's legal department replied: "You would have to get your cat certified like a Seeing-Eye dog gets certified. So if there is a training school that certifies cats as mice catchers, I think that you'll win your case." So tenant leaders are asking state officials how to go about certifying a "mouse catcher."

Now I'm in trouble because I ran an editorial saying the power plants are the best way to slow the rate of gentrification. The environmentalists are mad at me, the Tenants Association, the politicians, the Silvercup Studio people, the real estate people — they're all mad at me.

H WORSHIP CENTER
BEA FUCHS
TeL.(718)446-6170

LOOSE
END.
BARBER SHO

We're walking around Queensbridge Housing when we meet a woman from Nigeria sitting at a table outside the Loose Ends Barber Shop, which is now a Worship Center. Queen is an evangelist for the less-than-year-old church. We ask if she knows people with asthma. She tells us about her daughter.

QUEEN

Even the doctors gave up on my daughter. She was in a coma from a very wicked attack of asthma. After seven days, there was very little hope. So I began to pray in the spirit. I told God, "You say you saved me, and you said we're not going to die young if we believe in you. And I surrendered faithfully." He told me not to sleep with men for five years. I did that. Faithfully! The Lord Jesus Christ appeared to me in a vision, "You are a Queen of Jesus." That's how I got the name Queen. He is the King. I am the Queen.

I was born in Nigeria to a Muslim family who named me Sonata from the Qur'an. Then I got a call and the Lord Jesus showed me many things in heavenly places. But when my daughter was asleep for seven days, I couldn't accept that. She didn't have asthma when we came to this country. She was a baby, healthy. Nothing wrong with my daughter until the age of sixteen. It was the day we moved to Long Island City. She could barely breathe. I said, "Lord, what is this?" At the hospital they told me she has asthma. I say, "Asthma! Where all this thing come from? Nobody have asthma in my family." That was the first time I experience what that disease can do in someone's life.

296

It can take your life just like that. Since then we've been to the nurse. They gave her the pump and the medications. Twice she couldn't breathe. When my daughter was young, she could carry anything. But when this asthma thing happened, she can't do many things. Nothing heavy.

The third time it happened was a year ago. I was in Chicago when she fell into a coma. Nobody called to tell me, but I had a dream about it. In my dream, my daughter was in the hospital and I began to pray, "No, my daughter won't die." When I woke up, I kept calling her apartment. I left messages but she never answered. Day after day I said, "Lord. Where is my baby? I leave this girl in your hands." On the seventh day I was weeping. "Lord, this is the seventh day I can't hear from her. I always go to church to please you and to pray with the others. If I'm going to be your evangelist, then today, not tomorrow, today I want to talk to my daughter. Alive!" I quote his word to him. Like you said in Ezekiel, "Speak life to the bones and they will become human." When you serve God for real, you can ask him for anything.

I called my cousin in New York, and he say, "Your daughter's been in a coma. We didn't want you to know, cause we didn't want you to panic." "Panic! For what? I already know what's going on. I saw it in a dream. If you don't tell me what's going on, the Lord will." She said, "We were sitting, waiting for the hospital to call for us to pick up the dead body. But something happened today and she woke up from the coma." Glory be to God. The day I spoke life to God was the day he returned my daughter back to me. Even the hospital said it was a miracle. They thought everything was finished. Now they were saying she needed to start therapy. But I told her, "It's Jesus that heal you. You don't need no therapy. Ain't nothing wrong with your brain, your body. You'll be fine." And you know? She's fine now. She's living here with her own daughter. Only when the weather change, she has to use the pump.

Long Island City Community
• Pediatrics • Asthma and Allergy • Internal Medicine • Obstetrics a

Queen insists we speak to her pastor to see what she has to say about asthma. Pastor Bea Fuchs has several books in her hands. Her name is Fuchs because she married a Jewish man, who is also "born again."

You want to know about asthma? One of the reasons the doctors have not found a cure is because it's a spiritual condition. Asthma is a spirit! An evil, nasty spirit that gets inside you and tries to take your breath.

All these diseases, they all spirits. See this book? *The Demon Hit List.* It lists all the demons that can get inside you. And this is *The Book of Healing* by Carlton Frances Hunter. It tells you on the back: Cast out different spirits.

> **Abuse**
> **Acne**
> **Addiction**
> **Adrenal Glands**

Then it tells you how to minister. These things I've learned over the years. That's why I'm alive today. Cause I tell you brother, I was a goner. A lot of preachers don't believe in demons. They full of them, that's why they don't believe in it. See all these:

> **AIDS**
> **Alzheimer's disease**

And how to do it. How to grab arms and legs. How you lay hands on the front and the back of the head and command the apostate to be opened. You know, the opening at the top of the head. That's the apostate right there.

Let's see... **Asthma!** Cast out the spirit of asthma. Do TNT. Rock the Arms. Speak the Peace of God to their life. . .

All these spirits are running rampant. In my dream the Lord showed me how to eat these diseases. The cure for everything is the word of God. He says, "Medicine, the Word. Medicine to your flesh and health to all your bones." He said, "Speak the word when you lie down and when you get up." Don't take my word for it. God is going to hold me responsible for teaching the truth, but he's going to hold *you* responsible for living it. The hard part is maintenance. He said, "Once they go out and your house is empty, even more will come back and fill it, and they'll be worse than those before." So we fill ourselves with the Holy Spirit and the tongues. First Corinthians 13: "Though I speak in the tongues of angels and have not cherub," which means love, "I become like a sounding brass or tinkling cymbal."

> *We ask Bea if she's heard of all the power plants around here being a contributing factor to the high asthma rate. Surprisingly, she never noticed Big Alice, which looms like Mount Fuji over her church and all of Queensbridge Houses.*

Well, I don't know about the power plants because I've just been in the neighborhood about a year. I do know there's something back there, but I have not stopped to look. I'm sure it can contribute. Too much smoke in the air is evil. Any abundance of anything is bad. Even if you get too religious, you can become a nut! God wants balance in the world. Ecclesiastes 3:1-2: "There's a time to live and a time to die." *All* that has to do with balance. Otherwise the world would be much overpopulated.

Demons need a body to work in. They find their way inside politicians and preachers and people who run power plants. It comes from a mindset of, *I want, I need, me, me, not yours, mine.* Regardless of the risks, they do what they want, which usually is to make a buck. The love of money, that's at the top of the demon list.

I've seen so much and done been to hell and back so many times, the only thing I'm about now is salvation. Don't care who walks in the door. Had a Jewish brother here with a yarmulke and the curls the other day, praising Jesus! A Sikh with the yellow wraps – praising Jesus! One nation under God. We have Bulgaria, all the Latin tongues. We have a Spanish Pastor, Pastor Cruz. We're non-denominational. Pentecostal experience, because we can't go without the power of God. But no one denomination. Denominations divide people. It's not going to be your way, in the end it's going to be God's way. And this is the endtime now. The Enemy wants to steal as many lives as he can. So we have to get on the right side. The Enemy tried to steal my mind. Had a young lady come to me one night. She said, "Pastor, I need help. I'm under attack." I start to do battle warfare on her. Whatever she had, lodged in my arm, then it came up and lodged in the back of my neck. I didn't know what I was dealing with. All I knew, something terrible was inside my flesh. This went on for quite a while until one day I was praying in the Spirit, and the Lord let me see what was tormenting me. I saw a big black sea monster come up out of the water. The Lord allowed me to see what it was. It felt like my whole chest was embellishing outward. Up and down from my belly to the inside of my chest. I kid you not – we all have demons. They appear in threes you know. Now it's time to be delivered.

> *As we left Pastor Fuchs and Queen and the Living Church Worship Center, we couldn't help but look up and see the three smokestacks of the Big Alice power plant, looking like some kind of monster coming up out of the murky waters of the East River.*

we
shook
the bridge

The adjacent neighborhoods of Laurelton and
Cambria Heights in southeastern Queens are
home to the largest population of Haitians in
the borough. We walk down Linden Boulevard
in Cambria Heights past one- and two-story
brick buildings occupied mostly by mom and pop
storefronts: a Creole Bakery, a West-Indian
shipping company, Haitian-owned real estate
agencies, churches, and community organiza-
tions. We walk through surrounding streets lined
with small one- and two-family houses into
Laurelton, a somewhat more upscale residential
area. We come to a white stucco house where
the former leader of a much-feared Haitian
paramilitary force resides, the site of several
protests organized by Haitian exile and human
rights activist, Ray LaForest.

No stranger to political adversity, Ray LaForest
actively resisted the Duvalier dictatorships
before and after moving to New York in 1968.
A Queens resident for thirty years, Ray works as
a union organizer for home health-care workers;
serves on the national board of the "progressive,"
grassroots Pacifica Foundation; and remains
active in the Haitian community.

CAMBRIA HEIGHTS

THE BAHAMAS

LINDEN BLVD

CUBA

DOMINICAN
REPUBLIC

HAITI

Port-au-Prince

LAURELTON

HERRICK BLVD

FRANCIS LEWIS

RAY

When I first came to New York, I discovered a great little park near Queens College where people played soccer. A group of us from Haiti would go there on the weekends and play against people from other countries. There was a flagpole at the park. This was 1972. I don't remember exactly what was going on at that time, but something very political is always going on in Haiti. So we put up the Haitian flag right next to the American flag. The Haitian flag we put up was blue and red. The blue represents the blacks who are the majority in Haiti, so the blue is on top. The next week, some guys came and took our flag down and put up theirs which was the Haitian flag of the Duvalier regime. (Papa Doc considered himself more of a true African, so he changed the blue in the Haitian flag to black.) Well, this was a surprise to us, that there were Macoute in Queens. Maybe they were working for the embassy or the consulate. Maybe they got into an internal fight back home and were forced to leave the country. Or maybe they stole enough money out of Haiti that they could come here and open their own businesses. Whatever reason they were here, they were definitely Macoute. And once again they were trying to assert authority over us.

Macoute refers to the Tonton Macoute, the notoriously vicious paramilitary organization that ruled the streets of Haiti under the (Papa Doc and Baby Doc) Duvalier dictatorships. Named for a child-snatching bogeyman found in Haitian fairy tales, the Macoute [according to the U.N., the Inter-American Commission on Human Rights and others] carried out tens of thousands of extra-judicial executions over a period of 33 years.

My brother Henry cut the rope, took their flag down, stepped on it, and put our flag back up. The Macoute guys were shocked. That's when the fight broke out. We tried to leave but they cornered us. We're fighting and punching, and I remember my brother was dating a young Italian girl and she got punched in the nose. What a bunch of cowards. We could have beaten them but they pulled weapons on us. Handguns. In our faces. The Macoute were always good at killing Haitian people who are unarmed. What saved us is that we're a community here – of people who love Haiti and left Haiti because of what the Duvaliers have done to the country. And there were many more of us than them.

That was the first time I'd seen Macoute in Queens. We saw them before at demonstrations in front of the U.N. in Manhattan and noticed they would show up and take our pictures. Some of the demonstrators who have family in Haiti would cover their face with a bandanna out of fear of reprisal against their families back home. When you live in

Haiti, you know that Duvalier's people are ruthless killers. You know they have weapons. You are afraid. Then you come to this country and you pick up the phone one day and the guy on the other end says, "Si oupa sispan, sa oupran se paw" [If you don't stop, whatever you get you deserve]. Then you know the reach of Macoute is not restricted by borders.

My older brother Gerard and I got involved in the resistance movement when we were young teenagers in Port-au-Prince. Our organization was committed to over-throwing the Duvalier government one way or another. In the beginning, the fight against Duvalier was a bookish affair. People sitting around reading Che and Marx and Lenin. But our group knew how to bring peasants in and work with them in a respectful way. We knew if we were going to build a new society, violent action was a possibility. We'd defend ourselves first, take power by force if necessary – all with an intelligent program. At least that's what we thought. We trained in food and literacy programs and the use of guns. One time a member of another cell made a mistake. He picked up a .38, didn't check to make sure it wasn't loaded, and fired a round into somebody's chest. Gerard went and took the wounded guy to a safe house. The Duvalier government was so greedy, the phone system wasn't working. By the time the military came, the house was cleaned up.

In 1968, news came from a connection inside the government that I had been targeted for arrest. The message was very cryptic – *You have to get out.* My brother Gerard got out first, and then I came to New York to live with my father who got out a few years before us. I was lucky because I had a job waiting for me and a green card. As soon as I got here I started working in the accounting department of a hospital. That's all I could do because I didn't speak much English. I'd say things like, "It's high time to go," because they taught us what they called French-Canadian English back in Catholic school in Haiti. In New York people were saying things like, "The dude is cool man." Or, "Here come the fuzz!" I had no idea what they were saying. I thought fuzz meant something under your nose. And pot was where food in your belly went.

I was 20 when I came here. Within six months I had to register for the draft. I was not a citizen. I couldn't vote, but Uncle Sam could put an M16 in my hands and send me to Vietnam. When I went to the draft board I tried to fail the test by pre-tending I was deaf. You're supposed to press a button each time you hear a tone. Whenever I heard something, I didn't press the button. When I heard nothing, I pressed. I thought I fooled them good. They said, "Okay, we'll call you." In a little while somebody called my name, kind of softly, "LaForest." I said "Yes." He says, "Ah! You passed the test!" They had more experience than I did obviously. One of the officers asked me, "Suppose the U.S.A. got attacked by Russia, what would you do?" I could have said, "Nothing, I'm against war." But I wasn't against war. I had just come from fighting a war. Something clicked in me and for some reason I told the truth – that I don't want to fight and die in a war I don't believe in. Luckily I had started college and a student deferment saved me from going to Vietnam.

After I graduated from Queens College, I worked for three years as a social worker for Queens Family Mental Health Services. Social work is like trying to empty the ocean with a teaspoon. I'd help someone get a job so they could provide for their family, and the next week President Reagan would end a program that would lay off 100,000 people. Two weeks after my daughter was born I lost my job because of budget cuts. It was traumatic. What was I going to do, go to a social worker?

I became more involved organizing in the Haitian community. First there was the whole AIDS issue. Remember the four H's? Hemophiliacs,
Hypodermic needle users,
Homosexuals,
and Haitians.

In the early '80s, those were the people they said were spreading the AIDS virus. Haitian kids were coming home from school crying because they were told they were carriers of AIDS just because they are Haitian. It was very insulting. So we

got a permit to walk over the Brooklyn Bridge. It's a scary phenomenon – when you have 75,000 people walking on the bridge – it literally shakes. I thought it was an earthquake. We marched right up to City Hall chanting in Creole. We closed the financial district! At that moment, the Haitian community found its voice. Now we have a saying: "Nou souke pon an." We shook the Brooklyn Bridge. When it was time to organize the democracy movement to bring Aristide back to Haiti, the community was already galvanized.

The U.S supported both Duvalier dictatorships until 1986, when widespread protests lead President Reagan to arrange a safe haven for Baby Doc and his family in France. Four years later, Jean Bertrand Aristide emerged from the progressive branch of the Catholic Church as the first democratically elected leader of the island nation since 1804. Within seven months of being sworn in, Aristide was overthrown by a military coup, headed by Duvalier cronies.

By the late '80s Baby Doc was not only ruling with terror, but stealing and spending money faster than he could print it. A lot of companies like Disney came to Haiti bringing products to be assembled. The workers

got paid pennies while Baby Doc gave BMWs to his friends for Christmas and spent the citizens' money on horses and mansions. The infrastructure was so rotten and corrupt, eventually the companies couldn't even do their exploitation properly. There was no reliable phone system, no roads. The electricity was so unreliable, many of the factories had to have their own power plants built. Baby Doc became too much of an embarrassment. Things were so bad – the murders, the misery, the poverty – that the Catholic Church in Haiti started talking about justice, not just in a different life, but in this life. Saying that children have the right to eat. All those swollen bellies and cracked feet and runny noses are not part of what God planned for us as human beings. People unified in church, sang religious songs, and the movement slowly built up. The Pope came and said, "Things have to change." And the people went wild. Nobody can ignore the Pope. When real elections finally came in 1990, people walked for miles, then waited seven, eight hours in the sun to vote, without eating. People passed out. They were shot at. And still, Aristide won the election with almost 70% of the vote. My brother Gerard dropped everything and went back to Haiti and became an advisor to Aristide. He was one of three people who wrote the program for the new government. When the coup happened against Aristide, Gerard urged him to signal the people to rise up. There is a proverb in Creole: *"You say good morning to the devil, he's going to eat you up. You don't say good morning to the devil, he's going to eat you up. So, man, put your pants on and do what you got to do."* Aristide is a powerful figure and an eloquent speaker, but he didn't understand how many people would've put their lives on the line in a second.

Ray reminds us of Haiti's tradition of dissent, most notably, the successful slave revolt against Napoleon and the French in 1791. By 1804, the island became the first black independent nation. "Unfortunately, with power comes abuse." Self-declared emperors led to assassinations, and years later the splitting of the island into two countries, Haiti and the Dominican Republic.

After the coup against Aristide, the Haitian military junta took power and a man named Toto Constant emerged. He was the son of one of Baby Doc's top generals. Toto made himself useful because the military leaders needed to keep the people from rising up, but they didn't want to be tainted by killing thousands of people. Toto did the dirty work for them. He created a group called "FRAPH" [Front for the Advancement and Progress of Haiti]. The word fraph in Creole means *smack*. At one point if you were living in a poor neighborhood, you could not sleep in your bed. Everybody slept on the ground because FRAPH would come in the night and open fire on the level where your bed would be. I have pictures of young people with ropes around their necks, tied, covered with blood, slaughtered for nothing. Often they would come to a house with machetes, burning the houses and forcing the population into the sea. One of their favorite tactics was skinning their victim's face from ear to ear and burying them in shallow graves where dogs could eat them. This was a death squad that operated openly and on a very large scale. They held press conferences, received money from the government and the CIA, and it was plain to see many in their ranks came from Tonton Macoute.

Some Haitians believe "facial scalping" traps the spirit eternally in Purgatory.

Here in New York we were doing everything we could to get the word out about the situation in Haiti. Some of us in the Haitian activist community were invited to be on the Phil Donahue show. We brought a woman who had recently gotten out of Haiti to talk about what had happened to her at the hands of FRAPH. I met her for the first time in the green room before the show. Time just stopped for me. Before my eyes stood a ghost of a person. And she already had several surgeries by then.

She had a scar that went from one side of her face all the way to the other. When she showed me the pictures of what happened to her, I just melted. If you could see that woman's body – the way she was mutilated and left for dead. She had no business even being alive. Her nose was cut. They cut her jaw. They cut her tongue. They hit her with a machete so hard, her face was shifted to one side! Why did it happen? Because she was married to a guy, just some nobody living in a slum who was a supporter of Aristide. When FRAPH came to the house to get him, he climbed through the back window. They took her instead and sliced her like a salami and dropped her in a dumping ground called "Ti tanyen" that FRAPH loved to use. She crawled somewhere that night and some brave soul took her to a doctor. And the doctor decided to take pictures and make a record. Eventually the doctor had to cut her arm off completely. And on her other hand, she's missing all the top digits. As a human being, I had to say, "I'm sorry that another human being did that to you." It was clear that it wasn't just physically that they had hurt this person – she was hurt to the deepest part of her soul. And she was lucky because she's one of the few who could tell her story.

I was committed to changing the situation in Haiti. One of my dearest friends had been dragged from a church and shot in broad daylight by Constant's men. And when my brother went back to Haiti he was tortured by the military to within an inch of his life. There is an old Creole proverb, "Bay kou bliye, pote mak sonje." It means, "Those who give the blows forget. Those who bear the scars remember."

The emblem of Tonton Macoute, "The son of a tiger is a tiger."

Ray's brother Gerard, a.k.a. Tije, was killed in Haiti in 1998 under circumstances that were, in Ray's opinion, suspicious. This poem by Berthony Dupont was written for Ray after his brother's death:

Tije pa mouri!

Itswa Tije
pa itswa zonbi
Tije se linet nou
Tije pa sa mouri
Tije nan je pep la
Tije nan je tout moun
Tout moun k ap goumen
pou le lalin monte
sou povant soley
pou nou pa aveg
okontre pou lavi fleri.

Tije pa mouri, Ray!
Tije vwayaje
L al nan syel
L al chanche fyel
pou nou kenbe pi dyanm
pou n ka fe yon bal kanaval
pou n ka fe yon bal kanaval
apre revolisyon an
apre liberasyon an.

Tije we lwen
lwen pase nou
se sa k fe l
pran devan nou.
Ayiti se yon fore
Tale k pral rebwaze
Ko Tije se fimye.
San Tije se lawouze.
Tije pa mouri!
Tije tonbe nan lari
pou l ka leve tankou dyondyon
nan tout kwen lari.

Berthony Dupont

Tije is not dead!

The history of Tije's life
is not that of a zombie
Tije is our eyeglasses
Tije cannot be dead
Tije is in the eye of the whole people
Tije is in the eye of everybody
all of us were fighting so that when
the moon rises above the sun
we will not become blind
on the contrary so that life can flourish.

Tije is not dead, Ray!
Tije traveled on a journey
he went into heaven looking for spleen
[something that is bitter]
so we can be stronger
so that we can have a carnival ball
so that we can have a carnival ball
after the revolution
after the liberation.

Tije saw far
farther than most of us
that's why
he went ahead of us all.
Haiti is a forest
that any time is about to bloom.
Tije's body is fertilizer
his blood is the dew
Tije is not dead!
Tije fell in the streets
so we can rise up like mushrooms
on every street corner.

After dragging its feet for a long time, the Clinton administration sent in troops and brought Aristide back to Haiti [1994]. Shortly after, Toto slipped across the border to the Dominican Republic and somehow ended up living – with the consent and protection of the CIA – right here in the heart of the Haitian community in Queens, where many Haitians live who had been forced to flee their home precisely because of Toto Constant's brutal activity. No matter what the rationale of the U.S. government, it was a flagrant violation of anything decent to have this individual living in our community after what he had done. President Clinton himself called FRAPH "a terrorist organization." We lobbied to get Toto extradited to Haiti. In 1996, the INS did detain him for a little while, but then he threatened to spill the beans about the details of his involvement with the CIA. That's when the U.S. government said that it would be destabilizing for him to be sent back to Haiti, even though there is an extradition mandate from the Haitian government that he be sent back. The conditions of his release mandated that Constant must live in his mother's home in Laurelton, and he cannot travel outside the borough except for his weekly check-in with the INS in Manhattan.

After The Nation *magazine first reported the CIA's connection to Toto Constant [Oct. 1994], several government officials went on record to acknowledge the connection. Still, the U.S. government continued to harbor Constant under what appears to be an unprecedented agreement.*

At first Toto kept a low profile. By 1999, he was seen dancing in neighborhood clubs all dressed in black. He knew there was a good chance people would recognize him, but he didn't seem to care. Then we found out he got a job in a real estate firm right here on Linden Boulevard. A Haitian man had a For Sale sign in front of his house. The doorbell rings. The man answers the door and there's Toto Constant asking if he can show the house to a few clients. The guy knew who Toto was. He couldn't believe his eyes! Our organization, the Haiti Support Network, immediately went to the real-estate office and demanded that the owner fire Toto and denounce him. "How can you have this man showing houses?" The broker was afraid to fire him or say anything. We started raising hell. After we demonstrated in front his office, he had a change of heart and Toto lost his job. We organized three demonstrations in front of Toto's white stucco house. Some people started receiving death threats and were afraid to demonstrate, but a lot of us were so outraged, we didn't care. We carried photographs of the victims of FRAPH and passed out flyers informing neighbors who this man was. A few times we saw a black BMW come by, roll down the window, and take pictures of us. This made some people very nervous. So what I did, I took my camera and took their pictures too. I could show you those if you'd like. We initiated a resolution with the New York City Council demanding Toto be removed and sent back to Haiti. They passed the resolution, but the State Department has done nothing.

In September 2000 a Haitian court began prosecuting Emmanuel "Toto" Constant and the leaders of the junta in absentia for the April 22, 1994 massacre in the village of Raboteau. Surviving victims testified to the robbing, torture, and murder of countless villagers. The case was based on the same legal precedent used to prosecute Nazi leaders after World War II. Constant was sentenced to life imprisonment and to hard labor and the court took over all of his property in Haiti.

After September 11th, the United States says we are routing out terrorists everywhere. Meanwhile, we are accommodating a terrorist *right here in our own territory!*

We made frequent attempts to contact Toto Constant. He finally agreed to meet with us for an interview, but never showed.

the
latimer
senior center

SOLAMEN ZHANG
MARY GOLDMAN
HELEN WU

Originally named "Vlishing" by Dutch colonizers, Flushing became associated with the first declaration of religious tolerance in American history when its citizens defied Governor Peter Stuyvesant's order that colonists not let Quakers into their homes. "The Flushing Remonstrance" of 1657 asserted that every man be "let to stand and fall to his own Master." The village of Flushing eventually became a dense urban area teeming with apartment buildings and busy commercial streets. After the 1965 Immigration Act, Asians began filling the downtown Flushing apartments once occupied by Jewish, Italian, and German immigrants. According to the 2000 census, 54% of the population in Flushing is Asian, the lion's share coming from China. Many of the stores, banks, and groceries have signage with no English at all — a source of much consternation to some longtime Flushing residents who have expressed to us their feelings of having been "invaded." Other non-Asians are delighted by the sensation of walking out their door and feeling like they've been transported to "the other side of the earth."

We conducted a storytelling workshop at the Jacob Latimer Senior Center which now serves an aging Chinese population who came to Flushing within the last three decades. We heard stories of the Cultural Revolution, World War II, and acclimating to American life. Solamen Zhang, Mary Goldman, and Helen Wu were three of the people who participated in the workshop.

On Tuesday I go to Latimer Senior Center. They give us lunch. Wednesday I volunteer at a nursing home, read a scripture. Sing a song. They give me lunch. Thursday I go to St. George's Church, all Chinese people meet in the morning. Then they give us lunch. Friday, First Baptist Church. Mostly Chinese there too. Saturday I spend time with my grandchildren. My third son is living with us in our small apartment with his wife and two children. The two-year-old is my teacher. I say to him, "Will you show me how it is to be lovely like you? I want to learn what is the innocent love." He doesn't answer. He just smiles. Since I'm 70, I want to go back to my children's style. Especially their pure heart. That is my imagination.

An incredibly sweet, humble, and religous man, this former music teacher always has a play on words or a prayerful song ringing in his head.

All the years of my life, my name was Shru Zhang. My family name, Zhang means where we were lost, where we will be found. My first name, Shru means book. That was my name until I went for American citizenship interview in 1985. The officer ask me, "Do you know English?" I say, "If I become citizen, I want change my name to Solamen. I make poetry to find my new name." He writes down Solomon spelled like King Solomon in the Bible. Means wisdom. But I am not wisdom, I am very simple person. I say, "Not Solomon. Sol*amen*. First four letters, *Sola* means the sun. Last three letters, *men* is a creature living under the sun." The officer laughed. I say, "We cannot live without the sun. Also *Sol*." I sing, *"Do Re Mi Fa* — next one is *Sol*. Because I like to sing. The last four letters spell *amen*. When you finish a prayer, you always say *Amen*."* I passed the exam.

Shantung is a dialect of Mandarin.

My grandparents were Buddhist, but when I was a boy in Shantung province [Mainland China], my father was teaching American missionaries how to speak Shantung. That's how I come to accept Jesus at a revival meeting. Now I wonder if the Prince of Peace can make peace on earth or not. The history of man is always fighting. All my growing up, there was war around me.

The church was a sanctuary for my family until Japan bomb Pearl Harbor and the missionaries went back to America. That's when I left my parents, 14 years old. Chinese government promised to support students with school and housing in Western provinces. But this was not true because all bombings, all fightings, fightings — I became refugee. Never know if my parents are alive or where they are. By foot I ran from Jiangsu to Jiangxi to Hunan, many many provinces. All I had was a coat, two pair of pant, long soldier's shirt, a towel and wash basin. Even I don't have a toothbrush. For five years we did this. The government would give us some rice. Very often we would sell the rice to buy vegetables.

All those years I didn't go to school. Older people, not qualified would act like teachers. One man, so evil, teaching us English. If one word mistake, he would hit you with a board. Had to repeat by memory Dr. Sun Yat-sen's Will. Sun Yat-sen is like George

Washington of China. First President before Chiang Kai-shek and Mao Tse-tung. I can still remember:

"For forty years, I have devoted myself to the cause of national revolution. The aim of which is to secure for China a position of independence and equality among nations. The accumulated experience of this forty years has fully convinced me it is necessary to awaken the masses of our own people and associate ourselves with those people who treat us equally in writings, plans of national reconstruction. Fundamental of national reconstruction: three principals of the people. And the manifesto issued at the first national congress of our party and work increasingly for the confirmation above all the convocation of the people's convention and the abolition of unequal treaties, with least possible delay. This is my last will and behest."

Even today in Taiwan, in Mainland China, and in Flushing Chinese Cultural Center, they frame Sun Yat-sen's will on the wall.

When Second World War finish, the Communists occupied Mainland China. I jump on a big ship with many soldiers and guns. I don't know where this ship is going. Hundreds and hundreds of people trying to get on. The ship carried everyone to Taiwan.

At 26 years old, I pass examination and go to Teachers College in Taiwan, study music. All regular students are younger and normally growing up with pianos to practice on since they were children. I'm so poor, I don't have piano, but I stay in the program and got my degree and was music teacher for twelve years.

Me and my wife had four sons. When they start getting older I was worried. At that time all boys who reach 15 years old have to join Taiwanese army. I didn't want my boys to be in any war because I take objection to war. In 1979 there was preference for nurses to come to America. My wife is a nurse and she could emigrate with her family. We hear Flushing, Queens is a good place to come for Chinese. I got my green card, very lawfully. We don't have any cheating.

Seven years ago, Solamen saw someone playing music with a saw on TV. It reminded him of an erhu, the Chinese violin bowed between the legs. I got an old violin bow and took out my saw and found the scale. *Do Re Me Fa...* How to make it lower, how to make it higher. Found a song in my head, *Amazing Grace,* and very quickly I can play it. *Home on the Range.* Any song I can sing, I can play on the saw.

When I got here I'm thinking more and more about my parents. For 40 years I didn't speak to them or know how they are. The two governments of Taiwan and People's Republic of China don't let us connect. No phone, no writing. Very like a drama for me. My life. So I ask a church member here can he help me. Many many months and he find my parents' address. I write a letter and my parents write a letter back.

1984 I went back to China to see my family. After I left home, my parents had two more sons. So I didn't recognize them at the airport except they hold up a sign with my name, and I know the holder of the sign are my brothers I never met. Next to them are my elderly parents. Oh, the tears. For hours we cannot speak words. My parents have since pass away, but my brothers and I write like we always a family.

Many many jobs I had since I came here. I work in Swingline Staple factory here in Queens. I was messenger, dishwasher, I clean floor, overnight security guard. I was home attendant. I take care of sick people in wheelchair. Now I'm retired. America is much better place for my kids. For me, anywhere is a good place, because I have a living principle. **THE THREE S's.** *Simplicity.*
Serenity.
Satisfaction.
Serenity comes from being quiet. Not too much thinking. And simple life. One dollar is quite enough for me to buy a bagel and drink some water. Satisfied is I don't have any big ambitions. That's why I'm happy. That is my invention — the three S's.

My childhood in Shanghai is very happy. But my middle, during the Cultural Revolution, very suffering. Mao Tse–tung closed the country door. Make his face like sun. Everyday you look up, it is there big and round. When I was in school had to read Little Red Book. Always say, "Chairman Mao, Chairman Mao. Long Life. Long Life." I was saying that in 1950. Now I'm 70 years old.

Cultural Revolution start in 1966. If you had a rice farm, they take it away and you become criminal. You landlord, you become criminal or very poor. My husband was manager of his father's jewelry store. We had a happy life. One night in summer–time, we hear the drumming, *boom boom boom.* I open the door. Sixty Red Guards and the drummer. *Boom boom boom.* In tune with my heart. The leader say, "Now you will see the other side." My eleven–year–old son they put in bathroom. My thirteen–year–old daughter they put in another room. They bring me to bedroom. My husband to kitchen. He get whatever money we had, some pieces of gold. "That's everything." The Red Guard didn't believe him. They take me to the kitchen. The guard holds Mao's book in the air. "You are lying! Where do you hide the gold?" They go through our drawers. Stuff our coats and all jewelry into suitcases. Make me stand in the kitchen till five o'clock the next morning. After that, every time I heard a drummer, my heart is jump. The government take over the jewelry store, make my husband work as cashier with very small salary.

My husband joined underground. Mao Tse–tung put him in jail. After he came out, he drank. He beat me, have girlfriends. Broke my heart. My parents say, "You have to divorce." But family is good for kids. I stay with him ten years, then I divorce. Move back with my par–ents till 1993. Never have boyfriend, because I hate the men. Just doing low worker job. Then retired to take care of my parents. My children marry, have their own families. I'm waiting, when my government going to change? I decide to join my cousin in New York.

Sixty-two years old, I come here alone. Every Sunday I go to Chinese church. The minister's wife is English teacher for new-comers like me. I study one year. A classmate say to me, "You always stay with Chinese people, no chance to practice English. I have neighbor, this senior man is very nice. Wife is gone and I ask him if he be your conversation teacher."

Every Saturday afternoon, three hours talking with Mr. Goldman, first basic sentences, then about my life. About his life. He always ask me about my family situation in Shanghai. Every week getting very good feeling talking. Six months later, he say, "You don't have to stay your cousin's house. You move in my house." I don't know what to say because he is so much older than me, by sixteen years. His life way very different. Because he is American Jewish. But after we talking about customs, I see Jewish people and Chinese people very similar.

Next time I go to his house he asks if I will marry him. He says, "I am un-happy. Maybe you are unhappy." I say, "I'm student. You are teacher. I respect you." We have the good feeling and we have the spirit love. Not so make love, this is young people do that. Senior people, we don't think about this. We take care each other."

It's possible Mary married the only Jewish man in New York who doesn't like Chinese food. To please him, she taught herself how to cook what she calls American Jewish food: matzoh ball soup, chopped liver, baked potato topped with mush-rooms. Little by little she sneaks Chinese ingredients into her cooking. Instead of cooking a baked potato, she'll bake a yam. Just recently Mary cooked Frank some Chinese fried rice. He said, "Mmmm. Tastes good."

Five years now, I live with Frank. I got second spring. Second spring is beautiful. My husband say, "Yeah. I got you, I'm so lucky." It's hard to translate to English. Chinese people say, the feeling has no words – *I love you. You love me.* Highest spirit love don't need words like that.

When we met Helen Wu, she was 82 years old. At least she thought she was 82. Helen had a memory problem. Like Mary, she was a loyal student of Latimer's beloved English as a Second Language teacher, Evan Ginzburg. Helen was determined to regain her memory and finally get some control of English, which was new to her when she came to the U.S. in the '70s.

A few weeks after the workshop, we visited Helen in her apartment. The windows were shaded and the room was filled with (mostly) unopened boxes. Although she couldn't cook, she served us tea with exquisite hospitality and grace. Her long hair was tied up in a bun by a chopstick. Occasionally strands of hair would loosen and fall on her remarkably preserved skin. Anxious to tell us about her life, Helen prepared a handwritten history that she wanted to read to us. Instead, we spent a wonderful afternoon talking. A few weeks before we were going to photograph her, Helen disappeared and hasn't been heard from since.

If you work hard / America doesn't care where you come from / I come here almost 40 years old / I am here / no money / no relative / no friend / no English / Only talk to my husband / and to my God / I work many job / Go to the Chinese restaurant work / Do the hostess in Japanese steakhouse / American people don't know difference / Chinese / Japanese / I good looking / Then Italian restaurant / hat check girl / I work the beauty parlor for manicure / I learn hairdresser / I learn to do the finger wave / I do laundry job / Jewish customer from laundry have 89 years old mother / She has eyes cannot see / Ears cannot hear / Hip broken / Husband dead / Daughter give me home attendant job / I take care of her mother / I stay three days / three nights / I wash the hair / Push on glasses to read newspaper / Push the wheelchair / Find the sunshine so she comfortable / I don't know how to cook / Her daughter next door / she cook chicken / hamburger / tell me how to warm it up / They say I'm such good aid / I get nice reference letter from them / You see / I was nurse back in China

I born Mainland China / Japanese fighting that time / I'm just a kid / Don't know anything / We go to school / Come home / Play / We just young kids / Did I tell you? / I'm sorry / My life / accident / Back of the brain / Adema / Little by little / many people talk to me / This is my life / My lifetime past / I car accident / Big story / Sometime can't remember

Japanese take over Nanking / Capital of Chiang Kai-shek / Japanese fighting fighting / My mother have twelve children / Three girls / Nine boys / First sister die / My father was teacher in other province / He come back / give my mother one baby / Come back / give my mother another baby / Come back / give my mother another baby / She has all children alone / Three inches her feet / Tied up so small / This was the fashion / She was particularly Chinese lady / Woman stay home / Marry / Take care children / Don't need to (like in America) work / You just take care the home / My mother take care everybody / I want to help her cook or sew clothes / She say, "Go play" / So I never know how to do the home job / I just go to school / Come home / Play

For my mother it was tough time / Very poor / Had to leave Nanking / Japanese soldier everywhere / We are refugees / Chiang Kai-shek move capital to Chun King / All the children and worker follow Chiang Kai-shek / Not much school / This is my past / My life / I'm a refugee / Go to study nursing in Chung King / My mother say / "That is terrible / Nursing is like servant job" / When war finish I go back to Nanking with family / Everything destroy /

Buildings black and empty / Tears everywhere / Nanking hospital still there but nobody control / We nursing students learning with hands on patients / Graduate 1949 / Work three months nurse / then meet my children's father / My sister introduce / I'm in twenties / He is rich single old man / 50 years old / legislator / "Marry me" / I like him / He's the third way politician / He don't like Mao Tse-tung / He don't like Chiang Kai-shek

1957 / I had car accident / very big / Daughter is two years old / Son is four / I rode bicycle / This is my life / Always rode bicycle / The cars cross the street / In Formosa that time not all streets have traffic lights / Big America army truck drag my bicycle / I flying in sky / *Ahhhhh* / When I come down / No memory / Very no memory / Adema / Water on brain / In hospital I look at my daughter / Not sure is she my daughter / Little by little / many people talk to me / My husband see I cannot take care of myself / He get baby sitter / I just a wife / she take care my children / I have everything / chauffeur / chef / servant / Always the servant complain to my husband that I forgot where my handkerchief / That the reason he knew I am a total changed person / He have liver problem / He scare when he die nobody take care of kids / I cannot take care of myself / He saw that I'm young / I'm good looking / He better let me go find someone take care of me / He wrote letter to my family in Mainland to send me back to them / They thought husband threw me away / I explain / "No / he's worry about the kids / Cannot blame him" / He divorce me / Little by little many people talk to me / Every time I listen / a little more my memory brings back

Second husband American citizen / Friends say to him / you go to China / find Chinese lady / My husband friend say if you want your wife learning English or go working or shopping / New York is better than California / You don't have to drive / This my life / I'm lucky woman / Two husbands support me / Second husband / we had a good life / He cook for me / I never know how to cook / Since my husband die I'm very independent / Next door there is Senior Center / Take English class with Mr. Evan / then eat lunch / In the morning coffee something / bread / In the evening eat in friend's apartment / Never hungry / Day by day I improve / Go to English classes with Mr. Evan / Monday / Tuesday / Wednesday / Each day different Senior Center / I don't want to be old lady only read kid's book

You call me / even you are Chinese I want to speak English / English / You call me / my name is Helen / My Chinese name is Chyuan-Ming / very hard for Americans / When I went to immigration they want American name / I saw the blind woman Helen Keller when she came to Formosa to speak long time ago / I go to hear how a blind and deaf person can speak / I feel she has strong mind to stand up against obstacle / My life is full of obstacle / I take her name / And American call me easy

You want my life / I'm not finish / I feel myself / I'm a strong woman / I have a big story. But how do you think is my life? Is all right?

LABIB SALAMA
NASSER EL GABRY

labib's café

After the attack on the World Trade Center, there was a lot of talk in the city and on the national media about a new spirit of cooperation and neighborliness in America. We knew the experience for Arabs and South Asians was not quite as cozy. We visited Ali and Moustafa (pages 180–195) to see how they were faring. Business was particularly slow for all the Middle Eastern restaurants and shops on Steinway Street, and nerves were on edge. Ali and Moustafa were okay, but they suggested we go speak to Labib who has an Egyptian coffee shop across the street. A half-dozen men are sitting at tables playing chess, drinking coffee, smoking shisha. The sound of popular Egyptian music fills the apple-scented smoky air. Labib calls his cab driver friend Nasser over to talk with us about what happened at the café five nights after September 11th. They're sitting in front of a wall-length mirror that looks like someone threw a rock at it. A large crack in the mirror radiates out like a spider web.

MEDITERRANEAN SEA

ISRAEL

Cairo

EGYPT

Nile

ASTORIA

SAUDI ARA

SUDAN

Three o'clock in the morning. We're sitting around minding our own business, when four guys came smashing into the coffee shop. Two white American. Two Hispanic American, around the age 20 to 25. They bring a lot of anger with them, throwing with their hands and feet all the tables and chairs bent over to the floor. They break a lot of things. Break the windows, break the mirror and all the glasses. We call the police. The cops come right away. Actually they were very helpful.

I said, "No. Denied."

I understand the feeling they have. Everybody hurt. Everybody angry. We don't want to make more hatred than what we already have. They didn't steal from me. They didn't take from the cash register. They just angry. I tell the police not to do any– thing. They say if I don't press charges, they can't arrest them. "Do you want any money back for the damage you have?" I said, "No."

So the police let the guys go. And the police leave too. Five or six customer and the two guys working here, we start to clean up the place. There's broken glass all over. Tables everywhere. I'm thinking now we are between the two sides. I'm afraid from the terrorist number one, and now I'm afraid from the American too.

NASSER

The police lay the guys on the ground. They searched them out. IDs, drivers license. Everything. They asked them why they did that. Then they asked Labib if he wanted to press charges.

Not the first time Steinway Street was the site of violence against "foreigners" — our friend, Bunzy Sherman, grew up in Astoria in the 1930s, and remembers the anti-immigrant, anti-Semitic rabble-rouser Father Coughlin, "coming into the neighborhood, preaching hatred against the Jews," resulting in rocks being thrown into Jewish-owned stores along Steinway Street. Bunzy's father was so shaken by the unfriendly climate, he moved his family to the Bronx.

An hour later,
        we're cleaning up
                and I see the four guys coming again inside the door.
                They came back to the café.
For what, I'm thinking. What's going to happen now?
It's 4 o'clock in the morning. The first thing out of their mouths,
they say, "We are sorry."
They apologize!
They say, "We can fix for you whatever is broke. If you want some money
to buy something back." They help us with the cleanup. They offer to buy
drinks for everybody. Then we sit here until eight o'clock in the morning
talking what is on our minds – from both sides. They want to know first
of all why I didn't press charges. We want to know why they do this to us.

They said, "You are Arab. You are speaking the same language as bin Laden. We thought he is someone who belong
to you." We told them we don't have nothing to do with
this guy. "To you we all look alike. You know how many
Arab are in this country? We carry American citizenship
too. You know, the Spanish people also looks like us. The
Portuguese, the Brazilian. We're all Mediterranean. Do we
all have to be blamed for something we didn't commit? We
cannot change our face. We can't make plastic surgery just
for the time being and when the next terrorist is Chinese
or a white guy, we can come back to our original faces."

Large-screen TV in Labib's café airs Egyptian satellite programming

They said they're sorry, "but you have to understand
our feeling. We are angry for the people who die. We
are afraid, are we going to be next? Are we going to
lose our way of living?" I told them we understand
your feeling very well. I drive a yellow cab. From
that day until today I don't make one dollar. Let me
surprise you. I've been here since 1989 and I never
once been up in the World Trade Center. But that was
where I make my living. Twelve times a day I was
dropping people off, picking them up there. When a
tourist comes to New York, the first thing they say,
"Where is the World Trade Center? If you're coming

from Pennsylvania or uptown at 195th street, you point with your finger and you find those two buildings. They were the same for me as the pyramid of Giza or the Sphinx. When you're in Egypt, anywhere you go you see them. After 7,000 years to see them collapse, it's like a part of my soul collapse.

LABIB

They think because we smoking shisha from a water pipe, we are celebrating. We told them there's nothing to celebrate about. We don't drink, so we smoke and watch TV. Since the World Trade Center attack we watch news all the time. I tell the guys, "Next time you want to come and be friendly with us, you don't have to hit us and then say you're sorry. Just come and be friendly in the first place."

The two groups of guys were together for four hours talking and cleaning the café. As the night turned into day, fear and rage turned into forgiveness over broken glass, conversation, and freshly-brewed Egyptian coffee.

It's time right now to bring the anger down. You have to inhale everything bad. You have to take the blame sometime even if you didn't do anything. You have to forgive for the people to forgive you. That's what the Qur'an tells us.

The prophet Mohammed, peace be unto him, he said a long time ago, if a man stand in front of you and curse you and you fight back, you will only end up having a fight. But if you stand there and talk to his hatred, you can melt it. There will come another time somebody will forgive you when you did something bad. Who will have the guts to say I'm sorry? The coward only will start the fight. This is what Islam is all about. Islam doesn't say, "Go kill somebody and you'll go to heaven." Heaven is not a nightclub. You've got to earn your way in.

The page from the Qur'an illuminating this page (Chapter 41, verses 34–36) contains one of many passages where Mohammed speaks of peaceful reconciliation and neighborliness.

It doesn't matter Muslim or Christian or Jewish. All religions tell you to forgive. I am Christian. Nasser is Muslim. You can't tell who's who. The guys who attack us were just walking among the Arab to pick a fight. They pick a fight with us. But we showed them something else.

I hope somebody got the guts and the money to rebuild the towers even higher than before to lift the spirit of America up! Slap the terrorist in the face. If I had the money I would do it tomorrow. But I'm just a cab driver. I have the guts but no money.

LABIB   *Six months later*

Since September, I lost 75% of my customers.
Number 1. People scared to be seen in Egyptian coffee shop.
Number 2. So many people lost their job, they can't spend money.
Number 3. Some of my customers got arrested.
The first customer got arrested for driving his hot–dog car with international driver's license. Used to be nothing wrong to drive with international license. After September 11th they put a lot of new rules affect everybody. A month in jail, he calls me, "Oh, Labib, I need $5,000 bond." Then another four customers got arrested for expiration of green card, things like that. They put them in jail with–out telling anyone. This is part of the new rules. First we don't know what happened to them. Then the phone starts ringing. "I need $5,000 bond." I say, "Fawad, you need $5,000, and Alah, you need $5,000, and Adal needs $5,000, and Mohammed needs $5,000, and another guy needs $5,000. That's $25,000! I don't have that kind of money."

Six weeks after the attacks on the World Trade Center and the Pentagon, the Congress over-whelmingly approved the USA PATRIOT ACT. In the name of national security, the Act confers vast powers to the executive branch including the ability to conduct unchecked surveillance, the creation of new crimes and enhanced penalties, and the authority to detain immigrants without notification or legal council for an indefinite period of time. Within six months of passing the Act, thousands of Middle Eastern and South Asian immigrants had been detained without charge. Some were deported; some were released on bond; all were interrogated and many held for months without legal council or access to their families; practi-cally no one was indicted of any terrorist association or activity.

"If you don't pay, they're going to send us back to Egypt."

Some of these guys are still in jail. Some got sent back to Egypt. Some we don't know where they are.

A few of my customer when they heard the FBI need Arab people to help track down terrorists, they went right away to FBI office. They give their phone number and fill out the application. None of them got called back for a job. We are the ones have the double angers to want to find out who did this. Then we can be free. Because right now we're on the hook. Everybody point their finger at us.

NASSER

Only an Arab can think like an Arab. Don't try to drop Americans in there. This is two hundred years nation. Arabs have seven thousand years nation. In Arab world we care too much about the little thing. It's the itsy-bitsy thing going to slide under the feet and that's how you can catch him. Americans depend too much on computers and science and human beings always blinking at the computer. In that one blink, many things can happen.

LABIB

FBI agents have come to the café, ask us if we seen some car, who do we know. Journalists come too, ask a lot of questions. I can't tell who is who. FBI never show a badge. They come like you. They say, "I'm making an interview for a book. For a radio program." Now every-one I see, I think, *that's FBI.* Maybe the two of you are FBI. Even if you are FBI, I am happy to help. I wish I could do more, but I have less time than ever. Since my coffee-shop business is struggling, I had to go back to driving a cab. Ten years now I haven't driven a cab.

NASSER

Sometimes a customer comes into my cab, they see on my nametag
NASSER
and they say, "Oh I'm sorry. I forgot something,"
and they run out of the cab. I've been driving a cab since 1989.
I'm the same cabdriver as before. What can I say? "Don't worry, I'm
not a terrorist." Some people come into the cab and they assume I don't
speak English. They say every kind of thing about every kind of person. I
won't even begin to repeat. Whatever anger a customer brings into my cab,
I try to calm him down. If a customer is late, I try to get him there on time.
It's not just about money. I love to serve the public. The public who are
decent. Some people want to show you how tough they are. I had a woman
once, she jumped the line at Kennedy airport. She say, "Take me to Woodhaven and Metropolitan Avenue." She give me directions. I tell her, "That's
the wrong way." She say, "Do what I say." After a while I say, "This is the
wrong way." She say, "You don't know where you're going to." I turn
around. She say, "Why you taking me this way?" She pushed me to the
limit. I told her, "Lady. Listen to me. I'm a cabdriver. I'm not your husband.
Whatever it is, don't take it out on me."

I think I'd rather be a dishwasher. Less hassles, especially from the police. The police were good when the kids came to my café. When they do their duty, they do their duty excellent. But some cops, when they are working by quota to write 20 tickets a day, they wait in a corner till they see you go through the yellow light and they pull you over. If they hear you are a foreigner with a strong accent like me, they will treat you like shit. "Say one more word I will lock you up." I drive a cab because I was not born in this country. If I speak good English I'd have a job as a professor.

Let me tell you one thing — being a police officer is a big-time curse. They don't like to run around just giving somebody ticket. They have to do it. If you get to know them face to face, most are nice guys. It's the media that makes me mad. **The media is worse than atomic bomb.** How many American news reporters opened a book to read what is Islam before they come to judge people they never seen? They say bin Laden is Arab. They say he is Muslim. Ok. Arab Muslim — that's their description of the new enemy. That's a big mistake when they say that. I will tell you who is bin Laden. An angry soldier whose heart turn cold against his old boss. He never think about all the innocent souls, a wife that just got married she don't have her husband anymore to open the door and say, "Honey, I'm home." He never think about all the two-years-old kids waiting for Baba or her fireman Dada or Mama to come home from work that day.

He only think, oh, I hate America because the CIA pay me for nine years to kill Russians and when they got what they wanted, they dump me. He's not thinking I do this for Allah. It has nothing to do with Muslim anything. Who trained this man? He got his guns and weapons and power from America. And now it explodes in our faces. Don't tell me this is Arab problem. Arabs didn't build him into a monster. Nobody want him in Saudi Arabia. His own family don't want him. He's more a graduate of what CIA teach him than anything he read in the Qur'an. 99.9% of Arabs in America, the most we can do is just living peacefully. My girlfriend's name Islam. Imagine the problems she has now with a name like that.

I just want to say one more thing — LONG LIVE NEW YORK AND GOD BLESS AMERICA! This is the place where we are. Where we make a living. Where we want to be. This is where I'm getting older. This is where I drive 200 mile a day. I know every block, brick by brick, number by number.

TAXI FARE
$2.00 Initial Charge

N.Y.C. TA

LABIB

For ten years we are side by side on the block with Italians and Greek and Spanish, Yugoslavian, Albanian, Colombian. We have no problem with them. Everybody is shaking hands and friendly. Now the others are a little bit cool with us.

NASSER

There's a lot of things missing from home that we need all the time. So you hang around in the coffee shop with the people you love. When you see a friend you have a warm welcome to him. That's what home is. A lot of people in Cairo now, they know if you go to America you will go to Steinway Street and you're never going to get lost.

Every week I go to mosque. I do regular thing like everybody else. I go, pray and leave. I thank God. I don't know if God hear me or not. I didn't get any disaster relief money, but at least I'm alive. Every morning I wake up around four o'clock. Used to be downtown beside the World Trade Center by five. On September 11th I didn't wake up till nine o'clock. I don't know what happen. I can't say it was this reason or that. Thank the angels. I could be part of the dust down there. No thanks to George W. Bush. What a mistake I made to vote for that man. I would like to sit him in front of me and ask him one simple question, direct:

Why it happened?

Where have you been when it happen?

Where were the most intelligent security people the world ever known? Were they busy laundering money from selling drugs? And what the hell you doing right now? You running after whom with billions of dollars just for one guy? And you tell me you can't get that guy?

Helloooooo!

We didn't realize it, but we were visiting Labib on Valentine's Day. He gives Judith a long-stem rose.

I wish I could give a flower to everybody who lost someone on September 11th, but my connections are not that high around. I got you so I give you a flower. Everyone who died left a person who is torn up. If she's a lady who died there, there's a man who can't give a flower to her. If he's a man, the woman can't give him a flower. A very big part of us has disappeared. I am hurting with my business, but that is minimum when we see people lost someone they love. You can do some other business,

but a life cannot be switched back on.

unlikely bedfellows

- champion ping pong
- international high school
- democratic club for new americans
- gogol bordello

champion
ping pong

SHI LI MIN

O.J. MAGNUS

GEORGE BRATHWAITE

RENATA PELUCHOVA

TAHL LEIBOVITZ

JIDONG LU

I [Warren] used to think I was a pretty good ping-pong player. Then I came to Champion Ping Pong (a.k.a. Champion Table Tennis Center), located alongside the incessantly rattling elevated subway tracks on Roosevelt Avenue in Jackson Heights. This no-frills, second-floor, seven-table-and-a-juice-machine hall is a haven to several dozen professional and semi-professional level players from all parts of the world. Anything that might ordinarily separate these people disappears when that 40mm ball is in motion. To some it's a sport, others a pastime, or a very pleasurable means of staying in shape. Still others approach the art of table tennis as a way of being.

I'd love to come back more often, just to play, but I feel guilty. Both Jidong Lu and a man known as "The Professor" gave me lessons and said I have a lot of potential. If I came back three, four times a week, I could begin to gain control and in time play semi-professional. As a teacher myself, I want students to listen to me, to take the craft seriously. How can I come back in a few months with a little more of a belly and the same bad habits? Judith also thought she was a decent player, but she's too embarrassed to even take a lesson.

JACKSON HEIGHTS

Haifa ○ ● Georgetown

GUYANA

ISRAEL ROOSEVELT

CHINA Shanghai ○

JAMAICA ○ Frýdek Místek
Kingston ●
CZECH
REPUBLIC

I return the paddle to the club owner Min. He sees I'm sweating a bit more than I ought to be. He's looking at me, this guy and his "project." Half-shaking his head, Min says, "Ping pong good for heart. Good exercise. Good for mind too, to let go." I know he's right. I need to change my life and come here at least five days a week. Half-smiling, he says, "And if you're Chinese, it's good for your inner."

The club's manager, Shi Li Min, competed in the Olympics for the Chinese national team in the '70s. He came to New York after coaching the national table tennis teams of Spain, Chile, Ecuador, and the United States. Tired of living the life of an itinerant coach, Min now spends ten hours a day, seven days a week at the club. The chairs are a bit beat up and the floors are scruffy, but Champion Ping Pong is always busy. His English is rough; his Spanish, fluent; this interview was translated from Mandarin.

MIN

For ping pong, I left my wife and five-year-old daughter to coach in different countries on behalf of the Chinese government. Ten years my wife waited for me in China and supported me while I was away. Because of me, ping pong is much more popular in South America than it used to be. My goal now is to make popular the sport here too. That is why I came here — for adventure and to change the attitude about table tennis in America.

During the Cultural Revolution in China, the sport was forbidden. Most major sports were banned for some reason — I will never understand why. By the early '70s, things were much better and table tennis was back on track. When George [Brathwaite] and the U.S. team came to China in 1971, it was a major event. Two important international countries got to know each other better through this sport. Two years later I was selected for the national team.

Opposite: detail of scuff marks on the floor of Champion Ping Pong

Min came to Queens after hearing from friends that it's a home away from home for many Chinese people. The previous manager of Champion Ping Pong was struggling to keep the ping pong business afloat. Since taking over, Min added a few tables, brought tournaments to the club, and attracted more top players. He teaches six or seven private lessons a day.

MIN

A lot of people coach here. Most of them are not that great, but teaching is the only way to make a living with ping pong in this country. As long as you are a member of the club, you are free to teach and you are free to learn. The problem is, not too many people in this country know the essence of this game. They regard it as a simple sport. That is a distortion. Ping pong is the most complicated sport in the world! It is a science. How to keep the ball on the table — that is the basic challenge. To do that there are many techniques. Forty different kinds of paddles, dozens of spins, a mind that can focus. Play it right and you will:

- Know how to concentrate on just one thing and never be distracted.
- Develop agility. The only way to succeed is to respond to things very quickly.
- Improve your vision because you have to watch the ball all the time.
- Stay in very good shape because you're going to run most of the time, and you're going to sweat a lot.
- Live a happy life because you will always hang around people. Through ping pong, you can see a lot of different faces with different styles. Spiritually speaking, you will see we're all connected. There is no difference. We welcome people from all over to play table tennis in this club.
- Relieve a lot of tension. No matter what is bothering you, when you play ping pong, you forget about everything.

Up until 1999, Otis Magnum, aka O.J., was ranked among the top 60 table tennis players in the U.S. A Jamaican with no perceptible Jamaican accent in his English, O.J. got his job as an Assistant Manager with a large Chinese furniture company, due in large part to his fluency with the Chinese language (Mandarin and Cantonese). He also speaks Spanish and French. Born and raised in the capital city of Kingston, O.J. came to the U.S. with his mom and three siblings at the age of thirteen in 1982. Extremely athletic, he practices Tae Kwon Do, has a black belt in Wu Shu (a Chinese form of karate), and does freestyle dancing whenever he can.

O.J.

Table tennis is like chess. You have to plan three moves ahead. The best players know what's on every ball coming at them, where it's going, how to return it; exactly where to place it, and how to return the return of what they're hitting now. Look at George Brathwaite. He's my coach. He's in his mid-sixties and plays with a lot more technique and strategy than someone like me. I try to crush you with the ball, get it past you however I can. But he'll skill you out of the game.

O.J.

If I'm going to serve a ball with a topspin that means I'm serving with a mix of spins. Make it turn this way and that. A loop is a forehand or backhand stroke that produces a lot of topspin. The ball is arched so much it looks like it's floating, like a gyroscope. A loop drive has more forward motion than a loop. It goes a lot faster, less floaty. A drive is kind of like a tennis shot where you kill the ball. A chop is more defensive. Of course the Chinese are the best at that. They're the best at everything in table tennis. If I use the "anti" racket, it returns the exact opposite of whatever kind of spin you hit to me. So a topspin comes back as an underspin. A dead ball has absolutely no spin. Normally you can see the brand name of the ball and you know which direction it's spinning. But a dead ball just comes over. That tricks a lot of opponents. You can push a ball long or put it short. You can play a fast game, like the top player from Korea, Kim Taek Soo. When that guy hits the ball, it's like a gunshot. First time I heard the sound, I almost hit the ground. My favorite player is Jan-Ove Waldner, from Sweden. The guy creates a new shot every time he plays. Everybody says, "That's not in the book! How did he do that?"

Right now my job is sitting on a chair looking at a computer all day. Then I go home and I'm in front of the computer or the TV. Before I got married I used to play six days a week, sometimes seven. Now with the baby I'm lucky if I play once a week. Champion is a great place for me because it's on my way home from work and there's ONLY table tennis here. Nobody's socializing around a food counter. Easier to concentrate. Because when you're playing table tennis and a pretty lady walks in to play pool, it's very easy to get distracted. Here, it's just tables and mostly guys who want to play.

In Jamaica, everybody had to take table tennis in seventh grade. Soccer, track and field, volleyball, and table tennis. I wasn't a natural at table tennis. Then I picked up the racket again in the U.S. when I went to City College. One day I wandered into the game room at school. I thought, oh, I'll just hit the ball around a couple of times. I was stuck on it like a drug! A few times I've tried quitting, sold all my rackets – and after two weeks my hands actually start shaking. I start pacing and getting like, "Oh man, I have to play this game!"

At City College there were quite a few players from Africa and the West Indies, but mostly from China. So I started going to the table tennis clubs with them in Manhattan. First two occasions I went to a serious club, I could not play. I was stunned. It's like if you're

walking through Queens and you go to a park and you see guys playing basketball,
and you think, these guys are pretty good. Then you go to
an NBA game, and it's a totally different level.

After a while I picked up things about the game and
I also picked up a good number of Chinese phrases
and swear words of course. One Chinese friend said,
"You pronounce Chinese words like a real Chinese per-
son." Then he told me about an exchange program with
China. I was accepted and I went. Everybody thinks all
Chinese people do martial arts – a universal misconception.
If everybody in China knew martial arts, they'd rule the world. But almost every-
body plays ping pong. I went to this club once and this guy had to be at least 70.
It didn't even look like he was moving. I could not beat him! My hardest defeat was
a nine-year-old kid. His head barely reached over the table and he kicked my butt.

For a lot of people in China, I was the first black person they ever saw. A few
people actually rubbed the skin on my arm to see if the black would come off.
You hear different things about how the Chinese get along or don't get along
with black people, but the Chinese in China treated me just like they did any
other guest to their country – almost like a king!

The second time I went to China I really immersed myself in the language. When
it comes to language, I've always been a quick study. Whoever I'm around, I begin
to speak like them. I don't know if it's an ability or a flaw. To me Chinese is easier
than English because Chinese has no past tense, future tense. In English we say:
I eat. I am eating. I ate. I have eaten. I will eat. Chinese? One word: eat. That's it.
I eat today. I eat tomorrow. I eat yesterday. Very direct.

I got quite popular on the table tennis circuit in the U.S. being the only black guy
who speaks Chinese. But I'm not the weirdest thing in table tennis right now. I'd
say Tahl is weirder than me. He's calmed down, but he used to miss a point, pick
up a table and throw it. He's banned from a club in New Jersey because he lost
his temper and threw his racket out the window. Broke the window. Broke
the table. Normally the other guy likes it when you're mad because
you're losing your concentration. But throwing tables,
that's something else.

Born in Haifa, Israel, Tahl Leibovitz has several hundred medals in "Disabled" and "Able-bodied" categories, including an Olympic Gold Medal in the "disabled standing" category. We spoke to him a day before he was going to China to play with the U.S Paralympic team.

TAHL

There are ten classes of disability. One through five, you've got to be in a wheelchair. Five is you're in a wheelchair, but you can stand up. Four is you don't have much movement in your legs. Three is you're a quadriplegic. Ten is the least disabled.

That means, if you're playing say with your right hand, you might have a disability with your left. Nine would be somebody might have a spinal problem, or they're missing a leg. Eight could be someone is missing both legs and maybe an arm, but they've got plastic legs and a plastic arm. I'm a class seven, because I have a disability in my playing arm. I also have benign bone tumors all over my body. In both knees, in my back, in my right ankle and my right arm. They're all benign. At least I got lucky on that. When I was thirteen I had surgery to take out a huge bone tumor that was messing up my hips. You want to see the scar? Eight hundred stitches! It goes all the way around. That was painful. But the real problem is, I can't turn my right arm. So according to the system, I'm more disabled than a guy with one leg and one arm! In 1996, I won a Gold Medal in the Olympics. Class seven. Then they moved me up to class ten, because I was beating all the sevens pretty easily. In ten I won a Bronze Medal at the World Championships.

None of the other players knew I was homeless. For seven years, on and off, I was playing tournaments, walking out with a trophy and I had no place to stay. The trophies had places to stay, but I didn't. When you win a table tennis tournament in this country, it's not like reporters are clamoring for an interview, and you can take the microphone and tell people, "Hey, I'm a champion and I'm homeless! Anybody out there got a place for me to live?" I was only interviewed once for a paper at the U.S. Open. But that was after I was already living someplace.

When I was 14 years old I had a lot of trouble with my mom. I wasn't really going to school and she kind of forced me out of her place. The first ten months I was sleeping on the **E** train. It's a relatively safe train because it doesn't go through any really bad neighborhoods. Sleeping on the **J** train, that causes a little bit of a problem. Back before they fixed up Grand Central, me and a couple guys used to sleep down in the tunnels. There's seven levels under the street you know. Five years ago there was probably 150,000 people living under the subway. There's still about 40,000 people living underground in New York.

When it wasn't cold out, I'd sleep on the beach or the roof of an apartment building. Sometimes in the summer, it was so hot, I'd wake up soaking wet. When you're living on the street, there's never a set place that you're at. You might stay somewhere for a few days or a few months. Then something happens and you have to find someplace else. I went to Covenant House for a couple of days. I've been to the shelters, but they're extremely dangerous. The most difficult thing about not having a place to live is boredom. So you go to a hall to play table tennis. It's a good way just to pass the time. Play a little bit. Stop. Play a little. Then go back on the street.

I lived with my father for a while, but he doesn't really like me, so that didn't last too long. He told me living on the street in New York is easy. He never did it but he was sure it wasn't a difficult thing to do compared to being homeless anywhere else in the world. For me it was pretty tough. I'd get into fights every couple of days. Once in a while I'd steal some food from a 7-11. Who knows, maybe it would be easy for my dad. He left Communist Romania and went to Israel and fought in a couple of wars. The Six-Day War, a few others. That's where he met my mom. That was another war, the two of them. My father does a lot of drugs and stuff. He's got a lot of different philosophies, none of which have much to do with child-rearing. There is one good thing about living on the street — Nobody has anything over you. As long as it doesn't cost anything, you can do just about anything you want. And you're not afraid of anything because you don't have anything to lose.

Now I'm an athlete. I got lucky with table tennis. I've had so much bad luck in my life, I think it's finally balancing out. I started playing when I was 15 years old, which is extremely late. Most really good players start when they're five or six. After a few months I was eligible for the Junior Olympics. I didn't go because I didn't have any money, but I kept playing tournaments. My main goal was just to be competitive against the top players in the U.S. In the beginning nobody would play with me. They were like, "You stink." You know, this little guy with a messed-up arm. Within two years I was able to beat a lot of them. They hit the ball much harder and faster than I can. So I have to place the ball just how I want it. Or I make them hit it as hard as they can and then I use their force against them. So many people in the U.S. play with no strategy at all. They're much better than me, but they're just putting the ball in the same place in the same way all the time. In one point, I can loop it and smash it, then chop it. Nobody can anticipate what I'm going to do. I've really never practiced. Most of the top players train one stroke, ten hours a day. They practice their serve, then their forehand loop, then their backhand. For me it's very boring to keep doing the same thing over and over. I just like to play matches and have fun. The truth is, I'm not as pumped up about the sport as I used to be. I really used to love to play and play and play. Now I play just for the exercise and to hang out.

Tahl teaches table tennis on the Internet and is working on three how-to books on the sport as well as an autobiography.

One of the few women we ever see playing at Champion Ping Pong, Renata Peluchova was a professional table tennis player in the Czech Republic and Germany.

I came with a couple of friends to New York only for vacation. Then I found this club here in Queens and one in Manhattan. When I enter the door for the first time, I had never seen so many guys. No women. Everybody stopped playing. All eyes looking at me. I said, "Oh my goodness, what did I do?" A man who used to be a top player in Africa explain to me how it works in United States. "If you want to play, you have to play with the guys. Same thing in tournaments." I said, "Why? Why should I play with guys?" He said, "There aren't enough women players in this country." When I told him I used to play for Czech National Team, he told me, "Go play that guy over there." The guy says, "Oh, this girl, I'm going to beat her bad." I took him down so easy — a few matches in a row. From that moment everybody start to respect me. I met some nice people. They offered to help me stay in this country. I start thinking why not change my life? If table tennis is your work, you never know what can happen next day. If you're going to be injured, you're finished. My goal in life is not only to play ping pong. That's why all during my professional level in Europe, I was studying in Economic College with a specialization in traveling and tourism management. I had really good life over there, but I'm the kind of person looking for change. The next year I came again to the U.S.

No longer able to support herself by playing table tennis, Renata works as a medical biller for a sports doctor by day. By night and on the weekends she's a fitness trainer, a table tennis coach, and [the week of our meeting] the fourth-ranked female player in the United States. She lives in Ridgewood, Queens and comes to Champion Ping Pong to practice.

For me it is unusual that clubs like this don't have facilities for showers. If I practice, I sweat. The whole system of table tennis in this country took a little getting used to. Like in competitions you don't have an exact time schedule. You just wait till they call you to play. You have to warm up. Then again wait. Then you could be playing in the finals on the worst table, people walking around, talking very loud. You cannot say, "Listen, be quiet, I cannot play." That is why I have to improve my concentration even more. Especially you are a woman playing all the time against guys.

In the beginning I thought how can I play against guys. After a while I figure out their weaknesses. They might show me, this day they're not playing so good. An opponent like me will take advantage of that. In the past few years I beat so many guys. Some of them cannot handle they got beat by a woman. They want to break their rackets. You have to come to the table and look very confident. You are not scared. Doesn't matter if this player is bigger than you. That is something my coach taught me. Because I used to have a problem of the mind. Sometimes I couldn't move because I like to win too much and I was really so tight.

As member of the Czech team, the government pay my school scholarship, they pay my boardinghouse, food, equipment, and I had the opportunity to travel. That was Communism time and most everybody wasn't allowed to travel. My first trip was to Austria. I was 13 years old. None of us could mention, "Wow, in Austria they have shopping center where you can buy so many things!" When I was 18, there was a great revolution and everything changed from that time. Vaclav Havel got out of prison and we elect him President. I consider him one of the very best Presidents. But after Communism, the government stopped support of sports. Now it's the same system as America. Everything is based on money. If your family has money, you can do many things. If not, there is little opportunity for a girl or boy to succeed.

All of my friends from the Czech team are already married and have kids. I am the only one single and don't have family. It's different life, yeah? I prefer little bit enjoy myself right now. What I miss most from Europe, after we practice, or after competition, we would go together for dinner and hang out. But in this country, everybody is in a hurry. I am getting that way too. If you work in the morning until evening just to pay the rent, then you take subway again to give table tennis lessons for two hours, and you know you have two subways and a bus to get home, you don't have any energy left to hang out.

If George Brathwaite is any example, fifty years of top-ranked ping pong playing may not make you rich, but it can keep you in excellent shape and disposition. Originally from Guyana, he's a two-time winner of the Caribbean and Central American championships, a five-time winner of the U.S. Senior Championships, and a former member of the U.S. team that went with President Richard Nixon on his ice-thawing trip to China in 1971.

GEORGE

We were naive in the beginning about the overall purpose of the trip. For us it was an opportunity to practice with Chinese players, try and learn some of their techniques. Soon as we got to Hong Kong, we were being ushered through side doors to get away from reporters like yourself. That's when we first realized the political significance of this trip. The original invitation came from playing with the Chinese at the World Championships in Nayoga, Japan the year before. We would get together with them on occasion, and the President of our associ–ation got to talking to his Chinese counterparts and the end result was an invitation for us to come to China. That's what we thought anyway.

The funny thing is, I was employed at the United Nations, but I never thought of my ping–pong playing as having anything to do with diplomacy. One day, we were on the bus to the Great Wall, and one of the Chinese interpreters discov–ered that I worked at the U.N., and he said, "I understand you work at the U.N." I said, "Yeah." He said, "Do you think that China will be accepted as a member nation at the next meeting of the General Assembly?" I said, "Well, I'm not really in an official capacity to be able to answer that question accurately." So he said, "Well. If you were in a capacity, would you vote in favor of China being accepted?" I said, "Well, if I were, I would definitely vote that all nations become member nations of the U.N." When I got back, I found myself in a conversation with the Secretary General, which wasn't all that frequent a thing being that I was just an accountant clerk for the Accounts Department. I told him about what happened on the bus and he thought that was a very nice answer I gave. He was very pleased. Of course today you know, China's a permanent member on the Security Council.

Jidong Lu came from Mainland China to the U.S. as a student of applied linguistics in 1989. He worked as an English as a Second Language teacher at first, then as a school administrator.

JIDONG

Working as a dean in a public high school in the Bronx is a lot of stress. When the students are fighting out of control you have to stand between them. Sometimes they're biting and you have to call for assistance. That's why I come to this club five nights a week. Two nights I stay with my family. Ping pong is an excellent sport to relieve pressure.

Playing ping pong, one rule you have to keep in mind — to be flexible. And in life, in whatever kind of job you take, you have to be flexible. We come to this earth with nothing, and when we leave, we cannot take anything with us. In between you just have to find a way to enjoy yourself. Not to be bothered by petty things. When you hit the ball, each one coming at you is different. In your life too. There are different stages, different ways of life. When I was in China ten years ago, I would never have imagined I'd be here in America. And everything changed after I came here because you have to start from the very beginning again. Like playing table tennis, you do not know what kind of angle the ball is going to be hit to you. So you just have to remain flexible.

queens international high school

MOHAMED ATTIA
JONATHAN BARBA
JOANNA PITTNER
MALY FUNG
ADIS NUHANOVIC
ELIANA GARCIA
ANTON KONET
JUAN CARLOS

Drive over the 59th Street Bridge from Manhattan to Queens and you end up in the (once) industrial area of Long Island City. Hundreds of high school students walk briskly across a superwide three-way intersection to building E of LaGuardia Community College. They descend to the basement, where they attend the Queens International High School, which admits students who have been in the United States for less than four years and have limited English proficiency. I [Judith] have been an artist-in-residence at "International" for five years, teaching writing and storytelling workshops and directing original theatre pieces. Many kids don't know why their parents left their country. Early in the semester I ask them to find out. A girl from Ecuador comes back to class, "You know Miss, this is the first time I talk to my father. He left home when I was two and didn't bring me here till I was ten. Now that I ask him questions he thinks I want to listen to his stories all the time and he won't shut up."

The kids are from over 50 different countries. Cultural differences sometimes erupt in clashes, but usually dissipate over time. In the hallways you can hear Chinese kids learning Spanish and Hispanic kids learning Russian. The eight young people we are featuring here were all part of a year-long theatre workshop. One thing they all have in common is that they, like all immigrant teenagers before them, are becoming more American than their parents ever will.

LONG ISLAND CITY

Valencia
NEZUELA
Rivne
UKRAINE
ECUADOR
Ambato
MEXICO
Tlaxcala

DOMINICAN
REPUBLIC
Santo Domingo

BOSNIA
Zenica

POLAND
Rzeszow
Kuwait City

KUWAIT

Mohamed Attia was born in Kuwait. His family went back to his father's homeland of Egypt after Iraq invaded Kuwait in 1990. His older brother applied for the visa lottery and the whole family came to New York in 1996 when Mohamed was 13 years old.

In Egypt the other kids used to shout, *"Kuwaitee boy. Hey Kuwaitee boy, come here."* When I came to New York the kids called me, *"Mummyboy."* So I use *mummyboy* for my e-mail. My first year at Ridgewood Junior High I couldn't understand any English. The teacher asked me my name. I told her, "Egypt." All the kids laughed at me. The worst thing was saying words with the letter C or S because of my lisp. When I say, "What's up?," the other kids tease me, *"Whasthup? Hey Wasthup Mummyboy?"* So I get pissed off and I start talking less and less and less. One day, I just stopped talking. To anyone. For a whole year.

That was a bad idea because I didn't practice talking. First year in high school I start quiet. When I begin talking again, I think of how to say a sentence without using a C or S before I open my mouth. It takes me longer to answer, so some people including teachers think I don't understand. But I understand very well. In Egypt I was one of the big guys. I'm very good at soccer. In America I became quiet and a little bit scared.

That's why I decide to take the acting class – to show everybody that I am the man, that I can speak, even if I have a problem. Everything I said onstage was loud, because I said it with anger. The good news for me was that Judith gave me lines without S or C and it makes me look good in

JONATHAN

Jonathan Barba came to the United States when he was eleven years old. He now lives with both his parents in Ridgewood, Queens.

We always saw American tourists in Ecuador when I was a kid. Tall, white, blonde, blue eyes. And with big, big backpacks way above their heads and down to their knees. There's a place in Ecuador that's really famous – it's not that great – a volcano and pools of hot water. All the gringos go there. When I came to the U.S., I thought I'd see gringos all over the place. Instead I saw people from every-where *except* the United States. Because I live in Queens! There's lots of gringos in Manhattan, but where I live there are no white people.

Born in Poland, Joanna Pittner lives in Maspeth, Queens with her Polish-speaking parents and an older brother. She came to New York in 1997 when she was 13 years old.

JOANNA

No one told me we were going to stay in America. First six months in Queens I threw up every day. Diarrhea. Crying. Everything. My entire world was turned upside down.

front of the rest of the school. People give me more respect. Two years ago, nobody knew me in this school. The more I win in soccer, the more I get famous and see girls come to me. That's why I am not religious. I wouldn't be able to give a girl a hi or bye kiss. Maybe when I'm older I'll be religious. I do believe in Mohammed as a prophet. I do believe in God. It is not a problem for me in science class because I can believe that God created the big bang and from there we have people. But I don't believe we came from monkeys. If I have to take a test and there is a question about evolution, I will answer what my teacher wants me to say.

After September 11th, some guys in school call me Mohamed Atta – you know, the guy who flew the plane into the World Trade Towers. *"Yo, Atta! Atta!"* Some kids call all the Arabians in the school terrorist. I have only one other friend at school also named Mohamed. In Egypt we had many boys named Mohamed. In my class of 60 students, all boys, 54 were named Mohamed. Of the other six, two were named Ahmed, three Mamod, and one person named Shedi. We had to use three different names to call all the Mohameds because sometimes kids had the same two names. Sometimes they had the same three names. My name is Mohamed El Sayed Attia. My cousin is Mohamed El Sayed Attia. My father's name is Hasan, so they called me Mohamed El Sayed Attia Hasan.

It was always my dream to be a pilot. Not a normal pilot, I wanted to become something exciting like a war pilot. After September 11th, the war is against the Muslim people, so I changed my plans. Right now, all I want to be is maybe a mechanic for airplanes.

The first time I see war was in Kuwait. We were in our house packing to go to Egypt for two month vacation when my mother called from her job and told us to look out the window. Smoke was covering the sky. Airplanes and bombs and lights. I went to the roof that night and could see lights coming up and down in the sky. I wasn't scared about war. I'd never seen it before, only in a movie or cartoon. It was exciting. I was too young at eight years old to know any better. I wasn't scared to die. My father met with all the other Egyptian men in the neighborhood. They were looking at the map, making plans to leave by car.

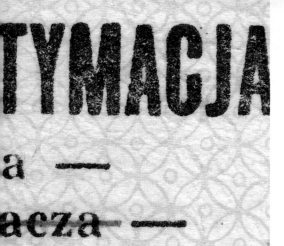

JOANNA

At the end of sixth grade, my mother put me and my brother on a plane without her. I just took one bag of clothes, thinking, we're going on vacation to America and I'm going to meet my dad. After so many years I thought it was going to be awkward to see him, but right away we started talking.

When he took us to where he lived in Maspeth, I thought the house was going to be this huge mansion like in the movies, but it was just an apartment in a long skinny building divided into two rooms and a kitchen with a thin hallway. You don't see small dark apartments like that on TV. My mom came a few weeks later and my parents started talking about me going to school. Without even asking! I felt betrayed. They did say, "If you don't like it, we're gonna go back." The thing is, I didn't like it! I hated it. So I just closed myself out. I didn't speak to them, nothing. They asked me something, I would answer, but I would never start the conversation. Just "Yes. No. No. Yes."

JONATHAN

My father came to the U.S. when I was two because he couldn't make enough money to feed all of us children. We were very poor. The kind of poor that meant we didn't have anything to eat. My mother joined my father when I was five and she'd visit us in Ecuador once a year. My older sister was the one who raised me but she was only seven years older, so I started to hang out at a friend's house and it grew into a family thing. Eventually I started living with them. They had a restaurant, so I had plenty to eat. They liked having me there because I was with their son and he was the only boy in the house. But it wasn't really my family. Every time there was a parent/teacher meeting in school, my aunts would come or friends. Sometimes nobody came.

Six months later my mom and I went back to Poland for Christmas. My friends were all mad at me, "You didn't even say goodbye." I told them I didn't know! That's when I finally got to say goodbye and when I brought this little box from  my grandma back to America. It's the one thing I have to remember her by. She died when I was five. She gave the box to my mom, and Mom gave it to me at my First Communion. I'm probably going to give it to my daughter. Things are going to be totally different with my daughter. For one, I'm not going to lie to her. We're going to have like a best-friend, best-friend relationship.

A week later we left at four o'clock in the morning. We only brought
a few photographs and small things we could fit in the car. Our car led
a caravan of maybe 25 cars following. The day we left, the sky was

smokey. Dark. You couldn't see the sun
out of the smoke because Iraq was
bombing the airports. The fuel tanks
and planes were on fire. My dad saw
some Iraqi soldiers far ahead on the
road, so he took a left turn and started
to drive over the sand.

a photograph of Mohamed in Egypt

We had no choice but to drive through
the desert. Every time I look back I see
less and less cars behind us. If they slow
down, they get stuck. We drive three or four hours when my uncle's
friend got stuck in the sand and we all stopped to push the car out.
Then my uncle got stuck. So we help my uncle out. Then *we* got stuck.
My father tells the other men to keep going. We had no choice but to
build a tent in the desert. My father, my mom, my fourteen-year-old
brother, my eighteen-year-old sister and me. My brother tells me there
are snakes in the desert that bite. I get scared and sleep in the car. The
next morning I wake up and everything is yellow outside. The wind is
going very fast. I open the door a little but I had to close it right away.
Sand was moving all around. I'm crying and calling for my daddy but
he can't hear me. About five or six hours later the sandstorm calms
down. My father picks me up and my brother starts laughing at me so
I hit him. I got beat up in the end, but I was happy because it was the
first time I fought my older brother.

The next day a big truck passes by. We had to give the driver all our
Pepsis to get him to help us out of the sand. My father steps on the gas
and we run like the wind. Maybe 200 miles an hour. If we get stuck
again, we know it's all over. We made it to the check point, stayed in
Saudi Arabia two days, then took a ship across the Red Sea. I really
liked that ship because it was big as a building. In Egypt I watch the
war on TV. All I wanted was to stay in Kuwait, because at that age
I didn't care if there was a war or not.

Maly's parents emigrated to the city of Valencia in Venzuela where there are many Chinese immigrants. Maly came to the U.S. to study when she was 14. At 16, she lives with her mother, brother and sister in
MALY *Fresh Meadows, Queens.*

Basically I'm a quiet girl but I'm a freak wannabe; a rebel, but in a peaceful way. There was a Polish girl at school who had her head shaved with only a very little bit of pink hair on her forehead. From her appearance she looked like a mean girl. She was interesting. That's the image I want. I want to appear mean because people don't fear me. They think I'm friendly and nice and everything, and I'm not! At home I'm mean. I'm mean to those people that I'm close to. But basically, I am very quiet.

JOANNA

My parents will never understand how painful it was having to leave my school and start over. They were done with their lives in Poland. They're old. My dad is 51. He was a retired police officer who thought he could make more money here. Now I get along better with him than my mom. In Poland she and I were best friends. There was no curfew. She wasn't worried about where I am or who I'm with. Here, she doesn't know any of my friends because she doesn't speak any English. The real reason my parents brought us here is because of my brother. In Poland he was going downhill — smoking pot, drinking alcohol, and he got involved in a gang. They thought he needed a father figure. Nobody really cared what was going on with me.

After five years here, I dream and think in English. My parents are the only ones I talk to in Polish. The new Polish kids in school expect me to speak to them but I'm always messing the words up. The Polish kids are always in one corner of the student lounge. Spanish kids in another. Chinese another. Then there's a mixed group. Mixed is Polish, Spanish, Chinese, Bulgarian, Russian, Korean and Albanian. One day the other Polish kids started calling me "Streitze" [traitor] because I hang out with a lot of Spanish kids. They don't know what they're missing. I learn lots of phrases. You know how Spanish men stand on the street making kissing noises at girls? My friend taught me how to say "Deja de mirar mi culo," which means "Don't look at my ass" in Spanish.

353

My first impression of New York — I never saw so many Chinese people in my life! I thought I was in China, then I realize it's Chinatown. Most of the kids at International identify with their country. I'm Chinese and Hispanic and right now I'm in limbo. The Chinese kids from China are shy because the language and the culture are so different. Most of them speak Mandarin. There is only one other girl who speaks Cantonese. The Chinese kids from Venezuela, we have Latino culture in us. Like in school when we say hi, we kiss each other on the cheeks, but the kids from China would never do that. My parents are closed like that too. We don't see them show affection in front of us. Never!

I didn't know what an immigrant was until I realized **I'm two times an immigrant!** I'm an immigrant from Venezuela here, and I'm Chinese in Venezuela. I'd be three times an immigrant if we ever went to Hong Kong. In Venezuela I spoke Spanish at school, and Chinese at home. My mom used to tell us, "If you don't speak Chinese, you don't get dinner!" The Hispanic kids made fun of the Chinese. They used to say, "Chinita con arroz." That's "little Chinese girl with rice." I would yell back at them in Chinese, "What do you eat, shit?" I never understood their insult because Venezuelans eat rice too.

Most of the Chinese people in Venezuela ran supermarkets or little stores, like my dad. In the summer, the Hispanics went on vacation but the Chinese never had a break. I was always working with my mom. All she did from morning to night was sit by the cash register counting money. She said, "What do you want to do in the future?" I said, "I know I don't want to end up like you sitting as a cashier all day." She laughed, but I think she went home and thought, wow, my daughter really doesn't want to have a future like me.

That conversation had something to do with my parents sending me and my sister to stay in Miami with an aunt. They were afraid if we stayed in our country, we were just going to marry some guy and have no future. In Venezuela I barely talked to my mom. Then we came to the U.S and I talk to her on the phone every day. "Mom, I miss you." I wet the phone with tears. For the first time I told my parents I loved them. And they told me back. That was the most amazing thing. There's a saying in Chinese, if you're related to a person, the farther away you stay, the better the relationship.

MALY

We were supposed to be learning English, but most of the kids in Miami were Cuban, so we spoke Spanish all day. I didn't fit in at school. I didn't fit in with my aunt. My parents were paying her and she was using us like servants. We had to clean her house and cook. Then she'd tell my mom that we were lazy. When my mom found out that she hit my sister, that was the last drop that spilled over the glass of water. She said, "I know you're not learn-ing English there. I have a couple of friends in New York." My sister and I were like, "Oh, New York! Let's go!" We stayed with an old Cantonese-speaking couple in Astoria, Queens. Right away, I went to International High School and started learning English. Now I speak Chinese, English, and Spanish. Most of the boys that I've dated are Hispanic — one from El Salvador, a Colombian guy, and a Brazilian. Only once I dated a Chinese guy. Didn't like him. My parents want me to marry a Chinese guy so they can talk with the groom. But I tell my mom I'm a different generation. She laughs with a worried face.

The good thing about our school is you get to know people from all over the world and you have to adapt. Sometimes I don't understand someone, like Adis. He wants to show everybody in school that he's a bad boy. I never liked him. But in drama class I started seeing another part of him. I found out that hey, he's afraid too. Now I see him in the hallway, I say hi.

Maly helped organize a protest rally against the City University of New York's tuition hikes for undocumented immigrants.

I'm going downtown to the Global Kids office, make phone calls, make sure people are going to the march, make signs and get everything ready for the protest at City Hall. I've been handing out flyers in the school. A lot of people are affected by this issue and they're scared. We want to reverse the tuition hikes completely. Because City University of New York is supposed to be the college for immigrants. It always was and it always should be. But after 9/11, they doubled the tuition for undocumented immigrants. So they're charging out-of-state tuition to immigrants that are in-state residents. Even if you have your Social Security, you have to pay out-of-state tuition. This is how the American system works: you're allowed to work here with a work authorization and with that you get a Social Security number to pay your taxes. But you're not a resident, you're not legal, you don't have the resident card. That's pretty much where I'm at. My mother's brother petitioned me for the green card. But I have no idea how long that will take.

ADIS *Adis is from Bosnia. He came to the United States with his family in 1997.*

Some people say, "Boxing, oohhh, evil thing."
Like boxing will lead to Columbine. But for angry people like
me, boxing is good. It calms me down. I used to train in the nuclear
shelter. We wouldn't even feel the bombs down there. The wall is
lead. Then there's a wall of water. Then there's another wall of lead.
You know, Cold War design.

*Columbine here refers to
the high-school massacre
that took place in April
1999, in the suburban
Colorado town of Colum-
bine. Two students came
to school with shotguns,
assault rifles, and explo-
sives, shot up as many
students and teachers as
they could, and then
killed themselves. While
TV, teenagers, trenchcoats,
two-income families, the
Internet, rap music, and
video games were blamed,
only a few minor gun-
control laws were enacted
after Columbine and
other school shootings.*

I was ten or twelve when the war started in Bosnia. I think that was summer of '92. All of a sudden the Serbs started attacking the capital, Sarejevo. They put snipers up on a Holiday Inn Hotel and started shooting. First they started shooting at truck tires. The truckers didn't know what was going on. They killed one trucker and three escaped. One of them only had one arm and he was dragging his legs along the ground. From that day on it just escalated. Shooting people and kids. Anything that moved. In the beginning it was like the movies. You know, every day you see another war movie or karate movie. Then I see my mom crying, "Oh my God, those poor people." And I realize, *damn, people are really dying!* You play with your friends, you don't realize this one's a Christian or Serb or Muslim. I never looked at it that way before. They're just your friends. All of a sudden you hear people talk, "I hate Serbs. Look what they're doing to us." My mom is a Serb! She doesn't want to kill anybody. But a lot of Serbs have this hate in them against the Muslims. Five hundred years the Turks ruled Serbia, and they been carrying around the hate ever since. It's history, man! Give it up.

My father is Muslim and my mom is Orthodox Christian. In Bosnia we call Orthodox Christians, Serbs. We lived in Zenica, Central Bosnia. Winter of '93, the Serbs took 70% of our country. As other cities in Bosnia were taken like Prijedor, Banja Luka, Bosanski Brod, refugees started coming. So my city was in shock. They closed the theaters and kindergartens just to have places to put all the refugees. The first wave that came didn't suffer as bad. But the second wave of refugees, there were almost no men because men and boys my age were all killed or kept in concentration camps. All of them were Muslims except for the few Serbs who tried to protect the Muslims. The refugees made fires in the theatre and they would sit in a circle and talk about what happened to them. Sometimes the whole neighborhood used to gather around listening to stories about little girls being raped, and women and innocent children being killed. When I was listening to those stories, I remember feeling this hate building up in me. I'd never seen a man without an arm before or without both legs in my neighbor- hood. Even though my mom is a Serb and and her whole family are Serbs, I started hating Serbs.

At the end of '92 our city started getting bombed.
Suddenly everything was quiet.

Z
Z
Z
Z
S
h
o
o
o
Oop.
Bzewww,
Bzewww,
Bzewww,
Bzewww.

The War in Bosnia ('92–'95), gave us the phrase "ethnic cleansing," a euphemism for murdering, raping, and exiling the people you hate. The Serbs were portrayed as the clear perpetrators in this war, but Bosnian Muslims also took part in wiping out communities of indigenous Serbs in Eastern Slovinia and Western Krajina.

Shells came flying down around the city.

Fifteen people dead. Twenty people dead. Everyone was afraid.
We couldn't run because we were surrounded. At that time Croatia was against us too, so you had to stay put, hide in your basement like rats. Some people thought we're going to lose everything because the Serbs are much stronger than us. They gave up hope. Started killing themselves. They thought the war is never going to stop.

My dad was one of the first people organizing resistance. All they had in the beginning were hunting guns compared to the Serbs' bazookas. My job was to clean my dad's gun when he came back from fighting. You know those old guns in gangster movies with the circle on the bottom? You couldn't shoot the guy if he was at the end of the block. Eventually my dad was in the war as a tank mechanic.

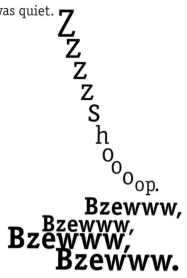

My sister was scared of bombs, but I actually liked it. It's stupid I know, but I liked war because it's so exciting to see those bombs going off. I ran out of the shelter to see how it looks, how it feels. My dad yelled at me, "What the hell is wrong with you? Get inside!"

He decided to take me with him to the war zone to show me. "Look what they did. They burned these houses. This is not a game!"

One day I was playing outside with some friends and a bomb fell on the other side of the building. We dropped because of the ringing noise in our ears, VrrooOOOOojjj. Out of nowhere, kRAK! Explosions, people aaaHHH! Screaming. Blood everywhere, pieces of bodies. My English teacher and a neighbor were playing chess and the bomb fell in the middle of the chessboard. That was it for those two guys.

Somebody found my teacher's head a half mile away.

The Mujahadeens came in '93 and '94, some from Saudi Arabia and some from Algeria. They were fighting for God and Muslim people anywhere in the world.

The Serbs would drop their coffee and breakfast and run because they heard when the Mujahadeens come, nothing is left alive.

My whole family lost a lot of weight during the war because the food supplies were short. My dad was skinny before the war but by '95 he looked like a skeleton walking down the street. We used to go to other people's gardens and steal apples in the summer, corn during the fall. We dug up potatoes and saved them for the winter.

As the war was ending we heard the country was going to be broken up with new lines drawn. My dad grew a mustache to look like a Croatian. He bought a fake ID with a different name and set out for Germany. Along the way, there were a lot of checkpoints. Soldiers would stop the bus and ask, "Who's Muslim here?" Some people were shot because they were stupid enough to carry both IDs. Two months later, my mom, my sister and I left with a trucker from Croatia. We all had different names and fake passports and just a few pieces of underwear and clothes. If you take too many things it looks like you're running away. I really really wanted my red fishing rod that my mother gave me for my fifth birthday, but we had to leave it behind. I wanted to take some bullets with me too. My mom said, "What the hell are you thinking?" I was collecting spent bullets to show kids that I was in a war. You could have shown a picture of them in your book!

detail of Adis' father's tank mechanic-brigade patch

At every checkpoint, my mom was smiling, but inside she was dying, afraid she'd forget all our new names. In one day I saw gray hairs coming out of her head. By the time we made it to Germany, almost every hair on her head was gray. She was 35 years old! When we got to our aunt's house in Germany my dad was so happy to see us, he started crying. That was the first time I saw him cry. I didn't want to show that I was crying so I held my teeth and sucked in the tears. To be a man in my country, you can't show that you are weak.

Adis' parents applied to the United States as refugees for protection against retaliation from either side as a mixed couple. The U.S. accepted them, along with 10,000 other Bosinian refugees.

In Germany I saw my first black person. I was fascinated. "Let me touch you. Please!" I found out the skin of a black person feels the same as mine. Then we land in JFK and drive through Jamaica and other neighborhoods in Queens and see how many black people are here! We had this stereotyped image in Germany listening to Tupac and Biggie and all the rappers. Now one of my best friends is black. He calls me whitey, so one time I called him nigger. I asked him, "Does it offend you?" You hear black people say, "Oh, what's up, my nigger?"
He said it was okay, but I'm not sure it really is.

Before eighth grade I used to be short, then I just popped up really fast like a tree. My height adds to my image that I have to keep up of being a tough guy. In my country, kids were constantly fighting. It wasn't a big thing over there. It wasn't personal. Except when it came to religion, that was war.

The whole thing with Jonathan was a misunderstanding. In my country you tell somebody, "I'm going to kill you," it means we're going to have a fight. But in America people take things really seriously. Especially after Columbine. A few weeks earlier, I told Jonathan, "We're going to kick your ass." I was making fun of him in class because of his touchy-kissy ways with the girls. In my country you don't touch a girl unless she's your girlfriend. Even if you're just friends, a kiss on the cheek is not good. That's why we have hands. To shake them. For four years I've been around all these Spanish kids, but still my culture is burned into me. It doesn't get erased like a tape recorder. Albanians are like us too. All the Balkans and Muslim also. You're a sissy if you show tears.

So me and two Albanian guys, I'll call them R and E, were sitting in the computer room downloading some rap songs. We were looking through my buddy list and R said, "Oh, look at this faggot online. Fuck him. Let's send him something."

I said, "Just make sure the screen name you use isn't mine." So R e-mailed, wut up bitch? And Jonathan e-mailed back, whos this? And we wrote, u dont want to know, pussy. All these insults. R started e-mailing, im gonna rip ur head off and scatter ur body all over the cemetery. Really violent things and Jonathan got scared. I would be too because he didn't know who we are. He actually said at one point, is this u adis? We wrote back, who the hell is adis?

Jonathan saved the e-mails and we got caught. They called us into the school one at a time. I confessed, wrote every detail down. E took the blame too, but R said he didn't have anything to do with it. R was my friend for two years and then thraW, I just wanted to go to his house and beat him up.

All three of us got suspended and banned from the computer room for a month. They weren't going to let me back in the theatre class either, because Jonathan was in there. So I apologized to everyone and let them know I was no threat. I didn't want all those months of rehearsing to go to waste over a stupid prank. I told Jonathan, "Listen bro, you know I didn't mean it." Jonathan said, "I know, but I was afraid it was somebody else." I never punched anybody at school, maybe push them around, cursing, making jokes. I have my limits. I would never kick somebody's ass just because I'm jealous of them. Maybe I was thinking, if I go up to a girl, hug for half an hour, she'd be like, "Get out of here you pervert!" When *he* does it, it's normal. I wish my culture was. . . you know, more affectionate. Guys aren't supposed to have feelings. We're supposed to be robots with batteries in them and the feelings shut off.

JONATHAN

I never fight. I learned Tae Kwon Do because it gives you discipline. I'm lazy and I needed to do something about my health and my body. I want to be useful. Not just a thing living on earth. This lady once told me, "You may be sixteen years old now, but one day you'll blink, or you'll wake up, and you'll be sixty." I don't want to waste my life.

When I met Adis, I knew he was jealous of me. He told me right in my face, "You think you're 'in love' because you hang out with all the cute girls." I wanted to tell him they're just my friends. They can be your friends too. But I didn't say anything. When I found out it was him that threatened to kill me, I talked to him and he was cool with me again. I didn't have to fight him or anything. Adis can't control himself, that's just the way he is.

At sixteen years old, Eliana lives with her mother, stepdad, and two brothers in what she describes as a "too-quiet" neigbhorhood in Woodhaven, Queens. She came to live with her mother in the U.S. in 1999, while she was in the eighth grade.

ELIANA

When I speak in class, everybody turns to look at me, like, *oh my God, she's speaking again.* I'm the loudest girl in the class.

I'm Dominican!

That's who I am, where I'm from, my family, my background. Wild, loud, music, dancing, beaches, rivers, GUYS! I'm American because I was born here. My mom came here and gave birth to me and she did that with my brother too. She was in New York working in factories, sending money back to my father so we could afford to live. Even though I'm an American citizen I consider myself an immigrant.

You want to know what I long for from my country?
The one thing I can't get here?

My dad!

I grew up with just my dad from when I was four till thirteen. I was this little girl hanging out with all these grown-up men and we would make parties at home, all these guys coming in and drinking and stuff. It sounds scary like, *oh my God, this is the only girl in the house with all these men!* But they took care of me. Not exactly role models, but now I know how not to get tricked. My dad's friends would say, "If a man tells you to go somewhere, always say no. If they give you beer, don't take it. They could put something in it." They were warning me about themselves. I've had four boyfriends in my life, and none of them has tried to *cross the border.*

Some things were strange like I had to tell my dad the first time I got my period. I was like, oh my God. When I told him, he hugged me. "You're a señorita now. Are you okay? Does it hurt?" Then he started calling all his sisters here in New York. I told him to calm down. He said, "Do you know how to..." I said, "Yeah, I know. Mom told me everything before she left."

The 14th Amendment states, "All persons born or naturalized in the United States, and subject to the jurisdiction thereof, are citizens of the United States." Groups in favor of tighter immigration policies, such as the Queens-based PROJECT USA, are fighting to end "birthright citizenship," which they call "anchor babies," saying the practice is a misreading of the Amendment. Others insist lawmakers were unambiguous on this point.

One day when I was twelve, we went to pick my mom up at the airport. When my dad went to say hi to her, she turned away. I thought, *what's going on here?* A few weeks later my dad said, "Your mom wants a divorce." I hoped it was just a bad dream or a joke. It wasn't a dream or a joke. I came here to live with her. I really didn't want to leave my daddy alone over there.

My mom got remarried two years ago. That was a big thing for me to move in with a strange man. In my country I used to walk around the house naked. Oh my God, here you can't do that. Everything is different. We live near a park but I don't ever go there because I don't know anyone in our neighborhood. In the D.R. I used to play outside all the time. I ran track and I won every single time I raced. Here my parents are scared for me to go out of the apartment. I get no exercise.

Anton came to the U.S. in May 2001. We interviewed him in May 2002. He says his biggest problem in school is the English language. He is learning as fast as he can.

I remember my country being born because that was when I start smoking. Ten years old. Most of my friends was older, so I copy them. I wasn't smoking like I am now, half-pack a day. Cigarettes cost like twenty cents and I always had some money from cleaning cars, selling newspaper. Lots of ways to make money. In the beginning everybody was happy with new Ukraine. "Oh we get our country. Now we make our life much better than in Soviet Union." By two years nobody had money. People still working but get no money for their jobs. When it is Soviet Union, if you have money, you could not buy something from empty store. Now it is independent country of Ukraine and you can find some nice things in stores, but everybody has empty pockets.

I was one of the best students of my school. But after eighth grade, my father start working in Poland. Only visit once a year and I didn't see somebody good in front of me that I can copy. I just went to the streets, dress like gangster in big coat. I was stealing from stores, drinking, doing bad things. In Ukraine you can buy alcohol if you're five years old. "Give me a bottle of vodka for my father." They just give it to you. This is so bad. In one week, eight of my friends go to jail. I didn't want a future like this.

When we first move here, we live with a friend of my mother's. One side of the street is Brooklyn. One side is Queens. It wasn't so bad, but it wasn't so good. I go to some school to learn English because I knew only how to say, "My name is Anton, I am from Ukraine, and how are you doing?" Also I knew bad words. Asshole, I heard from movies and rap songs. Shit, motherfucker, the basics. I know Russian friend who can't say "How you doing?" in English, but he knows how to say "Get the fuck out of here." Now I speak English pretty good for only one year ago coming, making everybody laugh in drama class, so Juan ask me to be on his election team. Other people running wore jeans and T-shirt, but I think for this I need to wear clothes like adult. Nobody saw me wear white man's shirt and tie before. They only think of me as a tough guy. After next year I will try to be President myself.

JUAN CARLOS

At 11 years old, Juan Carlos and his younger brother came across the border in a car with people they didn't know. Like many new immigrants from Mexico, his family lives in a tiny apartment. They came from a small town where they lived in a big house. Juan has learned to do homework in a room full of people watching TV. We spoke to him right after the end of an election campaign.

It's my dream to become legal. Especially now. Because of the immigrants who crashed into the Twin Towers, every other immigrant suffers. Your position in life is like stairs. Your background determines on which stair you're standing. I'm an immigrant and a teenager. Neither are very high on the ladder. People think teenagers are irresponsible. Being an immigrant puts me even lower.

Parents who left their parents and all their family behind, put their hopes on you. Do you know how it feels not to know if you'll be able to pay them back; to make their eager dreams come true; not to know whether coming to the U.S. was really the best decision? When the politicians raised the City University tuition, they took away our future. My mother said, "We're going to pay whatever we have to, even if it means we're going to eat beans every day." The tuition increase was reversed but it will still be hard for me to go to college because of my legal status.

The high school was getting ready for student elections and Maly said, "Juan, there's only one team running for office. That's not an election." In Mexico I was very active in student government, so I decided to put together a team here. I ran for President and asked Anton to be my treasurer, and he said, sure. And we won!

I'd like to tell someone from back home, but I don't know who. Of the few things I brought here, this letter is the only thing I kept. I didn't tell anyone we were coming to the U.S., but a friend found out, and the day before we left, she handed me this letter and ran away. She wrote, "You were born from hope. Your crib was the heart. Your mom is a rose. Your dad is a carnation. You are a friend I will never forget."

the
new
american
democratic
club

MORSHED ALAM
SALEHA ALAM
HARJINDER SINGH DUGGAL
ELIZABETH AIVERS

The storefront waiting room of a beauty salon may not be the most prestigious location for Morshed Alam's campaign headquarters, but it's affordable, and it gives Saleha Alam a wife's-eye-view from her laundromat directly across the street on Hillside Avenue in Jamaica, Queens. This is Morshed's third run for public office. A former student leader in Bangladesh's fight for independence, now a father of three and an environmental engineer, Morshed really doesn't care if he himself gets elected to the City Council. The important thing is making a few inroads within a political machine that does not reflect the immigrant population of the city.

A new term limits law, effective November 2001, opened up 36 of the 51 seats on the New York City Council. Morshed's New American Democratic Club is backing dozens of candidates who came to this country from Asia, Latin America, the West Indies, and Africa. He started the insurgent club after the county Democratic organization opposed his first run for the State Senate in 1998. Unlike previous immigrant groups who came to New York in the early part of the 20th century and rose to political power after a few generations, post–1965 immigrants come from so many countries and ethnic groups, no one group can add up to more than a fraction of the population. The coalitions forged by this club and others like it have been helpful in scoring some victories. Meet here Morshed and Saleha Alam and two other club members.

Punjab
Caracas
INDIA   VENEZUELA
Dhaka
BANGLADESH

I'm Indian first. Sikh second. Politician third.
No, I'm American first. I must be grateful to this flag.

Harjinder Singh Duggal is a Actually, I'm human being first. American second.
hard-working entrepreneur, Indian third. I mean, Sikh third. Indian fourth.
a proud Sikh-American, a Irish, maybe fifth or sixth. I may not look it, but
school board member, and a Duggal is an Irish name. Five hundred years ago
candidate for City Council. there was a mutiny in North India and the king hired some mercenaries from Ireland to fight for him. When the kingdom was saved,
the mercenaries settled in North India. Of course they didn't come
with their wives, so the blood started to mix. It's a very long tree. We
have Dugan and Douglas and Duggal and Atwal and Oswald.

American people are the best people in the world. Even the criminals are good.
When I first came here I was driving a taxi cab, and one time a passenger put
a gun in the back of my neck and asked me to hand over all my money. I gave
him all the money from my wallet. $13. He said, "You sure that's all you
have?" I said, "Yes. You're only my second customer of the day, sir." He made
me empty my pockets, and then he abused me, "Oh you're a bloody poor
fellow. I can't rob you." He handed my $13 back, reached into
his pocket and gave me a dollar. "Here," he said. "This is
to buy your coffee." I let him out at the corner
and thought, *wow! This is the most
incredible country in the*
whole world!

Maybe there's something in
the air that makes this country great.
The Pakistanis and the Indians are traditional
enemies. The Bangladeshis and the Pakistanis
also are not famous for getting along. But we
come here to Queens and we're all called Desi.
One word. There are always going to be a few
fanatics, but most of us are living here like
brothers and sisters. Before the British made
a deal with Nehru in 1947 to partition India
into different states, we were one country.
In Queens again we are one people.

*Desi is a commonly used term for
anyone from the Indian subcontinent
who is now living somewhere else.*

A graduate of Dhaka University with a degree in home economics, Saleha Alam runs a laundromat while raising three children with her husband, Morshed.

SALEHA

The first time I had a look at Morshed was the day of our marriage. Well, I did meet him once before, but I didn't know it. My oldest brother asked Morshed to come to a dinner party. He took a look at me and said to my brother, "Okay, no problem." We didn't even speak. The next week we were married. When they told me I was getting married, I said, "Okay." When I finally saw him I thought to myself, *not bad.* That was more than 22 years ago. And we love each other to this day.

MORSHED

The machine is melting!

Even if I don't win my own race, it makes me feel great about what I'm doing. Winning isn't everything. There's something like 40 of us running for City Council this year. Sixteen Asians. It's unprecedented. If we win two seats, that's progress. Nobody's going to give up power just like that.

A prosecutor with the Queens County Family Court, Elizabeth Aivers is actively involved with Latin-American and immigrant community groups.

ELIZABETH

My parents were horrified when I first moved to New York City. I came from a small village in Venezuela, which is a very close-knit, homogenous society. People care for each other, which is wonderful, but it also means everyone is always into your business. People know about things that are happening to you before you do.

HARJINDER

Many of my friends signed up to run for the City Council. I thought why shouldn't I? When I came to know about term limits, I thought, I should run because this is my nature to serve other people.

My campaign headquarters is in my apartment. I haven't raised any money, but I'm mobilizing the opinion of many people. It's helpful that I speak Hindi, Urdu, Punjabi, Marathi, Gujarati, Persian, Sanskrit, Arabic, and English. Also I understand a little bit of Spanish, but I can't speak it because there's too many languages already in my head. One more and I'm afraid I'll scramble them all.

Really I'm not a politician. I'm a linguistic specialist. I do translations in the courts — city, state, federal. I've translated for newspapers, book publishers, even filmmakers. That's the work I do on the side. Really I'm a businessman. My business is Information Technology — I have four newsstands. You want the news from anywhere in the world, you come to my newsstand, I can print it out. You want today's St. Petersburg Press. We look on the computer for the dot-com and print the article out. New Yorkers always do things first in the world and I am the person with the first

MORSHED

In 1965, India and Pakistan were in a big war. Bangladesh didn't even exist yet as a country. At seven or eight years old, I really couldn't comprehend what I heard on the radio. Somehow I had a feeling it was just a few people making a big mess for everybody else.

Third grade was a big year for me. I won the position of class captain. In sixth grade I was elected to the student union, and in high school I was the Secretary General of the Bangladeshi Student League for the whole Cumala district of East Pakistan. I went to 39 high schools, organizing students to join the Bangladeshi liberation movement. If I couldn't convince the principal to bring all the students into one big room, I'd get them to meet in an open field with a microphone.

SALEHA

Arranged marriage is regular in our country. Only now some people get married by their own choice. Morshed and I are looking for a husband for our oldest daughter when she turns 20. All our daughters know we're from a different culture. If one of them marries an American that will be hard to take. As long as they marry a nice person.

Morshed wants Nusrat to go into politics. My dream is to help my daughters finish a good education and then they will get married. Even though there's no money for women in my country, there is less stress for us there. In America the woman works outside *and* inside the home *and* takes care of the kids. I had no idea life would be so tough here. We came in 1984 when I was 22 years old and eight months pregnant.

For eight years I worked as a technician for a printer, leaving at seven in the morning and coming home exhausted. Then Morshed saw an ad in the paper for a laundromat. We bought the business so I could have more time to be with the kids. Only now I think I spend a lot more time at the

HARJINDER

cyber-newsstand in the world. Now it isn't working because someone stole my computers. Soon as my financial situation is better, I'll restart it. I know the man who took the computers. He got involved with drug people and out of curiosity he tried drugs and then to get some more, he robbed my newsstand.

So I've been robbed and mugged a few times. New York is still the greatest city in the world! Instead of arresting the man who robbed me, the city could do something for people who are mentally upset.

I am hoping soon to raise some funds so I can start my campaign rigorously. Maybe being a politician is not for me. Really I'm an engineer by profession. Did I tell you that? Until I came here and took any menial job I could find. That's how I got started in the newsstand business, from selling newspapers on the street. Where else but America can a person go from street peddler to company owner? You dream it. You do it in America. Doesn't matter who you are.

Indian-American, that's what you can say I am. Not American-Indian. Indian-American. Or just American or just Desi. Doesn't matter what you call me. As long as you call me.

MORSHED

Oh man, the speeches people made! They weren't like speeches you hear politicians giving today. We had so much at stake – life and death and freedom or no freedom! When I hear the speeches of Martin Luther King, I'm reminded of the spirit of our rallies. We never had anything against the Pakistani people. It was the government who imposed their culture on us in a very oppressive way.

I was trained to fight as part of the revolutionary army, but I am not a physical fighter. I never killed anyone. My part was going to people's houses collecting money, food and clothes, signalling when the coast was clear for the freedom fighters to cross the street, relaying information to the front lines. December 16th, 1971, Bangladesh won its independence from Pakistan. I'm very proud of the role the students played in that.

After the liberation I went to the University in Dhaka. Everybody was boiling over with dreams of what kind of society we're going to have. I came from a remote area and nobody in the city knew who I was. So I had to figure out ways to promote myself. The college had an annual sports event at the stadium every fall. Even though I am not a sportsman, I put my name as a competitor on all the events. Soccer, running, long jump, gymnastics. At the start of each event they called the names of the participants

SALEHA

laundromat than I ever did at the printer. We're open seven days a week from 7:30 in the morning to 10 at night. It's a lot of work but I like being my own boss. Sometimes people read about Morshed or see his campaign posters in the window and they want to talk to me about politics. But I never talk about politics with them. At first I was going with him everywhere he was speaking. Tell you the truth, sometimes I feel he should get out of politics. I'd rather he not run for anything anymore. I'm tired of it.

to come to the field while 2,000 students sat watching in the stands. When they called **Morshed Alam** on the loudspeaker, I didn't come. They announced my name again, **Morshed Alam**. Still I didn't come. By the time they announced my name six times, Morshed Alam Morshed Alam everybody was wondering and looking, who is this guy Morshed Alam? That's Morsh when I ran onto the field. I did this for ten different events. I wasn't good at any of the games, but by the end of the weekend, everybody knew my name.

I graduated and started my Master's degree in chemical engineering. Before I had even one class, the leader of the liberation movement who had become the father of our country, Prime Minister Muzra Rahman, was assassinated by the army. That terrible nightmare happened on August 15th, 1975. Immediately the head of the army declared martial law. Most of our leaders were killed, thrown in jail or forced to leave the country. I was one of seventeen student organizers working very quietly against this military takeover. It was my job to go to the six universities and organize new elections for the Bangladesh Chattra League. The League sent me to every district in the country. Some places are so remote, it takes two days to get there. You have to take a train, then a bus, then maybe a sheep or a rickshaw, sometimes in rain and wind, then you have to walk miles through rough terrain, take a boat or swim.

Morshed and Saleha live in Jamaica, the most ethnically diverse neighborhood in Queens, and by all accounts the most colorful, polyglot, multi-ethnic location this side of the Milky Way.

Except for one arrest, getting pelted by stones and a beating in the head, I managed to elude the police all those years and finally I got my Master's degree and married Saleha. Neither of us ever dreamed of coming to the United States, but we were sick of living under an oppressive government and I got a technical expert visa to the U.S. So we left.

After arriving in New York I got a job with a pharmaceutical company and Saleha and I started making a family. Soon we had three kids going to public schools, and naturally I wanted to make sure they're getting a quality education. I became the first South Asian ever elected to a New York City School Board.

Detail of a poster depicting Prime Minister Rahman, as the "Father of the Bangladeshi Nation"

I could tell you, after eight years working for the pharmaceutical company, that I took a job with the Department of Environmental Protection because I

সরবরাহ ও স্বাস্থ্য রক্ষার পক্ষে। এ ছাড়া ও রয়েছে সুলভে ভাল ব
ইস্যু ইমিগ্র্যান্টদের সুবিধার্থে উত্থাপিত হয়েছে। জনাব আলম ব
কবেন কিন্তু তিনি সাদা কালো

*Official Barbie doll from the
Democratic Convention 2000*

was tired of working for a corporation. I could tell you I
wanted to see that the environment and human beings and
the microbes are all protected. And all of that is true. But
also I was thinking with a government job I can participate in
the labor union and get their support if I ever run for political position. First I was a union delegate. Then I was elected
Vice President. Now I am President of 1200 chemists and
engineers of Local 375.

In 1996, the Republican State Senator from my district wrote
a book saying there are too many immigrants in America.
It's time to put a padlock at the gates to this country. Many
people in the community had
demonstrations against what he
said. I thought, I will challenge
this guy for his Senate seat.

A week after I announced, my
campaign manager said to me,
"I cannot be a part of it. It's a
dangerous thing what you're
doing." He was getting mountains
of pressure. I thought, what is
this? I contacted the Queens
County Democratic Party. They
said, "If you run, there will be a
racial issue in your district. In
the last election we ran a white,
Jewish guy and he only got 34%
of vote. There's no use wasting
time and money."

They challenged my petition in
the Board of Elections, claiming
irregularities with my signatures.
A columnist in the local paper
wrote an article saying, "Morshed
Alam is no Martin Luther King."

ELIZABETH

By the time I graduated high school in
1972, the Venezuelan government sent
in the army to shut down the universities
because of all the student protests. I
would have had to wait three years before
starting college. So I came to New York
City to be a pre-med student at NYU.
But my real education was with these
idealistic young professionals I met who
started an alternative youth program in
the Village called The Door. Any pregnant
teenager or runaway or drug-addicted kid
could walk in there and find help. Legal,
psychological, medical. I decided to be
a lawyer and called my mother, and she
said "You've always been a lawyer since
you were a little kid."

I got my law degree and worked for a
small firm in the private sector. Then I
fell down some steps and broke my ankle
and was laid up in bed for a few weeks.
During this time I got a call from the
New York City Department of Corrections,

Even when I won the Democratic primary, and was legally the party's candidate, the party machine didn't help me. I'm thinking, is this a real democracy? I went through every kind of hell in that race. A religious fundamentalist group hired three Hispanic guys to rough me up. I was sent to the hospital with two broken bones around my eyes. Everybody's telling me, "Drop out of it. Drop out of it." But I didn't quit.

I got 42% of the vote. We lost but we shook the system. My opponent spent over $500,000. I spent $35,000 with no backing from my own party. **To get that kind of result made a lot of people think about what is possible. No one ethnic group will ever have a majority again in this borough. Now you have to have a coalition.** My campaign committee was made up of a Colombian-American, a Jewish-American, a Black-American, a union worker and a conservative Republican. It's not like years ago when you were Irish in an Irish neighborhood, or Italian in Italian neighborhood. April 15th we are all paying taxes. Everybody eats. Everybody wants their kids to get a good education. It doesn't make a difference the color of your skin or the God you pray to. You need a decent place to live. You want to drink clean water and breathe clean air. There's nothing racial about those things!

In exchange for dropping out of his race for City Council, Morshed was given a statewide position as head of the Democratic Committee on New Americans. Two members of Morshed's club — the first Asian-American and the first Puerto Rican — won City Council seats.

asking me to come for an interview. It was a nine-to-five job so I took it. Then I got another job with the city, monitoring federal programs that helped immigrants, and because of that I got a call a few years later from Mayor Dinkins asking if I'd like to be the Director of Immigrant Affairs. For four years I worked with every immigrant group in the city, 180 nationalities. I come from the sixties, where the institutions of government were seen as *the problem.* And there I was, and here I am still — a part of the government. It's not a totally natural fit. I like to say that the only reason I started working for the government was because I broke my ankle.

You can call me a city employee or a prosecutor or a bureaucrat. I think of myself as a door opener. As a prosecutor, my favorite role is to advocate for people who think they are totally powerless: undocumented aliens, children, and all the women I see whose husbands or boyfriends have abandoned them and their kids. In many cases, the victims and their families don't want to come to court. I have to send them letters and call them up and keep calling. If I can get them to my office, the first thing they see are pictures of Venezuela all over my walls. Beautiful mountains and the little village where I grew up by the ocean. If they are from a Spanish-speaking country, then we speak Spanish. If they are from Africa, I tell them I've been to Ghana and they are surprised I've been to that part of the world. If they're

from South Asia, I might tell them my son's favorite place to eat is Curry In A Hurry. If they're not legal residents, I have to convince them that I don't have anything to do with immigration. "Aren't you concerned that your kid is not beaten up again? Don't you think, rather than staying at home afraid to go out, if your daughter faced the perpetrator in court, it would help her to heal? If we get justice for your child, she will be empowered by seeing that the system can work." In certain situations the law can't do much. A woman from Bangladesh has a husband who has been abusive for a long time. She finally came to court to get an order of protection. Then we discover the child has bruises because the father spanks her. The child can be taken away from the mother because she didn't stop him. I saw a baby who was still breastfeeding, taken away from her mother

who doesn't speak English. I was completely wrenched inside. The judge says to the mother, "You haven't been able to protect your child? How can you guarantee you'll be able to keep your husband out of the house?"

Elizabeth works in a family court system that is completely backlogged. Sit in the intake room and you can see 150 petitions for removal or protection in one day.

I joined Morshed's club because I like helping candidates. A lot of people have suggested I run for office, but I'm satisfied with my job. At 5 o'clock I'm free to do volunteer work, have a life, and be a mother to my kids.

One time when I was working for the Mayor, I was coming back on the ferry boat into lower Manhattan, looking at this magnificent city, when I had this realization that the government is like the janitor. You come into work every morning and the garbage cans are empty and the floor

is clean, and you don't think about how it got that way. The city looks like it's just standing there on its own. Millions of professionals and working people have come from all over the world at all different levels, with lots of money or very little money, working 24 hours a day, trading with other parts of the world, inventing, producing things, getting their children off to school, commuting back and forth. It made me feel humble about the role of government. We're not the ones that make the city great — it's the people: the ambition, the hard work, and the enthusiasm that is constantly flowing in and out of the city. And if the government is doing its job, it should all be practically invisible.

gogol bordello

EUGENE HÜTZ
YURY LEMESHEV
SERGEY RYABTSEV
PIROSHKA
ORI KAPLAN

We conclude this volume of crossing stories with some of the members of the self-described punk-gypsy cabaret band "Gogol Bordello." Like so many people we've met, their relationship to Queens is one of passing through. Whether sub-waying in from other boroughs in search of hard to find cultural treasures; or living here for as few as three months, or as many as thirty years; Gogol band members regard Queens with varying degrees of ambivalence, disdain, and fascination.

Made up of musicians from Ukraine, Russia, Kazakstan, Israel, and the U.S., the music of Gogol Bordello chronicles the immigrant/refugee experience in songs like "Greencard Husband, " "Passport," and "Occurance on the Border." During a sold-out performance at a downtown NY Club, Ukranian-born songwriter and band-leader, Eugene Hütz is surrounded by two "Gogol dancers" dressed in mock Russian border patrol uniforms. They take his passport, beat and tie him up with his microphone cord as he continues singing: "Where is your friend now officer? / That sharp good-looking lieutenant / That got vacation cause he shot my friend."

Offstage — Eugene and company are puckish, contrarian, and philosophical. With the help of beer and vodka, they share their own migration stories, reflect on Roma [Gypsy] identity, and make the distinction between being anti-multi-cultural and proudly "Multi-Kontra-Culti."

EUGENE

Gogol is one of the writers,
even though you HAD to read him in high school, you still love him.
During immigration years I read a lot of Gogol.
Immigration time is very depressing.
A lot of times you feel on the brink of going nuts.
I just left my girlfriend in Ukraine and I had this great band
that was really popular. There I was right in the midst of that moment which
is what every teenager strives for,
and suddenly I'm sitting in refugee hotel
eating macaroni, getting letters from my friends in Ukraine saying,

Hey, your song is in the charts. Where the fuck are you?

You probably picture refugee hotel like barbed-wire place, but it's like any motel or hotel that doesn't make any money, and is in some stupid faraway location that the refugee program rents really cheap for a year. I'm sitting with a dick in my hand in the middle of fucking nowhere, with no passport for any country, no money, and I can't get laid. I started reading Gogol because I thought he was going to help preserve my sanity, and the more I was reading, it actually did occur to me, his stories are totally normal. Only later, when I was 25, did I realize the whole grotesque position of his.

My dad was figure number 1 who brought me together with music and Western culture. He was a big Westernizer. He liked the Doors, Velvet Underground, Jimi Hendrix. But mainly spooky rock music with shamanistic touch. Ironically enough, I made my way to black market before my dad. I was fourteen years old when
I collected a month of school lunch money, 60 rubles, and went to black
market outside Kiev to buy my dad a present for his birthday
which was a **Black Sabbath** record.
He could not believe where the fuck I got it.

Only when **CHERNOBYL** blew up was I put face to face
with my actual heritage of Gypsy side because we were evacuated to
Western Ukraine for a while. It was April 26 and I was on a boat with my dad.
He secretly bought this small boat and would tell my mom we were going to
fishing market but really we were going fishing and boating. She would hate that

he would spend family money on something like that. **We were actually going up the stream to Chernobyl. It's only 80–90 kilometers away.** The only reason we didn't end up there is because it was storming that day and this boat was very small. We were always listening to BBC Russian broadcasting which was heavily polluted with a noise Russians were projecting onto it, trying to shut it down. Couldn't hear fucking shit... ~~the relik mmrek jdk jdk ji~~ Jimi Hendrix, ~~Cifk jfk jl w, ely the only~~ Jim Morrison. We recorded it and listened to it over and over and could gather what they were saying through the noise. On BBC they were saying, "WELL, TODAY WE HAVE TO BRING YOU MORE THAN JUST CULTURAL NEWS. THERE'S A BIG CATASTROPHE IN UKRAINE IN CHERNOBYL ATOMIC STATION." My dad called his friends and some of them also heard it. When the weekend was over, I went back to school and in school there was nothing. No press for five days. Only on the fifth day, the Russian news program said, "A little accident appeared at Chernobyl Atomic Plant, but everything is under control."

The 1986 Chernobyl nuclear power plant explosion is arguably the worst ecological and technological catastrophe in the history of mankind. In Ukraine alone, 10% of the nation's territory has been contaminated by radioactive fallout, over 160,000 people have been resettled, and 3.5 million have been exposed.

⊕ KIEV

It's like America exactly. Nobody's going to give you any news here either. You want to find out what's going on in America, tune in to Canadian or Mexican radio.

My dad called our relatives in Western Ukraine and told them we had to get out of there. He aquired an eximeter (geiger counter) to measure the radiation. I didn't know what the norm was, but it was totally blinking away, snap, snap, snap, snap, snap, snap, snap. We brought it to Western Ukraine with us and it was going, snap,

snap,

snap.

Two years later I went with my friend to St. Petersburg where they have a nuclear power plant. The thing was going snap, snap, snap, snap, snap, snap. Just like near Chernobyl, but nobody ever told these people anything.

I met relatives in Western Ukraine who were Roma and half-Roma. I thought, how come these people in my family are so fucking dark? Up until 13 years old, I was convinced I was totally white. That's when I find out my whole family is completely mixed. My mother is Roma; we've got Ukranian, Russian, German. Fuck! I'm like the walking United Nations.

When I went back to Kiev, I was 14, 15 and I got straight into punk rock. After Gorbachev came to power, all kind of creative movements were going on, kind of a renaissance time for the arts. I finished high school and applied to university even though I knew my parents already applied to leave the country. With help from Russian charity that had no money, we ended up in Austria and then we went to Italy, in refugee hotel with five people in every room. We had a family of three religious fanatics with us. A guy, his wife, and the pregnant daughter. These are people that sincerely believe that right now God is a guy with a big beard and he's sitting there watching. The whole hotel was like that. All these fucking freaks.

We went three times to American Consulate in Italy and got refused all three times. The Russian refugee program ran out of money. They ask us, "You want to go to South Africa?" We said no. "You want to go to Australia?" We said, "We want to go to America." And they said, "You're not going anywhere because America is too packed." We didn't want to accept any other country because all the music we like is from America. They call us a week later, "Okay, you're going to America." Our sponsor was a Czechoslovakian and Albanian program in a refugee house in Vermont. The winters are fucking terrible in Burlington. I was there for five years, started a band, made a lot of waves and decided to take a bigger assignment.

I decide to start anew again in New York, looking for musicians — not musicians who play their music only from these old notes, no improvisation, but deriving from the tradition and mutating it out.

Hützovina, as depicted in Gogol Bordello's debut CD "Voi-La Intruder," is an imaginary Slavic country where the cruelly feudal 17th century merges with the cruelly chaotic 21st.

Design: Eugene Hütz

I did the same route as Eugene, but 1989. I'm from east, east, east. From Sakhalin Island. Near Hokkaido.

He's practically Japanese!

Before the wall came down during Gorbachev era there was a little door open and we happened to sneak in. Or sneak out. I used to play keyboards with Soviet pop groups and met my future wife, feature wife still. So I moved to Moscow where she resided. When I got bored with music there, I thought it would be good to start something new from zero, so we jumped.

When he first arrived in New York, accordionist Yury Lemeshev lived in Queens. He now lives in Brighton Beach, Brooklyn.

I went through all the steps with my music from age of ten when my parents picked the accordion for me. I would pick something else, maybe flute. Now I think accordion sucks. But it's too late to change to flute. If I think about the embouchure, I know I'll keep accordion. I'm good at it naturally, so I hate it.

EUGENE

That's why I love what I do, because I'm not that good. I'm still learning.

I want to be much worse accordion player and I'm getting there because I believe there's no limit. It can get worse than the worse ever.

After you fall in the bottom, you can still screw a hole in it and crawl through and fly endlessly down. Especially with the accordion. Negative infinity.

When we left Moscow, we went to Vienna, then Italy for four months.
I was in Italy for a year man!
Lucky, yes because I got refusnik status in Italy. **You got super lucky.**
I was happy with that life there. I was playing accordion on the streets of Rome, making good money. I love Italy. In refugee hotel we were one family in one room. Me, my wife and daughter. **Not a real refugee. You were on the Jewish line. We tried to rock that gig, but we're not Jewish. Lots of Jews in America sponsored that shit. They gave you $600 a month.**
No way! $200 a month. I love refusnik status, but I was making $100 a day on the street. In Italy there is very high appreciation for street performers.
That's unbelievable amount of money.
I was unhappy a little bit at first when they let us into the United States. Because of uncertainty. There was Polish-American guy who was tourist in Moscow. He heard me play in restaurant and tells me if we're going to New York, he could help. Lucky break for us. He picked us up at the airport 31st October, you know Halloween. What other night could I come to America? Definitely Halloween. This guy takes us to his house. His grandchildren were dressed up in costumes. I was thinking, *oh, they do that everyday? I'd love that.* I find out it's special holiday. Too bad.

Refusnik in this case refers to a Soviet Jew who was refused permission to emigrate to Israel. Later used as a term describing Israeli soldiers who refused to serve in the Occupied Territories.

It was another starting-from-zero situation for me in New York.
I took my accordion, very bad piece of shit from East Germany, you
know masterpiece, but bad condition, to play on the streets.
Somebody saw me, and another, and another, and jobs start coming.
First it was playing with people who speak English. So my English
picked up a little bit. Then Eugene approached me. I told him I
want to check you out first. Audition you guys. I came to play and
talk a little bit with him and I fell in love kind of with this guy.
He's irresistible fucking musical person, and I want to give it a try.
After the first tour, I realized that this is the place to be.

*Sergey Ryabisev was the director of the state
theater in Kazakstan. He came to the United
States with his violin in 1994. His English is
rough, but beautiful to listen to.*

SERGEY

I'm from middle part of Russia. I can say basic, very, very basic English. I've
been here seven years, and problem of talking is all my friends are Russian
people, and in the band I speak Russian. I don't have to speak English.

My father was my first teacher when I was young boy, six years old. He give
me his old violin and said, "Let's start." I play classical music from school
to college, but my father very like Gypsy music. So all my life I listen Gypsy
music. One night Eugene came to restaurant where I played, *Moscow Club*.
Four-piece Gyspy band. Guitar, balalaika, singer and violin.

EUGENE

Sergey was the only good thing in the restaurant. The only musician
with any concentration. So I approach him, "We're having a CD release
show in three days and maybe rehearsing is not that necessary because
you'll find yourself swimming like a fish in this kind of music."

I said, "What kind of music you play?" He said, "Don't worry."
I came to this concert. And I said, "*Wow!*"

I forgot to tell him anything about what's happening on stage. It was one
of those nights when I was drinking candle wax and putting cigarettes out
on myself. It was a thousand percent Gogol Bordello show, people climbing
everywhere and people who are not even in the band being on stage.

It was a big surprise for me. I thought, *I can do something interesting*. I feel I can
surprise them. This extreme situation, I like it.

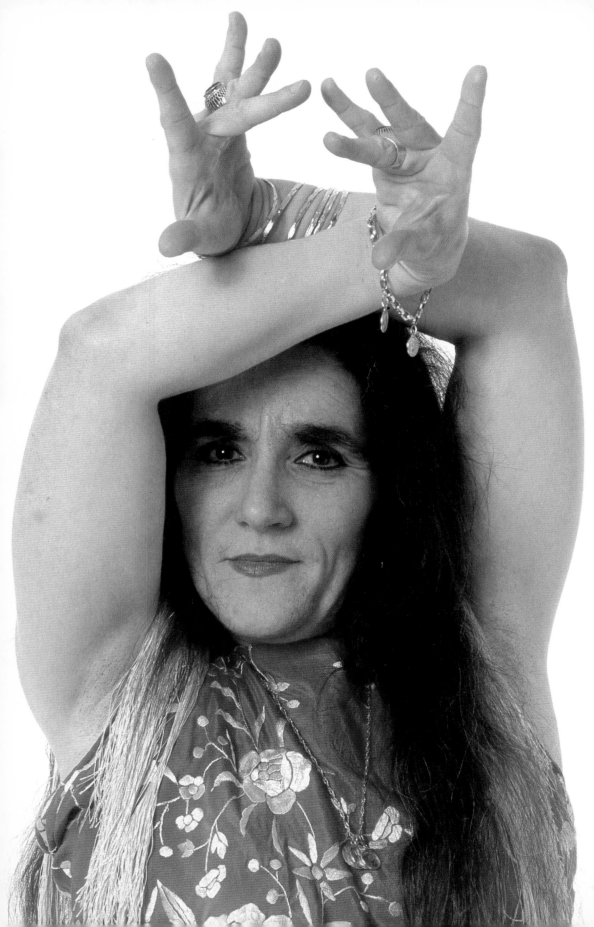

The only member of Gogol Bordello who was raised in a Roma-identified family, Piroshka lived in Queens for 30 years.

PIROSHKA

The other day, a girl asked me, "Are the Gypsies from Romania or Hungary?" You have to be patient. Even if it's a putzy question, you can't get angry. I told her, "We're not from any of those places." Originally we're from India.

But we settled in Macedonia and Bosnia, Spain, Germany, all those other countries, because wherever we were, we were forced to hide, forced to be ashamed, forced to leave. *The nomadic Gypsies* – it's a stereotype. Myself, I like to stay put. I won't travel with the band. I like to sleep in my own bed every night. Many Gypsies have been sedentary for centuries.

My grandma told us a lot of the Roma history; how we came into Hungary after escaping slavery under the Turks. Then in Albania and Bosnia, we were forced to convert to Islam. No matter what country the Roma went into, they'd keep the old customs and adapt the religion to suit their needs. Many tried to pass the way black people try to pass for white.

EUGENE

If you run into Roma in Ukraine, they say they're from Moldavia. Kiev espcially is very Russified. It puts them in a vulnerable situation to say who they are. In retrospcet I can see how my grandmother, who is Roma, preserved her ways without giving anybody a hint who she really is. She's a tailor. She never worked for the state.

Even today, I'm careful. If I feel threatened in some way, I won't give information. It's my duty to protect my family. Both sides are Roma and we don't have too many relatives at all. Hitler saw to that. I always tell people they should write Gypsy with a capital G. We're not an adjective. We're an ethnic group like anyone else.

The Nazis viewed Gypsies as racial "inferiors." In 1938, Himmler established a registration program to deal with the "Gypsy nuisance." By the end of World War II, approximately half a million Roma were killed, including virtually all 35,000 who lived in Greater Germany.

It doesn't matter if you use capital letter G! Of course they should get it right, but the public will never download it. I already gave up on correcting media and journalists about how to spell this and that. Fuck it. As long as we get the essence through, details don't matter.

There are different Gypsy communities in Queens. We each kept to our own group. My family group are Romongrey, known as the musician Roma of Hungary. We're not part of that fortune-telling kind, they're different. The Olashi, they are more what you might say, orthodox. Their marriages are usually arranged. Our people don't do that. And there's never any intermarriage between the two. It would be like a Hasidic marrying a Reform Jew. That would be a nightmare. Olashi keep two sets of dishes. One for the family and one for people who aren't Gypsy. Some of them don't go to school. I'm not saying they should study algebra and trigonometry, but it's important to know how to read and write, at least for protection if nothing else.

The biggest thing about Roma culture kept alive in my family was language and music. I speak two different dialects of Romanus. I also speak Spanish and Portugese. And English of course, that's my first language. But the music is what kept it alive for me. We were always making music around the house. Otherwise, growing up in Queens and later Long Island was a pretty assimilated existence. Mom and Dad had a lot of Jewish friends, Italian. Whenever they had dinner parties, I would hide under the tablecloth, steal food and listen to the adults talk.

You can't learn the kind of dance we do. You've got to be born into it. Have to really feel it. I danced at parties and weddings, all that kind of stuff growing up. If I like moves, even from other cultures, Indian dancing, flamenco, I take it and incorporate it into my own style. When I'm dancing I don't see the audience. I'm in a trance. I guess it's my kind of *flying*. I don't like to use the word, "high." I don't do drugs and I don't get drunk. I just give myself over to the music and everything else disappears. If your heart's not in it, better frickin' get out and not do it. Same like, if you're a shitty cook. Now, I'm a good cook. In my building on my floor, some of these people the smells that come out of their apartments. I'll stick my head out my door, and a lot of the people are deaf, so I'll yell,

"Take some cooking lessons, whoever you are. Your cooking smells like shit!"

There's a store on 14th Street owned by a Russian man. I've been a customer for years. Eugene was going around asking people if they knew a Gypsy singer and dancer. He went into this place and asked Boris and Boris told him about me. Two days later, I'm passing by the store and Boris signals for me to come in. He starts telling me about this guy. He calls Eugene and typical, I waited 45 minutes for him to get to the store! He walks in with his guitar. At first I looked at him and thought, *this guy? This young little string-bean punk?* He started playing. Right there in the store we're having a spontaneous party. I'm singing and danc-ing. Boris calls his wife and says, "Listen to this!"

A few days later, Eugene introduced me to the band for an actual practice at the studio. I'm the elder in the group. Anybody gets out of line, the only thing I might say is, "Who's more familiar with this kind of music?" That's why I would like Eugene to allow me to sing one or two songs. I'll just remind him that he came around the neighbor-hood looking for me. And I'm what he got. I like dancing for them. But my singing is a more pure form. I think it would make a nice contrast to the show.

This saxophone is from the '20s. I bought it from a guy who had cancer and he needed the money. It's been a working horn. It's a Holton. They used to make trumpets and tubas, Not so much saxophones. This color, you never see anymore. I bought it for a thousand dollars, Now I wouldn't even sell it for four. I always wanted to be a bass player and this is the closest I can get. I figured it would add to the sound of the band to have a low-end horn. Gypsy bands usually don't have saxophones.

At eleven years old, I was in Israel playing Klezmer music on my clarinet. I was very interested in Klezmer. But by the time I was seventeen, Klezmer was not cool. I was playing rock by then and then I was playing jazz and then after playing jazz seriously for eight years I was in New York and I started checking out Gypsy music, which turns out be a lot like Jewish music really. Klezmer is the same as Gypsy music except they use different ornamentation. The Jews don't use quarter-tone scales and they're less elaborate. I went to see Yuri Yunakov play at the Bulgarian bar, and that shocked me. That messed me up, so I befriended him, went to his house, studied with him. He lives in New Jersey now.

EUGENE

Do you know about Yuri Yunakov? **The guy went to fucking jail in Bulgaria because of his music!** In the '70s there was an official policy in Bulgaria of eliminating foreign elements from the culture. He's unbelievable and still he can't make enough money. He's driving a fucking cab.

Ori Kaplan left Israel for the U.S. with a variety of reed instruments in 1991. He acquired his baritone sax in New York where he lives on the border of Brooklyn and Queens.

ORI

After I saw Gogol Bordello, I told Eugene I wanted to play, and he invited me on a couple of songs as a guest. The rest I guess is history.

My own band is called *Shaatnez.* That's a Hebrew word that means material made out of two different kinds of wool. In the shtetl you couldn't wear any thing that was shaatnez. It's not kosher. We play some Gypsy tunes, Yiddish, and then we play kind of Tom Waits, pots and pans, abstract sounds. When I'm not playing or touring with either band, I'm home. I'm a Queens exile. I live right over the bridge in Greenpoint. I go to Queens all the time. P.S. 1 *[former public school converted into artist studio and exhibition space]* or I just go buy things. I don't like the post office in Greenpoint so I go to the one in Long Island City. There's nobody there. Queens is purgatory. Nobody wants to be in Queens. It's a stage for passage... Temporary lodging. A place to breathe and a place to leave. Brooklyn is a place to live. If you get a nice place in Brooklyn, you stay. People get old in Brooklyn.

EUGENE

My ex-girlfriend was a fashion designer. She went to Queens to get materials she couldn't get anywhere else. There's whole streets of that shit. There are places that have CDs of regional stars of rai, Punjabi, kwaito, flamenco, that no world music section of any stores carry.

Indian stores carry tapes which I cannot digest as
a DJ so I had to stop going. If I hear a track I like when
I'm in grocery store, I say to the Indian guy behind the
counter, "Come on, you know where to get it. You want to sell
it to me? You can get another copy. I don't know where to get it."
Usually they sell it to me. Queens has been absolute goldmine for
our musical collection as well as social sidekick place. However, right
now it is more of a much visited place. We might be doing our CD release concert at Bohemian Hall
in Astoria. The place is great except there's a group of Neo-Nazis that comes there. Young kids in
black T-shirts. I forget about that aspect in New York. Usually you hear about Neo-Nazis in Austria
or England or somewhere in mid-west. This whole universal redneck thing:

 exists everywhere,
but it's very well developed in America. Germany too.
Even Switzerland, most neutral country.

PIROSHKA

A couple of weeks after 9–11, I was walking at night and
three young girls passed by and said, "Why don't you
go take a ride on your magic carpet?"

YURY

A thousand and one nights. Dumb motherfuckers.
Don't know the difference between a Gypsy and an
Arab. They hate anyone who's different.

You can still feel that vibe if you go to Munich. If the people
get the chance, they'll do it again.

Kristallnacht!

This is part of why the whole globalization thing leaves the
public very confused. Because the same people will kill for your
Gypsy background then they'll go to the store and buy your
record. **ON THE ONE SIDE:** Globalization is a ridiculous-fabricated-
by-marketing-heads concept that helps sell things people don't
understand. It's killing the culture, watering everything down.
I was actually alarmed when descriptions of us started coming
out as multi-cultural. I hate some of these fucking bands. It's
like "Let's take Salsa groove or Arabic voice, then mix it up

The first four Buddha Bar CD releases are top-selling records in the "World Music" category.

Gogol Bordello CD, "Voi-La Intruder"

with a hip-hop beat and make a record." Like the whole Buddha Bar compilation thing. That's the most boring piece of shit I ever heard. And these Algerian Rai stars doing duets with Sting, trying to sell more records. People buy it and think, *oh, I'm so culturally enlightened now.*

ON THE OTHER SIDE:

You have anti-globalization artists. And some people think we're about being secluded in our own culture. It's not about that.

It's about preventing the sameness of the world!

That's what global culture is bringing — complete confusion. "Is this Brazilian or Arabic?" Eventually you won't be able tell. It'll be

THREE HUNDRED MILLION STATES OF AMERICA AROUND THE WORLD.

Music made for the fucking mall where you can buy all these idiotic souvenirs and shirts that you can't tell where the fuck they're from either. Globalization is about making everything the same. Like when you drive through America: Okay, this is Massachusetts and this is fucking Connecticut. What's the difference? I don't fucking know. Gas station, McDonald, McDonald, gas station, Shell, Esso, McDonald, Mobil. Pretty soon you'll go to Slovenia and see the same shit.

Gogol Bordello is not multi-cultural. We're Multi-**Kontra**-Cultural. That's the layer where the culture still lives and remains to be prolific. It's underground layer. People said there is no more underground. But there is underground! Everything that is not signed and is still struggling is underground. In that layer of the culture, all the best mutations are happening. That's where people are not relaxed or comfortable. Maybe some of them are struggling to get sold out. To become big rock star. Just seeing someone setting up their ampflifier and electric guitar, you kind of don't want to see it already. Okay, what the fuck is going to happen now? Is this guy going to plug in his pedals and start jerking off in my face? Fuck you. Being in CBGBs is boring. I don't want punk rock. I grew up with that shit. CBGBs is a souvenir store. They should be selling dolls of Joey Ramone. When we got a gig there, we play once and they kick us out. They say we're too wild. *Hatched in the '70s, the Lower East Side club, CBGBs, is still considered a hotspot for punk rockers.*

We might be popular but that doesn't mean we're not underground. We're not signed to a major label.

Most people are underground really. Because the finance people, the globalization people, they are not most people. They're most rich, but they're not most people.

Most people gravitate to music that takes them out of their melancholy. All the great music, even if you take a traditional folk standard or Gypsy song, it starts out slow and then it goes apeshit by the end. Because Roma are very poverty stricken people up until this day, so they make music to bring them up from there. For market-players, it's a very easy formula. It's Coca-Cola. You drink one and you want another. It leaves you thirsty because it has so much fucking chemical shit. Soon as you drink it, you want another one. It's preprogrammed to not be satisfying. Only for the moment you drink it does it satisfy. So is the music you hear on the radio. It leaves you three seconds after. Everything including education is mass-marketed in America. Many immigrants come here thinking their kids will get a better education. They're just victims of propaganda.

I'm a victim of propaganda. After ten years of living in America you understand what this system is all about. Everything is for sale. It's a country of no education, no culture. There's a lot of cultures, but not in mainstream. There is no history. People talk about Britney Spears.

A pop musician who achieved superstar status in her teens, Britney Spears is known as much for her recordings of other people's music as she is for her belly-button exposure and mega-million dollar appearances in Pepsi-Cola ads.

There is fucking culture here. Look at jazz! But it's not promoted. Look deeper and you'll find good stuff.

EUGENE

Where we all meet is our own version of Gypsy music.
Everyone in the band is about knowing your tradition.
You already rejected it,
      acquired a distance from it,
                  inhaled all this new stuff,

        and from those two,
        you go into third position
        of making an entity of its own.

    That's how you keep the tradition — by making it new.
Freely deriving from whatever the fuck you like.

1740 central government leaves recruitment to local government and entrepreneurs.
Goal of immigration policy is the recruitment of labor.

1790 Any free white person who resides in the U.S.
for two years can acquire American citizenship.

1847 Ireland in grip of Potato Famine; over one million die.
Ellis Island is proposed but not used as a depot to
house thousands of Irish immigrants.

1849 Drive for federal regulation of immigration originates in California
where Chinese immigrants are arriving for gold rush and as contract
labor to build railroads. In 1852, state courts declare Chinese ineligible
1852 for naturalization on the grounds that they are not "free whites."

1875 Supreme Court decision declares all existing state laws regulat-
ing immigration are unconstitutional on the grounds that they
usurp the power of Congress to regulate foreign commerce.
Decision calls for federal supervision of immigration.

1882 Chinese Exclusion Act bars foreign-born Chinese from acquiring
citizenship. First comprehensive federal immigration law dele-
gates immigration authority to Treasury Department.

1891 Bureau of Immigration formed as large influx of new immigrants from
southern and eastern Europe arrive. Popular journals are filled with
hostile references to newcomers as innately inferior and racially inassim-
ilable. Debate rages over need for a more or less regulated system.

1892 Ellis Island becomes gateway to America for millions
of immigrants. Three quarters of newcomers from
1892-1932 enter the U.S. at the Port of New York City.

1906 Authority to manage immigration is transferred to
Department of Commerce and Labor and a separate
Bureau of Immigration and Naturalization is established.

1917 Immigration Act of 1917 mandates literacy test. All new immigrants
over 16 who do not pass are turned back. No laborers are allowed
from "Asiatic Barred Zone," including India, Indochina, Afghanistan,
Arabia, the East Indies, and other Asian countries except China and

U.S. immigration policy expands and contracts with economic good and bad times and with war and peace. We began *Crossing the BLVD* at the peak of a thriving economy and immigration boom. We send this book off to press at a time of economic freefall; a declared war on terrorism without end; dramatically reduced immigration quotas; mass registration, incarceration, and deportation of Arab, South Asian, and Muslim men; and recently-enacted federal legislation placing the Immigration and Naturalization Service under a massive new Department of Homeland Security. The future of America, its posture in the world, and its embrace of "the huddled masses yearning to breathe free," remains uncertain. Will its tradition as a beacon of democracy, freedom, fairness, and inclusion prevail over its tradition of unequal justice, excesses of power, and hypocrisy? Or will the paradox that is America continue into another century?

Written in 1883, Emma Lazarus' celebrated poem "The New Colossus" is engraved on a plaque on the Statue of Liberty. Born in 1849 to a fourth-generation Sephardic Jewish family, Lazarus died in 1884 never knowing the impact of her poem.

As New Yorkers, we feel particularly susceptible these days to pangs of homeland insecurity, and wonder if the time has come to migrate ourselves. But the spirit, intelligence, ingenuity, wit, and generosity of the many people we have met over the past three years has transformed the place we live into a home. We embrace the serendipitous polyphony of Queens as *our culture*, and hope this volume of anecdotal evidence, images, and sounds helps to unveil some of the mysteries and misunderstandings that too often separate neighbors, strangers, and "aliens" from each other.

1924 Congress makes all native-born American Indians citizens. It also passes Immigration Act that provides for a national origins system favoring Northern and Western Europeans. This Act becomes the basis of restrictive policy until 1965.

1930 During the Depression, President Hoover pens executive order excluding anyone who might become a public charge. Only the wealthy are issued visas into the country.

1933 President Roosevelt moves Immigration and Naturalization Service to the Labor Department. In '36 he revokes Hoover's order, but existing (1924) law fails to distinguish between

1936 immigrants and refugees, effectively limiting the entry of Jewish émigrés fleeing Nazi and fascist regimes.

1940 INS moves to Department of Justice in order to provide more control over aliens at a time of international tension. After Japanese attack Pearl Harbor, Roosevelt signs Executive Order 9066 resulting in the internment of 120,000 Americans of Japanese

1944 descent. Roosevelt rescinds order in 1944. From 1933–44, more people are leaving the U.S. than are coming in. Smallest numbers of newcomers since the 1830s.

1968 Major source of immigration begins to shift from Europe to southern and eastern continents after the far-reaching 1965 Immigration and Nationality Act Amendments go into effect, reversing a two-century trend.

1980 1980 Refugee Act codifies procedure to admit refugees of "special" humanitarian concern. 1986 Immigration Reform and Control Act curbs illegal immigration by sanctioning

1986 employers of undocumented workers. Amnesty given to three million "aliens" who have been in the U.S. since '82.

1990 Immigration Act of 1990 increases set-asides for economic purposes tripling visas for immigrants with "extraordinary ability."

1996 Immigration Act tightens border enforcement and barriers faced by refugees seeking asylum, including "expedited removal" and detention. Food stamps and other services for immigrants curtailed as part of Welfare Act.

2001 In an effort to fight terrorism. The Patriot Act gives federal agencies sweeping powers that affect the civil rights of citizens and non-citizens.

Immigration quotas slashed. INS placed

EXIT

to the many people and organizations who helped us with this project over its three-year labor before birth:

Crossing the BLVD Project Partners – Elders Share the Arts,
the Lawyer's Committee for Human Rights, the Queens Museum of Art,
New York Public Radio (WNYC), the Queens Borough Public Library, the Brooklyn Arts Exchange;
New York City businesses – TEKSERVE and New York Filmworks;
our editor at Norton, Jim Mairs, who believed in and championed this project;
our agent, Sarah Jane Freyman, for *seeing* this book from the beginning;
Jonathan Masterjohn, for his care and skill as photo assistant;
additional photography assistance – Rayoon Choi and Jack Ramsdale;
EarSay assistant Brook Wilensky-Lanford for her help with research and transcribing;
Donna Chang for her able design assistance on map overlays;
Susan Perlstein at Elders Share the Arts for her steady partnership;
Michaela Baldwin for her generous, comforting and almost all-knowing computer consultation;
Leonard Seastone for his hands-on help and insight;
Jake Messing for the thanx graffiti on this page;
Camille Massey and Christie Constantine at the Lawyer's Committee for Human Rights for introducing
us to political refugees and for helping us navigate the maze of ever-shifting U.S. asylum law;
Jesús Canchola Sánchez for help with translation and transcribing;
Daniel Berlfein for translation and people research;
Chiara Batistello for help with the original high school workshops and transcription;
Emily Botein, Dean Olsher, Judith Kampfner, Dean Capello
and Brian Lehrer at New York Public Radio;
Doris Jones at the Queensborough Public Library for coordinating
storytelling workshops in libraries around the borough;
Sharon Vatsky, Jean Paul Matinsky, Tom Finkelpearl, Valerie Smith at the Queens Museum of Art;
Marya Warshaw at the Brooklyn Arts Exchange; Steve Zeitland at CityLore;
our proofreader, Ben Reynolds, for his close attention;
our colleagues at SUNY Purchase, School of Visual Arts, and NYU Gallatin School –
Phil Zimmermann, Steve Heller, Lita Talarico, Laurin Raiken, Michael Dinwiddie, Dean E. Frances White;
John Meyer, Offir Kilion for color and pre-press consulting; Elizabeth Elsas for design consultation;
additional sound and computer consulting – Andy Teirstein, Derek Davis, Caleb Clausen, Gary McDonnell;
additional transcription – Mariam Singer; Susan Leeman;
EarSay college interns from NYU and Queens College – Lisa Amato, Cale Brandley,
Hannah Fox, King Fung, Christine Ghezzo, Elizabeth Isaac, Dorit Kashi,
Spencer Riviera, Crystal Sershen, Lauren Shpall, Mimi Stauber, Georgia Tan;
the students in Judith's Cross-Cultural Dialogue Through the Arts project;
our friends and supporters Brian Clark; Marsha Becker; Marsha Gildin;
Chela, Rita, and Irwin Blitt; Dennis Bernstein; Liz Phillips;
Mark Shepard and Carlos Tejada of dotsperinch for their brilliant work on our website;
composer extraordinaire Scott Johnson for his alchemy of voice into music;
and most of all, the people we met Crossing the BLVD, who let us into
their homes, their lives, their documents, memories, nightmares, and visions.

The voices of **CROSSING the BLVD** are cast in an ensemble of type families: Nofret, Interstate, Rotis, Futura, Clearface, Stone Serif, Officina, Base 9, Goudy, Franklin Gothic, Matrix, and Barbera; with special guest appearances by Garamond, Clarendon, Mrs Eaves, Barmeno, Tema Cantante, The Mix, The Serif, Keystone State, Triplex, Weiss, and Century Expanded. The book was composed on a Macintosh computer using Quark Xpress, Adobe illustrator, and Adobe Photoshop. All scans were made by Warren Lehrer using Flextight Imacon and Heidelberg Saphir Ultra 2 scanners. Photographs were taken with a Hasselblad 501CM, a Hasselblad X-Pan, and a Minolta SRT 201. The book was printed on acid-free paper and bound at Mondadori Printers in Verona, Italy.

Judith Sloan is an actress, oral historian, writer, and radio producer whose work combines humor, pathos and a love of the absurd. Her theatre works, portraying a wide spectrum of characters, have been produced throughout the U.S. and abroad at theatres and festivals including La MaMa Experimental Theatre, the Public Theatre, the Theatre Workshop (Scotland), The Smithsonian Institution, the Knitting Factory, and the Jewish Museum. Her solo performances include *Denial of the Fittest, The Whole K'Cuffin World and a Few More Things,* and *A Tattle Tale: eyewitness in Mississippi,* written in collaboration with Warren Lehrer; and *Responding to Chaos, Solitary Days*, and *Anecdotal Evidence.* Her commentaries, plays, poetry and documentaries have aired on National Public Radio and Pacifica stations. She has received grants and fellowships for her work from the National Endowment for the Humanities, the Paul Robeson Fund, Franklin Furnace, the New York Foundation for the Arts, the Connecticut Commission on the Arts, the Puffin Foundation, and the Money for Women Fund. Sloan is an Adjunct Professor of theatre arts and oral history at NYU Gallatin School of Individualized Study. She is a frequent guest lecturer and performer in universities, and conducts arts in education workshops in the New York City schools.

Warren Lehrer is a writer, designer, and photographer whose books and theatrical works celebrate the music of thought and speech, the complexity of character, and the relationship between social structures and the individual. His books, acclaimed for capturing the shape of thought and reuniting the traditions of storytelling with the printed page include *The Portrait Series: a quartet of men; GRRRHHHHH: a study of social patterns; FRENCH FRIES; i mean you know,* and *versations.* With Dennis Bernstein he wrote the play *Social Security: the basic training of Eugene Solomon,* and with Harvey Goldman he co-composed a contemporary opera, *The Search for It and Other Pronouns,* and three plays with his wife and partner Judith Sloan. Lehrer has received grants and fellowships from the National Endowment for the Arts, the New York State Council for the Arts, the New York Foundation for the Arts, the Massachusetts Council for the Arts, and the Ford Foundation, and has received many awards including three AIGA Book awards, two Type Director's Club awards, The International Book Design Award, and a Prix Arts Electronica award. His limited edition books have been widely exhibited and are in many collections including the Museum of Modern Art, L.A. County Art Museum, The Getty Museum, Georges Pompidou Centre, and Tate Gallery. Lehrer is an Associate Professor of Art at Purchase College/SUNY and a graduate faculty member at the School of Visual Arts' *Designer as Author* program.

In 1999 Lehrer/Sloan founded EarSay, an artist-driven, non-profit organization dedicated to uncovering stories of the uncelebrated. Projects bridge the divide between documentary and expressive forms in books, onstage, in exhibitions, in sound, and in electronic media. **www.earsay.org**